understanding **feminism**

Understanding Movements in Modern Thought
Series Editor: Jack Reynolds

This series provides short, accessible and lively introductions to the major schools, movements and traditions in philosophy and the history of ideas since the beginning of the Enlightenment. All books in the series are written for undergraduates meeting the subject for the first time.

Published

Understanding Empiricism
Robert G. Meyers

Understanding Phenomenology
David R. Cerbone

Understanding Existentialism
Jack Reynolds

Understanding Postcolonialism
Jane Hiddleston

Understanding Feminism
Peta Bowden & Jane Mummery

Understanding Poststructuralism
James Williams

Understanding German Idealism
Will Dudley

Understanding Psychoanalysis
Matthew Sharpe & Joanne Faulkner

Understanding Hegelianism
Robert Sinnerbrink

Understanding Rationalism
Charlie Heunemann

Understanding Hermeneutics
Lawrence Schmidt

Understanding Utilitarianism
Tim Mulgan

Understanding Naturalism
Jack Ritchie

Understanding Virtue Ethics
Stan van Hooft

Forthcoming titles include

Understanding Environmental Philosophy
Andrew Brennan & Y. S. Lo

Understanding Pragmatism
Axel Mueller

understanding **feminism**

Peta Bowden & Jane Mummery

ACUMEN

First published in 2009 by Acumen

Acumen Publishing Limited
Stocksfield Hall
Stocksfield
NE43 7TN
www.acumenpublishing.co.uk

ISBN: 978-1-84465-194-8 (hardcover)
ISBN: 978-1-84465-195-5 (paperback)

British Library Cataloguing-in-Publication Data
A catalogue record for this book is available from the British Library.

Typeset in Minion Pro.
Printed and bound in Great Britain by
Cromwell Press Group, Trowbridge, Wiltshire.

Contents

Acknowledgements

This book has been generously supported through research leave, travel funding and editorial assistance provided by the University of Ballarat and Murdoch University. We are also grateful to the following colleagues, students and friends who have read chapters and provided moral support during the writing process: Rose Bishop, Brodie Cooper, April Jane Fleming, Helena Grehan, Trish Harris, Niall Lucy, Nell Newman, Marnie Nolton, Dick Ounsworth, Jodi Peskett, Lorraine Sim, Sam Stevenson and Anne Surma. Kate Machin has helped us enormously in getting the manuscript ready for publication and Acumen's anonymous reviewers and the Acumen editorial team, Jack Reynolds, Tristan Palmer and Kate Williams, have provided astute advice and professional assistance in the publication process.

Introduction

The history of women's struggle to change their lives is a long one. The term "feminism", which highlights their oppression specifically in relation to men, however, has been in use in English only since the campaigns for women's suffrage during the last decade of the nineteenth century. More recently, it has been the resurgence of women's movements in the late 1960s – the so-called "second wave" – that is usually associated with feminist strivings for women's equal rights, and freedom from oppressive constraints of sex, self-expression and autonomy. Most of the theoretical work of modern feminism has occurred during the period since this resurgence, and it is this work that is our focus in *Understanding Feminism*.

Second-wave feminisms emerged in the west in conjunction with the social contestations of student protest movements, anti-war movements and, in the United States, the struggle for civil rights for blacks. In this they echoed earlier challenges to women's subordination that characteristically reflected and radically extended wider social movements for change. British sociologist Sheila Rowbotham's *Women in Movement* (1992) traces some of these developments across the world during the period since the Enlightenment: from the struggles of women against the identification of human reason and progress with the reason and progress of men during the eighteenth-century revolutions in America and France, and their organization for women's rights during the movement to abolish slavery, to their mobilization on behalf of women in nineteenth-century social reform, the Russian revolution, the quest for Indian self-rule and Chinese communism. In all of these cases, women-specific activism and thought come into prominence with, and yet go beyond, the vision of other critical social movements for change. Practical and political imperatives on the ground shape and are shaped by theoretical insights concerning the possibilities of women's lives.

Some historical sources

One of the most important intellectual influences for second-wave feminists has been the philosophical vision of eighteenth-century Enlightenment thinkers in Europe with their focus on reason, individual rights and equality. Bourgeois women in countries such as England and France were at the time losing their opportunity to participate in society as paid employment was increasingly located outside the home and domestic activities were divorced from public significance. A divide between public and domestic affairs, in diverse formulations, has a much longer history, of course, but in the eighteenth century it left a group of middle-class women without any productive role in the economy and the opportunity to challenge their purported public irrelevance and dependence on men with new claims for a society ordered by reason rather than hierarchies of privilege. Mary Wollstonecraft's *A Vindication of the Rights of Woman* (1792) is the landmark expression of women's rights inspired by Enlightenment principles during this time. Wollstonecraft believed that individuals had natural rights to self-determination and that the reasoning by which liberal Enlightenment thought opposed the divine rights of kings and aristocracies should be used against "the *divine right* of husbands" (1967: 78) and women's obedience to men. The alleged inferiority of women on which men's rule over them is based had to be challenged, she insisted, by providing women with the education in reason that would allow them the autonomy and independence to participate equally in the opportunities in society.

Seventy-three years later, liberal philosopher John Stuart Mill reiterated this sort of equality perspective in his essay on "The Subjection of Women" (1869). Mill argued against women's inherent inferiority to men and for their rights to education, public office and political participation on a par with their male peers. "In no other instance", Mill explains, except in the case of women, "which comprehends half the human race, are the higher social functions closed against any one by a fatality of birth which no exertions, and no change of circumstance can overcome" (1970: 146).

Attacked in her own day for her unorthodox views of women's needs and capabilities, Anglo-Irish writer and philosopher Mary Wollstonecraft is now recognized as one of the mothers of modern feminism. Her best-known work, *A Vindication of the Rights of Woman* (1792), is scornful of the superficial lives of society women and their flawed education in trivial pursuits aimed simply at flattering men's sensual needs. Against Jean-Jacques Rousseau, Wollstonecraft argued that women deserved the same fundamental rights as men, in particular an education that would allow them to have independence of mind and to contribute actively to the progress of society as educators of their children and companions for their husbands. Her unfinished novel, *Maria: or The Wrongs of Woman* (1798), uses fiction to criticize the social exclusion and abuse of women of all classes, as well as women's own sentimentalizing of their lives. Other writings include her works educating children in reason and virtue, *Thoughts on the Education of Daughters* (1787) and *Original Stories from Real Life* (1788); her attack on aristocracy in response to Edmund Burke, *A Vindication of the Rights of Men* (1790); and another novel, *Mary: A Fiction* (1788), about a woman who is trapped in a marriage for economic reasons.

These views – that women's rule by men is a matter of social practice rather than a natural necessity, that women have the capacity for the kind of self-determining and independent engagement in social life that is accorded to men – resonate strongly, as we shall see, with second-wave feminist claims for equal rights. They also rehearse certain unresolved tensions for feminist understandings of equality that we shall see emerging again (in varying configurations) in the problems addressed by the second wave. For instance, the terms of reason and equality, articulated in the name of humanity but developed out of the interests of men, run into problems when it comes to women's distinctive roles in the family. While strongly critical of presumptions that women are naturally subordinate to men, neither Wollstonecraft nor Mill had any wish to take women out of their families. Rather, they contended that educated, autonomous women would make better wives and mothers. But just how these labours placed women in respect to their economic independence (of men) remained something of a mystery. Despite protests that "What is now called the nature of women is an eminently artificial thing – the result of forced repression in some directions, unnatural stimulation in others" (*ibid.*: 148), nature casts a long shadow. Wollstonecraft and Mill both conflate women's biological roles in childbearing with their social activities in child-rearing and, as a result, women's equality and emancipation still remain illusory.

Later feminists have grappled with the tangle of themes set in play by these Enlightenment thinkers: the limits of universal equality; the differences between women and men; the intertwined effects of nature and culture. In particular the question of women's differences from men, which Enlightenment thinkers could address only ambiguously, has remained especially perplexing for feminist thought. Against the opportunities for equal access to education and public participation that "sameness" positions offer is the idea that women's differences, their special qualities and virtues (as well as their domestic activities), merit a greater degree of social and political power. Despite the long tradition of women's subordination based on notions of their innate differences from the male standard, the denial of differences itself risks being little more than further support for men's monopoly on power. In the chapters that follow we shall see the problematic double binds of difference and sameness perspectives zigzag across numerous different contexts of feminist thought.

In addition, later feminists have challenged the presumptions of sameness among women that issue from the limited perspectives of the white middle classes. For instance, socialist feminists – influenced by the Marxian insight that liberal principles of reason and equal rights give little consideration to the material inequalities between people that greatly affect their abilities to exercise their rights – have stressed that white middle-class women simply do not have the same struggles as poor women (and men) do with the everyday grind of survival. And as we shall also see (especially as detailed in Chapter 4), anti-racist, third-world and postcolonial feminists draw attention to the racial and cultural limits of Enlightenment perspectives and their twentieth-century versions.

Another crucially important set of ideas for understanding modern feminism comes from analyses of sexuality and psychosexual development, primarily deriving from the work of Sigmund Freud in the late nineteenth and early twentieth centuries. Although Freud was by no means a feminist, his direct focus on sex differences and his insights into the processes through which sexual desire is constructed take feminist thinking straight to the action "of what women want" as it were (even though Freud himself admitted he could not answer this question). Basically, Freud's point is that human engagement with sexual drives shapes subjectivity, the Oedipal complex and the unconscious. More specifically, he argues that although each self starts to form within an undifferentiated infantile sexuality (the infant being pleasure-seeking with a close involvement with its mother's body), subjectivity starts to consolidate through the disruption of the Oedipal complex. Here, according to Freud's theory, the little boy is brought to realize that his continued desire for and pleasure in his mother's body is forbidden by his father (a threat the boy imagines to be backed up by "castration"), and the little girl comes to realize that she is in effect already castrated (not possessing a penis). This latter realization turns her from her relationship with her mother to a desired seduction of her father (who does possess a penis), failing which she returns to identify with the complex of mother and infant (the infant being a penis substitute). The Oedipal complex is thus the effecting of differently gendered subjects: men and women. In the course of acquiring adult sexuality girls and boys must also struggle to repress prohibited (incestuous) desires (a process that, Freud contends, results in the production of the unconscious).

Freud's apparent emphasis on biological determinants of gender difference ("anatomy is destiny") and the derivative status he accords female sexual development relative to that of males have evoked strong feminist criticism. Overall, however, his work in explaining the way the self develops through this operation of sexual differences has been hugely influential for feminist accounts of the significance of bodies, and conscious and unconscious desires, to women's oppression.

The Freudian heritage, later developments in psychoanalysis and their critiques have provided inspiration and resources for feminist engagement with questions concerning the nature of difference, the social and political implications of sexuality and desire, the relationship between cultural symbols and material processes, and the unconscious reproduction of patriarchy. In particular, Jacques Lacan's revisioning of Freud's theory of psychosexual development has been instrumental to a wide range of feminist projects. Lacan's basic point is that the child's development via the Oedipal complex is simultaneously a development in linguistic meaning-making, and he argues that both of these processes lead to the subject's realization that any identity (including her own) is inextricable from its relations of difference and similarity with every other identity. Lacan's contention, then, is that no identity (not even one's own) can ever be fully grasped or complete in itself. This in turn entails that the subject is caught up in a potentially endless process of deferral and substitution in so far as she is continuously desiring (and lacking) that which she thinks would "complete" her (e.g. a soul mate, a baby, wealth, celebrity, social or political power and so forth). As we shall see in *Understanding Feminism*, the significance of such psychoanalytic insights and approaches cuts across every chapter.

Finally, no account of the sources of second-wave feminisms can omit the philosophy and writings of French existentialist, Simone de Beauvoir. Beauvoir's 1949 classic *The Second Sex* with its famous pronouncement on women's lives – "One is not born, but rather becomes, a woman. No biological, psychological or economic fate determines the figure that the human female presents in society; it is civilization as a whole that produces this creature ... described as feminine" (1997: 249) – has become one of the most influential reference points for subsequent understandings of women's oppression. Rejecting notions of an "eternal feminine" nature as the determinant of women's fates, Beauvoir argues instead that women's subordination is due to their relegation to the position of man's Other, "the second sex". Maleness is the standard; men do not have to write a book on themselves as individuals of a certain sex since they are the universal, the positive and the neutral. Femaleness by contrast is the negative, what maleness is not: Otherness.

Beauvoir provides a striking analysis of the multiple factors – biological, psychological, sociohistorical, literary and anthropological – that have shaped femininity. In the process she takes up previously unmentionable dimensions of women's lives, examining their education from childhood, through puberty, menstruation, sexual initiation, lesbianism

---

Simone de Beauvoir (1908–86)

French intellectual, existentialist philosopher, novelist and writer, Simone de Beauvoir was a pioneer of modern feminism. Her major work, *The Second Sex* (1949), was one of the first systematic analyses of the oppression of women and was originally greeted with hostility by those who found its critique of sexism and exposure of male domination too confronting. Although Beauvoir did not write it as a feminist text, its astounding breadth of research and profound insights into the situations of women, their needs and desires, have made it one of the most influential works for contemporary feminisms. Beauvoir's other most significant philosophical work, *The Ethics of Ambiguity* (1947), is notable for its focus on the actual situations of individuals, their ethical responsibilities to each other and the constraints of circumstance on the possibility for living an authentic existence. Her emphasis on the concrete conditions of existence provides unique insight into the struggle for liberation in situations of oppression. Beauvoir also wrote several volumes of fiction exploring human struggles with personal and political turmoil, including the award-winning *The Mandarins* (1954). Her other writings include her four-volume autobiographical work, *Memoirs of a Dutiful Daughter* (1958), *The Prime of Life* (1960), *Force of Circumstance* (1963) and *All Said and Done* (1972), her attack on the treatment of the elderly, *The Coming of Age* (1970), and several memoirs.

and childbearing and their roles as mothers, wives and prostitutes. But with her existentialist commitment to the fundamental freedom of the individual, she also insists that women are in some senses complicit in their own subjugation because of apparent benefits and the escape from responsibility it offers. This analysis of the complexities and ambiguities of the bodily, social and psychological contributions to women's oppression, along with her focus on the concrete dimensions of individuals grappling with the meaning of their lives, remains relevant to subsequent feminist accounts of the construction of femininity and womanhood.

Understanding feminism

Given the diversity of these historical sources, it might seem reasonable to ask whether there is a project proper to feminism. That is, can we – and should we – make distinctions between various women-specific struggles and theoretical concerns, and see some as more properly feminist than others? If so, would that mean that, just as with many other domains of interlinked theory and practice, there is a feminist canon? Further, would there be criteria for the assessment of projects, texts and people as more or less feminist? These are vexed questions, and they cut to the heart of not only the feminist project (if there is any such single project) but what this book is all about. In fact, this book on understanding feminism is itself an attempt to tease out these questions and to demonstrate that, far from the popular understanding of feminism being a unified project with a single aim, the feminist project – or, as we shall see, projects – is constantly in flux.

This approach rests on two key points. First, the world does not stand still, meaning that feminist thinkers are constantly having to deal with new situations, new problems and new experiences. For instance, if Beauvoir was writing *The Second Sex* now, she would probably feel compelled to also consider such issues as eating disorders, new reproductive technologies, surrogacy, cosmetic surgery and perhaps even bioengineering. Secondly, the very grounds of feminist analysis are never settled once and for all. As Judith Butler has written, "What is incisive and valuable in feminist work is precisely the kind of thinking that calls into question the settled ground of analysis" (1994: 6). Indeed, as we shall demonstrate in the forthcoming chapters, despite the determination of feminists to focus on the inequalities, violence and oppression suffered by women simply because they are women, even that most obvious of feminist grounds – the concept of "woman" – is highly contested.

This unsettled state of feminist work is precisely what frames and drives this book. Hence, rather than following the lead of many other introductions to feminism and writing either a review of the major theoretical approaches to feminism (liberal, radical, socialist, anti-racist, psychoanalytic, poststructuralist, queer and postcolonial, for instance) or the chronological story of second-wave feminism, we have taken the unsettled state of feminism as our starting-point. In our view, then, feminism is best understood as a dynamic, multifaceted and adaptive movement that has evolved and changed in response to the different practical and theoretical problems faced by women. Feminism, in other words, is what has been done to counter such problems (feminism is as feminism does). Responsive to practical and theoretical issues that are themselves highly contextual, feminist arguments and indeed feminists cannot all be said to possess the same barcode.

In accordance with this problem-based understanding of feminism, our aim in this book is to show how every attempt to counter a specific problem raises further problems. Moreover, owing to these evolving transformative strategies in response to changing circumstances, and given the entwinement of women-specific struggles with other hierarchies of power, it should be clear that feminism is better understood as a project of multiple feminisms. Having made this point, however, it is also important to note that this book in no way aims to provide a complete survey of all the problems and responses constituting all the feminist projects. Such an aim would not only be beyond the possibilities of a single volume but it would forget that feminism itself has no proper boundaries; as an adaptive responsive movement it is still ongoing, still responding to new circumstances and problems. As a result, we have chosen to address six particular problems or sites of provocation that we consider able to demonstrate not only what are typically recognized to be key moves in second-wave feminist thought, but some of the diversity in response strategies encompassing both socioeconomic and cultural–symbolic concerns. At the same time, these problems – oppression; the significance of bodily existence; sex, gender and desire; the differences between and among women; the revisioning of agency; and the responsibilities of feminist thought – are by no means discrete, and one of our aims in working through them will be to show some of the ways in which they are interconnected and inform each other.

Telling this story

This brings us finally to a few pragmatic points. First, given that this is a story of second-wave feminism with origins in the western world, we have concentrated primarily – although not exclusively – on feminist thought as it has developed in the west. Given, however, that these formulations lead in turn to further issues and problems, we also identify challenges to this western-centric focus, and where feminist response strategies are either compelled to drop such a focus or have developed from non-western perspectives. Secondly, as part of a series on the major philosophical movements of modern thought, our story is biased towards more philosophical and theoretical feminist enquiries rather than towards empirical studies. Practical and empirical situations are of course a major impulse for all feminist thought and in *Understanding Feminism* our aim is to show how theory and practice are mutually informing, stimulating and shaping each other as social situations and theoretical insights shift and change. Indeed, the boundaries between the practical and the theoretical, or the popular and the academic, are never fixed. Overall, however, the sorts of moves we track are embedded in the terrain of critical theoretical enquiry and in this sense contribute to the kinds of concerns and issues that are common in academic understandings of feminist projects. This story, then, does not attempt to address cultural debates about who owns feminism, what it means, whether we need it or not or where it went wrong or right.

Instead, our focus is to introduce the complex strands of feminist thinking by way of an analysis of some of the central practical and theoretical problems feminists have sought to address in their diverse and sometimes conflicting attempts to understand the forms and mechanisms of women's subordination, how feminist resistance is possible and how women can lead lives that are fulfilling to them. In Chapter 1, "Oppression", we tack a course through some of the feminist responses to major socioeconomic and conceptual sources of women's oppression. More specifically, we discuss strategies for dealing with constraints on women's social opportunities in western societies in the organization of public and domestic activities, and in conceptual biases in the ideals of knowledge and the structures of language. Chapters 2 and 3 are concerned with the multifaceted problematics surrounding women's most visible aspects: their bodies, their sex and their sexual desire. Such problematics concern in particular the contested connection between biological sex difference and social and cultural norms of femininity and masculinity. In Chapter 2, "Embodiment", the problem of giving social form and meaning to the contradictions and ambivalences of female bodily existence is considered in light of tendencies in the western tradition not only to disregard the significance of human bodily existence but also to devalue females as somehow more bodily than males. Chapter 3, "Sexuality and Desire", explores feminists' concerns with those specific aspects of bodily existence related to sex differences, sex and gender norms, and understandings of sexual desire, including their expression in practices such as pornography, prostitution and sexual violence. The responses discussed here include contested perspectives on the norms of sexual behaviour, along with queer theory and poststructuralist insights into the plurality and mobility of sex and gender categories.

Chapter 4, "Differences Among and Within Women", focuses on a problematic that has led to one of the most influential transitions in feminist thinking: the move from a stress on women's shared oppression to a stress on difference – of race, class, ethnicity, sexual orientation, abledness and age. This change has resulted in strategies such as the recognition of intersecting oppressions, of multiple, fragmented and shifting identities, and the rethinking of the realm of feminist practice and theory to include the perspectives and concerns of other "Others". The final two chapters canvass problems relating to feminist agency and responsibility. In Chapter 5, "Agency", we investigate the problems traditional notions of subjectivity, agency and autonomy have created for women, along with feminists' attempts to develop alternative female- and feminist-friendly understandings of these notions. Finally, Chapter 6, "Responsibility", looks at the problems for an effective feminist agency with regard to broader issues of responsibility and emancipation, registering that, just as in their historical roots, feminist thought and action cannot afford to separate themselves and women from wider struggles against inequality and marginalization.

While a different cluster of concerns is discussed in each chapter, the problematics and response strategies that each explores also cut across and inform the others. Readers can thus expect to see key insights, theories and strategies emerge and re-emerge across different contexts and chapters, each time being sketched out a little more to show a different facet or application. Such spiralling is, indeed, especially pertinent to – and reflective of – feminist thinking, given the way it has both driven and utilized the insights from a diverse range of disciplines – sociology, cultural studies, history, philosophy, psychoanalysis, psychology and anthropology, for example – for a diverse array of projects. There is, for example, no single pick-up of poststructuralist insights by feminists, nor a single source for the important idea of essentialism; rather, they inform multiple projects in multiple contexts.

With all of that said, it remains for us to reiterate that this is only an introduction to some of the multifaceted concerns and projects of feminists. There are many other projects and thinkers that could have been included, and their omission is in no way meant to suggest that their contributions are uninteresting or unimportant. Indeed, given both the constraints of this text and the ongoing shifts and developments in feminist thought, we encourage readers to use this book as a jumping-off point, and to continue on to explore some of the richness of feminist thought in detail. (At the end of the text we provide some suggestions for such exploration.) Our aim, then, is that this text will stimulate further exploration and thinking, and that, by shining a light on some of the key developments in feminist work, it will show something of the rich resources and influential ideas that make feminist enquiries a major force in contemporary progressive thought.

one

Oppression

"The problem that has no name"

In 1963 American writer Betty Friedan published a book entitled *The Feminine Mystique*, which aimed to highlight what she termed "the problem that has no name". This book was to go on to be popularly credited with launching the second wave of the feminist movement. What was this problem that inspired women and men to new social insight and activism, and that spawned the new wave of thought that has developed into contemporary feminism? A white college-educated suburban housewife, Friedan claimed to identify a deep malaise among her female peers, a problem she diagnosed as based in the discrepancy between women's own sense of their needs and potential in life, and the feminine roles of wife and mother to which their society – husbands, doctors, experts, schools, churches, politics and professions – consigned them. Under the terms of the "feminine mystique", Friedan contended, women were living a lie, embracing a life that constrained and distorted their full potential. Subsequent thinkers have named the problems at the heart of feminism in different ways: oppression, exploitation, subordination, discrimination, inequality and exclusion, sexism, misogyny, chauvinism, patriarchy and phallism. Yet all of these terms circle around a common terrain: that of the restrictions associated with women's social opportunities. Some thinkers put these restrictions down to prevailing dispositions and attitudes, and others to social arrangements; some suggest they are the result of specific constraints, others more systematic problems. Perhaps it is better to understand the "problem that has no name" as a cluster of problems with many names.

In this chapter, we will map some of the key landmarks in feminist understandings of the nature and sources of the problem of women's limited social opportunities. This is a tall order as it requires taking on feminist analyses of not only the material conditions of women's oppression in both the public and private spheres, but also the impact of biases in the norms and ideals of knowledge, and in linguistic practices, on women's social situations. Alongside these critical analyses, we shall trace key feminist strategies for challenging these problematics, including those concerned with women's struggle for equitable recognition and participation in both the public and private spheres, and some of the revisionings of feminist understandings of knowledge and linguistic structures. In this process, we will also introduce what will be an ongoing thread of feminist discussion: the difficulties produced by the tendencies to pursue either an "equality" or a "difference" response strategy (strategies that assume either that women, having the same basic needs and interests as men, should be recognized as equal to men, or, being essentially different from men, should be recognized as having different needs and interests). As we shall see, both here and in later chapters, the contest between these strategies has not only shaped much of the work of second-wave feminists but itself presents a problematic that later thinkers have struggled to overcome or deconstruct.

Countering social oppression in the public and private spheres

In the Introduction we discussed how the work of eighteenth- and nineteenth-century thinkers such as Wollstonecraft and Mill challenged some of the social strictures on middle-class western women in their times. Friedan's twentieth-century articulation of the "problem with no name" echoed similar concerns. Friedan and her peers had greater educational opportunities than women of earlier times (and perhaps this accounts at least in part for the broader impact of Friedan's writings) but their frustration with their destinies as suburban housewives was diagnosed as the result of being excluded from developing their full potential through participation in the careers and decision-making of the mainstream public world (of men). Society, in other words, should allow women to have equal opportunity and independence to that enjoyed by men. Friedan also argued that women's engagement in public sphere activities of paid work and politics would allow them to see that the "feminine mystique" – with its requirements for sexual passivity, submission to male domination, and fulfilment in homemaking and motherhood – is no more than a giant ruse that prevents them from achieving freedom of choice, self-determination and dignity in an equal partnership with men.

A view like Friedan's, however, is seriously impaired by the limits of the experience of the particular women and men on which it draws. As a result, Friedan's analysis does not take account of the subordinate status of all those working-class women who were already engaged in arduous and often dispiriting labours in the public sphere; nor does it recognize that the self-directed life held up as the ideal for women was available only to a select group of men, or that there are racial and cultural differences when it comes to understanding the social situations of women. Nonetheless, its resonance for the dominant social class at a time of progressive challenges to the status quo in western societies ensured its popular uptake as exemplary for what feminism and women's liberation is all about. In understanding feminism, it is therefore important to understand how this particular version of feminism has developed and the problems and responses it has generated within its own (and the dominant strand of feminism's) white, middle-class terms. However, as we shall see in later chapters (especially Chapter 4), while views such as Friedan's have been influential in increasing the publicity and attention given to feminist ideas, the problems associated with their failure to recognize the differences in different women's social situations have forced feminists to rethink significantly their analyses and response strategies.

Friedan's diagnosis of women's situation and the means of its change is a version of what is known as "equality feminism". It demands that the freedoms of men's lives should be equally available to women, and that both men and women should have equal rights and responsibilities in all significant aspects of social life. At first sight this seems eminently plausible, at least if one keeps the lives of successful men in mind. In order to liberate themselves from oppression and exploitation, women need simply to refuse the conventions of female difference and fight for the right to live by the patterns forged for men. In such a view, a life comprising commitment to housekeeping, marriage and motherhood is inherently a second-class choice.

This position, that women should have the opportunity to fulfil the dominant ideal for (certain) male lives (taking that ideal as universal for all human beings), is also described as "liberal feminism". This is because feminists committed to this conception of equality tacitly endorse the liberal theory of politics with its accent on respect for individual choice and self-determination, its endorsement of capitalist economics and the sociopolitical distinction between public and private life. The question, however, is whether such equality or liberal feminisms are in fact effective responses to women's oppression. For a start, aside from the failure to take account of class and race differences in people's opportunities (a very big aside, as we have noted), a major problem readily becomes evident: who does the family work while women are in the marketplace? After all, the pursuit of a career is not simply a matter of putting on a business suit and getting out and about; it depends on someone taking care of both the family and those who are out and about. There is, in other words, a clash between participation in the public sphere and in family life, one that became obvious to many of the women who took Friedan's advice and ended up juggling paid employment and work for their families, or choosing one over the other.

The response of some feminists has been to jockey around the clash, encouraging women to fit their jobs into the periods when their children are at school, or after they have left home. (Of course, this can mean that women might struggle to meet the demands of some time-intensive professional careers.) For women who cannot afford this option, and when the demands of their work in the public sphere exceed the flexibility of family life, feminists demand rights to part-time and flexi-time jobs, maternity leave and reproductive control, and subsidized child- and elder-care provision. However, as more women enter the workforce and public life (whether through the impetus of feminism, or the breakdown of full male employment and the family wage), the stopgap nature of these claims becomes more apparent. Work–life balance, how to juggle employment and family responsibilities, is one of the most pressing contemporary issues for women.

Other feminists have responded to this clash more critically, noting that access to public life has not put an end to women's unequal social position. The experiences of women in marginalized socioeconomic and racial groups provide powerful evidence here. As African-American feminist bell hooks explains in *Feminist Theory* (1984), many of these women have always worked but this has not reduced their inequality or increased their opportunities for freedom of choice. For middle-class feminists in the west, too, terms such as "pink ghetto", "mummy track" and "glass ceiling" show how women's public sphere participation is still largely a second-rate affair. According to these analyses, while increasing numbers of women may achieve their dreams in education and employment, most are confined to the lower rungs of the marketplace and "pink collar" positions of caring and subservience to the needs of others. Such work, after all, holds the promise that it can be more easily fitted around family and household responsibilities, although conversely it often has little or no long-term security. For many women, participation in paid work and public life has also simply meant the addition of a "second shift" (see Hochschild 1989), where there is no reduction in household responsibilities to compensate for their additional obligations to employers (see also Summers 2003). Additionally, underemployment, increasing casualization and lack of affordable care services have all added to the difficulties of a growing number of women who struggle to support themselves and their families.

Challenging the structure of society

These difficulties suggest that the issues of equality of opportunity and freedom of choice are far more complex than as envisaged by equality-on-men's-terms versions of feminism. While there are varied responses, most liberal feminists agree that challenging women's material oppression depends on challenging the relationship between the public and the private spheres. British political theorist Carole Pateman in "Feminist Critiques of the Public/Private Dichotomy" (1989), for instance, shows how the two spheres do not simply distinguish different, but equally valued, realms of activity. Rather, women's and men's differential location in these spheres, allied with the emphases common to liberal theory, express "the patriarchal reality of a social structure of inequality and the domination of women by men" (*ibid.*: 120). Pateman's point is that the split between public and private in liberal societies is a hierarchical division that understands the private as subordinate and sometimes even irrelevant to the public. The dominant liberal social ideology holds that activities in the public sphere, the realm of economic production and political decision-making, are more significant and valuable than those of the private sphere of family nurturance and personal life. The accompanying designation of the public sphere as the location of men and their activities, and the private sphere as that of women, enshrines men's dominance in social life.

It is this rule of men over women that Pateman describes as "patriarchal". Although, strictly speaking, this term refers to the rule of fathers over their families, here it symbolizes the distinctive character of a sexual inequality that "rests on the appeal to nature and the claim that women's natural function in child-bearing prescribes their domestic and subordinate place in the order of things" (*ibid.*: 124). From here the idea that nature also underwrites a gendered division of labour (at least among the white middle classes) is only a short step away. Maternal and wifely work – caring for and nurturing the interests of others – then, is women's work and inferior, while the activities of economic production and political decision-making are men's work and superior. Along with these differences, of course, go those familiar ideals of femininity (nurturance, vulnerability, passivity, weakness) and masculinity (competitiveness, invulnerability, activity, strength) that are frequently used to measure and value women and men.

In other words, the liberal feminist argument here is that contemporary understandings of the public and private spheres rest on a gender ideology that naturalizes male domination and women's oppression. In addition, early attempts by middle-class women to cross the divide show that the two spheres are interrelated functionally. Far from being irrelevant to the public realm, it has become increasingly clear that women's domestic activities are vital to sustaining the operation of public life. After all, no one comes into the world ready to participate in the public sphere and, for everyone, the achievement of their full potential and independence depends on the provision of personal care and nurturance.

Later analyses thus demand "that if women are to participate fully, as equals in social life, men have to share equally in child-rearing and other domestic tasks. While women are identified with this 'private' work, their public status is always undermined" (*ibid.*: 135). This, however, would necessarily involve the structural reform of both families and workplaces so that work in each sphere dovetails with work in the other. Such a change would also require cultural changes in current understandings of women's and men's life possibilities and responsibilities. In this vein, American feminist Susan Moller Okin has argued that under what she calls "humanist liberalism" (1989a), equality presupposes changes for both men and women, including equal public sphere participation and equal sharing in child-rearing, care for the vulnerable and frail, and household duties. In this, as she contends elsewhere, justice and equity in the household are crucial, encompassing equal legal entitlement of partners to all earnings coming into the household and the same standard of living for both in post-divorce households (1989b). Indeed, it is fair to say that by prescribing a more androgynous model of life for all, Okin argues against the relevance of gender to social structures and practices.

It is important to note, however, that such analyses do not deny that there are at least two different dimensions to social engagement, or that women are naturally (biologically) bound to childbearing in a way that men are not. What they do reject is the sexual division of labour, the hierarchical opposition of public and private activities, and males' domination over females. All in all, this focus on the interrelationship of domestic and public sphere life reminds us that simply demanding women's participation in the public sphere will not allow for equality unless it occurs in terms that undo some of these hierarchies. Changes to the organization and norms of both spheres are necessary in order for women's participation in the public sphere to have any real impact on overcoming the problems of oppression and exploitation. Hence, while early liberal feminists such as Friedan suggested that feminists utilize existing social structures and standards of opportunity, respect and freedom of choice (initially developed in the interests of men) for their arguments for equality, later feminists have argued for new understandings of equality on the basis of their analyses of the public–private dichotomy, the gendered division of labour, and sexual, class and racial relations of domination and subordination.

Maybe men and women have different potentials and values

For some feminists, however, the emphasis on equality has seriously underestimated the significance of the very different values, interests and practices expressed by women in their private sphere, caregiving responsibilities. After all, while the dominant liberal capitalist tradition in contemporary western societies identifies and respects independence and self-determination in public sphere participation, it seems clear that these values are not appropriate in all of our activities. (For instance, while it is important to encourage independence and self-determination in our children, values of attachment, care and concern for others are also essential.) These thinkers also suggest that giving preference to public sphere values misses the very real differences between women's and men's lives, and the importance of private sphere virtues and activities as a locus for fulfilment and community-building. Additionally, such preference overlooks the aspirations of those for whom paid work is simply the means to support family and community life. According to this view, the real source of women's oppression is not their exclusion from paid work, but the marginalization and devaluation of women's family work in favour of the male-identified public sphere activities and values of instrumental work, profit-making, competitiveness and aggressiveness.

Known as "difference feminism" – or sometimes as "gynocentrism" or "cultural feminism" – these responses take a variety of forms (many of which we shall explore further in subsequent chapters). One argument is that feminine socialization in traditional roles of family nurturance and cooperation engenders virtues that can be a source of great strength for women. Another, neatly described by American political philosopher Iris Marion Young, is that "women's oppression consists ... of the denial and devaluation of specifically feminine virtues and activities by an overly instrumentalized and authoritarian masculinist culture" (1990: 79). Other feminists have argued that the promotion of these women-centred values is the key to overcoming the destructive (male) culture of violence, war and social, economic and environmental imperialism that many see as threatening global survival. Generally, however, difference feminists recognize that for many women, as feminist legal theorist Joan Williams explains in *Unbending Gender* (2000), family work provides meaning and empowerment in their lives; for others, especially those of working-class and racial minorities, paid employment is simply the necessary drudgery that enables them to support their families. Even those who aspire to enriching work in the public sphere, and for whom family work entails marginalization, may see private sphere responsibilities as more important than career demands. Responding to these women – and against the equality-feminist push to restructure society so as to promote careerist ambitions historically associated with upper- and middle-class men – difference feminists claim that revaluing and celebrating the strengths and virtues of womanhood, femininity and women's work is central to overcoming women's social and economic oppression.

More radical proponents of difference, however, have been dismissive of such attempts to gain greater social support for the virtues and activities traditionally associated with women. While they are concerned about restoring dignity and self-respect to women's activities and culture, they also call for sweeping changes to, and even the elimination of, existing social and political institutions. One of the most famous and uncompromising voices in this movement is that of radical feminist Mary Daly.

Daly's book *Gyn/Ecology* (1978), for instance, urges women to join together and exorcize patriarchal norms of femininity from their lives to make way for a "re-claiming of life-loving female energy" (*ibid.*: 355). In her view, women need to detach themselves from the seductions and tricks of a world that has been structured on the basis of their exploitation. Hence Daly critiques all moves for equal rights for women that do not challenge the male-designed world, roundly dismissing them as

---

Mary Daly (b. 1928)
American feminist philosopher and theologian Mary Daly can be credited with creating a philosophy for radical feminism. Her first two books, *The Church and the Second Sex* (1968) and *Beyond God the Father* (1973), are searingly critical of male bias in the Catholic Church and the phallic language of western religion. In *Gyn/Ecology* (1978), perhaps her most influential work for feminism more generally, she castigates men as necrophilic gynocidal woman-haters and urges women to throw off socially constructed notions of femininity to discover the "wild woman" within. *Pure Lust* (1984), *Websters' First New Intergalactic Wickedary of the English Language* (with Jane Caputi and Sudi Rakusin, 1987), *Outercourse* (1992), *Quintessence* (1998) and *Amazon Grace* (2006) continue this project, arguing for a new metaphysics and a new language that will enable women to escape the bonds of patriarchy. Daly's works are particularly notable for her startling and creative use of language aimed at turning misogynist meanings on their head and providing a "gynomorphic" language that reflects women-identified consciousness, experience and reality.

"tokenism" that "deflects and short circuits" female energy and power (*ibid.*: 375).

On a different tack, American Marxist feminist Nancy Hartsock argues that women's bodily experiences relating to menstruation, pregnancy and lactation, and their caring for others, give them a special understanding of social life, capable of development into a "feminist standpoint". Hartsock contends that if women are reflective and critical enough about their position in the sexual division of labour, this feminist standpoint can expose the biases and perversions of masculinist social relations and institutions. On this basis, Hartsock suggests, a feminist standpoint could have the potential to lead to "redefining and restructuring society as a whole on the basis of women's activity" (1983: 304).

All of these difference perspectives point to the fallacy of thinking about the possibilities of all human beings under the terms of a single universal ideal. The proposal to assess everyone according to abstract standards of equality and rights, they argue, is unrealistic and oppressive because it can never take account of all the socioeconomic, gendered, racial and bodily factors that affect people's different values, aspirations and opportunities. In contrast, difference positions can bring a distinctively women's perspective to bear on society and the changes required for women to be able to achieve their potential.

As we have seen, however, not all endorsements of the intrinsic value of women's work and values aim at overturning existing institutions. Some thinkers of difference feminisms stress, instead, the potential riches for women, and society more generally, if we could overcome our tendency to marginalize family work. On this view, the idea is that we should support the different norms and practices of both the public and the private sphere. As American political philosopher Nancy Fraser puts it, "the trick is to imagine a social world in which citizens' lives integrate wage earning, caregiving, community activism, political participation and involvement in the associational life of civil society" (1997: 62). According to this view, then, feminist positions that play into the devaluation of family work tacitly affirm its continued marginalization and perception as an obstacle to "proper" employment.

In their turn, equality proponents counter that exploitative traditions of family life and women's caregiving cast a heavy shadow over affirmations of women's difference. Indeed, they argue that it is impossible to know whether any of the so-called women's virtues and practices are anything more than the effects of an oppressive social system. Hence, as Okin explains:

So long as the ambiguity about the origins of these values persists, conservative forces that aim to keep women "in their place" could not have better ammunition than to be told (especially by feminists) that women are "naturally" well suited to caring for others, or that politics is a "masculinist" activity.

(1998: 124)

All of this means, then, that attempts to revalue female differences that themselves reflect the social stereotype of women's lives run the very dangerous risk of being re-appropriated by the same damaging tradition that they seek to challenge.

The equality–difference debate

So far we have seen a little of the complexity of what is known as the equality–difference debate in mainstream feminisms. More specifically, according to how respective thinkers challenge the problem of women's oppression, we have seen that it offers two unsatisfactory alternatives: women can either have equality on men's terms at the expense of the values and practices of conventional femininity, or they can affirm their difference at the expense of challenging subordination and marginalization. This dichotomy is, of course, a simplification and has been problematized by several thinkers, but it does show how the various arguments concerned with women's access to and participation in public sphere activities have struggled to understand not only what equality should mean, but the perceived differences between women and men, and their relationships to the public and private spheres. Nonetheless the equality–difference debate has been productive for the analysis of women's oppression. For instance, the call for equality with men, however problematic, has helped to uncover the inequities embedded in family work, and led to the development of what could be called a humanist conception of work that encourages the sharing of opportunities and responsibilities in both spheres. From the other side, understandings of gender difference, although they may be stalked by dangerous stereotypes, show how equality approaches tend to overlook the variations in women's situations and their substantively different needs and aspirations.

Yet it is clear to many thinkers that feminist strategies to overcome women's oppression and exploitation by revisioning the public–private divide are caught between the need, on the one hand, to do away with the subordinate place of women, and, on the other, to build up the political, social and economic meaning of women's activities. Such strategies also struggle with the recognition that achieving the former is a crucial dimension of the latter. With all of this in mind, then, it can be better seen how the various phenomena of the "pink ghetto", the "second shift" and the "glass ceiling" all reflect, in different ways, the binds of this central conflict for social policies that are aimed at alleviating women's subordination. Hence, although it might appear, in the western world at least, that women are now free to access and cross between the public and private spheres – women can, after all, be prime ministers and truck-drivers, surgeons and soldiers, mothers and morticians – such access and participation have not necessarily translated into the end of oppression and exploitation. Women are still massively under-represented at the highest levels of wealth and power in politics, business and religion; their full-time and average earnings are still less than those of men; they are over-represented among those living in poverty; and although more are working outside their homes, on the whole they are still working as hard at home as they were before (see Okin 1998; International Labour Office 2000; Summers 2003).

The epistemological face of women's oppression

What all of this shows us, then, is that while social and material inequities may be the outward face of the problem of women's oppression and exploitation, there must also be other facets to the problem. Of these, many feminists have come to realize that the issue of women's oppression is, at its most fundamental level, a matter of knowledge or epistemology (that is, ideas and theories concerning the origins of knowledge and how it is authorized). After all, many of the practices that have prevented women from achieving their potential are ultimately based on biased views or alleged facts about women's lives and aspirations. As Beauvoir shows in *The Second Sex* and Friedan in *The Feminine Mystique*, for example, the views of sociologists, psychologists and cultural anthropologists have all been used to confirm that it is (middle-class white) women's "natural" function to lead a life of dependence and servitude in the family. While such purported knowledge is false, it has nonetheless had a status of certainty that has authorized its justification of social and political policies that have prevented women from stepping out of such a life of dependence. For instance, physiological and psychological claims about women's mental capacities gave rise to laws that dictated that women could not own property or manage their own finances or even vote. Indeed, claims about the "facts of the matter" made by experts in the field have been and still are the most basic means of maintaining social practices that have consolidated gender inequalities. In other words, understandings of what knowledge is and the theories of knowledge that justify them have a vital role in determining women's possibilities. As Canadian epistemologist Lorraine Code succinctly explains, "epistemologies, in their trickle-down effects in the everyday world, play a part in sustaining patriarchal and other hierarchical social structures" (1998: 176).

There is, in other words, an epistemological dimension to oppression, where ideas about knowledge and what (or who) justifies it are not only key to better understanding women's oppression, but underpin a range of feminist attempts to counter this oppression in so far as presumptions and claims about knowledge and its justification are, of course, the basis of all political action and social policy changes. After all, without credible knowledge about who is marginalized, whose experience has been mistakenly interpreted, sidelined or left out of consideration, and whose has dominated and why, the unravelling of oppression is impossible. Unravelling and challenging the epistemological dimension of women's oppression is, however, extremely difficult. For a start, the problem is exceedingly wide-ranging, with claims from biology and the biomedical sciences, history, anthropology, sociology, economics, politics, psychology and philosophy – along with their far-reaching consequences for the ways human beings understand and organize themselves – all being implicated.

Importantly, the problem is not simply that these enquiries overlook, marginalize or misrepresent women, or that they have traditionally excluded women from engaging in them, although these have all been the case. (In the 1950s Daly, for instance, had to complete six degrees before she was finally permitted to study philosophy; and Virginia Woolf, of course, famously traces in *A Room of One's Own* [1929] some of the humiliations and rejections experienced by women of that time seeking to participate in intellectual enquiries.) Rather, at a deeper level, feminist analysis shows that the very practices of science and other authoritative knowledge-making activities – including their methodologies, norms and ideals – are themselves male-centred or androcentric. For example, in *The Man of Reason* (1984), Australian philosopher Genevieve Lloyd shows the links between rationality, a key component of the search for knowledge, and (white European) masculine characteristics in some of the most influential texts in philosophy. In a point we shall come back to in subsequent chapters (especially Chapter 2), Lloyd contends that understandings of reason and rational enquiry have historically been caught up in the pervasive gender norms that code the ordered pairs reason–emotion, mind–body, objectivity–subjectivity and universal–particular in accord with the male–female binary. And, she continues, it is on the basis of these conceptual constructions that ideals of knowledge are established that are hostile to traits associated with femininity and women, in turn making access to the realm of reason highly problematic for women.

This complex of issues concerning the content of knowledge – which facts or claims to knowledge should be seen as authoritative and why – has given rise to a range of feminist responses, many of which focus on the concept of objectivity in so far as it is usually seen as a symbol of authoritative knowledge. To unpack this briefly, the claim that knowledge is objective conventionally refers to its presumed impartiality, accuracy and certainty. That is, objective knowledge is free from any subjective prejudices, providing a neutral account of the world. Indeed, as American feminist Donna Haraway so memorably puts it, objectivity is associated with "the god trick of seeing everything from nowhere" (1991b: 189). This, in turn, means that those who possess objective knowledge are supposedly detached and neutral individuals whose social roles and personal dispositions have no effect on their knowledge. Their knowledge is the outcome of uncorrupted human faculties and provides independent access to the world its facts describe.

It is these kinds of assumptions that have made the epistemological dimension of women's oppression so hard to challenge. After all, if there is such a thing as objective knowledge, and if the knowledge claims made by biologists, psychologists, sociologists and so forth deserve this status, then feminist critiques of such knowledge claims relating to women's place in the world would clearly be unfounded and implausible. This, however, is the very crux of the issue. Are there really such unquestionable knowledge claims and knowers? Is it possible to challenge the assumptions and methodologies of objective knowledge? And if so, on what basis? After all, any attempt to challenge the objectivity of knowledge must itself be carried out from the basis of an alternative view: that objectivity is an illusion, a misconception or impossible, say. But why should anyone believe this alternative? What makes it credible? As we will come to see, these are difficulties that frequently haunt attempts by feminist thinkers to re-vision the most basic understandings women have of their lives.

Feminist empiricism

The beginnings of feminist work in epistemology, however, were not concerned with the complexities of challenging the objectivity of knowledge in general. Inspired by critical work in the biological, medical and social sciences, these first responses challenged the objectivity and truth of specific knowledge claims: claims such as those concerning the biological basis to women's supposed inability to use abstract reasoning; that women are naturally suited to care-based work; that clitoridectomy is a "'cure' for hysteria, nymphomania, lesbianism, and excessive masturbation" (Meyers 2004: 206). (More recently feminists have made similar challenges against evolutionary psychologists' claims about human sexual behaviours: for example, that domestic violence and rape are natural, genetically determined male behaviours; that women are naturally "coy" sexually, more risk averse and less competitive than men.) There is simply no strong evidence to support such claims, these critics have argued. Such questioning has been labelled "feminist empiricism", following the influential work of American philosopher Sandra Harding (1986, 1993), where "empiricism" stands for positions that rely principally on empirical evidence as the source of knowledge.

For feminist empiricists, then, biases and outright falsehoods as well as the exclusion of female perspectives, experience and issues from investigation taint the objectivity of so-called facts about sex differences. Objectively true knowledge, they insist, can be established only by extending the range of enquiry to include females and their interests, and by a much more careful scrutiny of so-called empirical evidence. Hence, according to Harding's explanation of feminist empiricism, "sexism and androcentrism could be eliminated from the results of research if scientists would just follow more rigorously and carefully the existing methods and norms of research – which, for practicing scientists, are fundamentally empiricist ones" (1993: 51). According to this view, objective biomedical science, for example, should include female as well as male rats in clinical tests for drugs; objective biology should use controls for sexual stereotypes in its examination of hormonal effects on "gender role behaviour" (e.g. Fausto-Sterling 1985); objective history should include details of changes in women's lives and not just the events and outcomes of men's aspirations; and objective economics should include the contribution of women's unpaid work in the family in measures of productivity (e.g. Waring 1990).

Importantly, however, these positions usually hold the ideal of objective knowledge intact. The notions that "brute" data, the results of unbiased observation, compel belief, and that knowledge is accountable only to this evidence, remain unchallenged. Indeed, for feminist empiricists, only such a vision of objectivity is able to invest feminist positions with the authority to promote change in both knowledge-making and, more importantly, the social and political policies enacted in its name. Further, given the feminist standpoint theory assumption that female practitioners are more likely than males to detect the mistakes, misuses and omissions made in what have traditionally been male enclaves, feminist empiricists also argue for the entry of more women into the laboratories, clinics and academies of knowledge-making.

This kind of corrective strategy has brought enormous gains with respect to the inclusion of women's perspectives and experiences in knowledge-making projects but, like the equality strategies discussed earlier, it also contains the seeds of a more radical response. In so far as the term "feminist empiricism" is an acknowledgement that some contextual and bodily qualities of knowers are significant to objectivity, some thinkers argue that the orthodox understanding of objectivity as neutral is itself an illusion. (Supporters of the traditional understanding of objectivity argue, on the other hand, that owing to its stress on sex difference, feminist epistemology is itself a contradiction in terms.) Of concern for us here, however, is the feminist empiricist idea that the way to address the incomplete and partial knowledge gained from traditional androcentric research methodologies is simply to add in missing components and perspectives. There are two issues here. The first is the question whether a neutral objectivity is still perhaps possible if researchers could simply find and add in every missing component and perspective. Most thinkers agree that even if this is in principle possible, we human beings certainly could not attain such a "god's-eye perspective". The second is the idea that bringing alternative perspectives to bear on enquiry actually challenges the guiding frameworks that posit male standards as the norm and male outlooks as the measure of significance.

A clear example of this latter idea is to be found in Haraway's (1991a) analysis of the field of primatology, where she demonstrates that when female scientists began studying primate behaviour they challenged the framework within which scientific observations and interpretation had been carried out. For instance, prior to the entry of women into the field, primatologists explained the characteristics of group cohesion among primates in terms of dominance hierarchies modelled on "man-the-hunter" (and European racial) power structures. Focusing instead on female–infant relationships, women primatologists challenged the significance of this explanatory framework. Haraway's point, then, is not to promote any particular framework but rather to show how scientists' sociopolitical contexts in fact directly shape their so-called objective findings regarding the primate world.

Reconceiving objectivity

As we have seen in the first part of this chapter, when the strategy of including women (or women's perspectives) in systems that have traditionally been seen as universal shows that those systems are in fact biased towards males, an obvious feminist move has been to champion alternative ideals based on women's differences from men. In the realm of feminist epistemology, however, the notion that women have distinctive ways of knowing that can be substituted for, or used within, dominant paradigms has been seen as problematic. The key critique is as follows: either the alternative plays into the existing terms of women's subordination ("we always knew that females thought differently, and/ or irrationally"), or it creates an enclave that cannot challenge the dominant tradition ("female thinking is so different that it is unable to be understood or used by anyone else").

Before we accept this double bind, however, there is a third possibility, albeit one that many feminists have found to be just as unsatisfactory. In this instance, women's knowledge may be recognized as valid in its own right, but it may not be able to provide any standards for assessing or challenging the validity of other positions. On this view, when different claims about the facts of the matter are pitted against each other (for example, when the claim that primate group cohesion is best explained in relation to male hunting activities is challenged by the claim that female–infant relations are the most significant factors for understanding the dynamics of group cohesion), both claims may be taken to have equal authority. This is owing to a view that suggests that as long as a particular group or individual expresses its views in good faith, its claims cannot be wrong as such; they are simply true relative to that perspective. That is, there is no neutral objective space or perspective that people can use to evaluate various claims once and for all. This is, of course, a kind of epistemological relativism or subjectivism. For many thinkers, however, while this kind of relativist "anything goes" view might allow people to recognize and celebrate differing perspectives, it is a non-starter for achieving sociopolitical change. After all, if sexist and non-sexist attitudes are equally right, being the views of different groups, how can anyone make a viable argument for policies that specifically enforce non-sexist attitudes?

The problem for feminists concerned with these broader issues of knowledge-making is thus to work out a response that recognizes both the maleness of a supposedly neutral objectivity, and that knowledge claims can be wrong. The title of Code's paper, "Taking Subjectivity into Account" (1993), neatly sums up what is required. As she sees it, feminist epistemologists need a working conception of objectivity that also accounts for the subjectivity of knowers. We cannot jettison objectivity, after all, because it is surely obvious that some aspects of our reality are independent of human knowers: "earthquakes, trees, disease, attitudes and social arrangements are *there*" (*ibid.*: 21). At the same time, human perspectives shape much of the world we live in, and thus knowledge claims should reflect this perspectivism. For example, for some kinds of knowledge (whether the earth is flat or round, say) the human context is so widely shared that it suggests that these facts are universal and that they comply with neutral objectivity. In many cases, however, and especially those concerning persons (whether women are exploited with regard to family work, for instance), the particularity of knowers, their social location and their perspectives all have a significant role to play in the construction of knowledge. This, then, is a project aimed at broadening conceptions of objectivity so that they can indeed "take subjectivity into account". And although it cannot yield fixed, universal and certain truths, it can avoid the twin dangers of hiding behind an illusion of impartiality and independence and the "anything goes" of radical relativism. Overall, thinkers such as Code accept that knowledge inevitably bears the marks of its human creators and their sociopolitical context, while contending that it is also constrained by the existence of an independent reality.

One of the most influential contributions to the project of reconceiving objectivity is Harding's feminist standpoint epistemology in which she develops a concept of "strong objectivity" (1993). Here Harding builds on Hartsock's work, arguing that the standpoint of the oppressed can provide special access to the task of revisioning objectivity. Briefly, as mentioned earlier, the idea of standpoint theory is that the roles and activities of those in the dominant class place limits on what they can understand about themselves and the world. In contrast, the experience of the marginalized can give them an epistemic advantage because their lives spark lines of investigation that are invisible to those in the top strata. According to this strategy, so-called neutral objectivity – or "objectivism" as Harding (*ibid.*) terms it – despite its status as

> **Sandra Harding (b. 1935)**
> An American philosopher and postcolonial theorist, Sandra Harding is one
> of the founders of the fields of feminist epistemology and philosophy of
> science. Her co-edited collection (with Merrill Hintikka) *Discovering Reality*
> (1983) is credited with bringing feminist analyses of knowledge construction
> on to centre stage for feminist theory; while *The Science Question in Feminism*
> (1986) provides definitions of various feminist approaches to the philoso-
> phy of science and epistemology that have come to be seen, albeit contro-
> versially, as paradigm-setting for the field. Harding's articulation of feminist
> standpoint theory and "strong objectivity" has also been highly influential
> as a research methodology in the social sciences, providing philosophical
> tools for those who are concerned about androcentric biases in research
> frameworks. *Whose Science? Whose Knowledge?* (1991) continues this work of
> unmasking the political effects in epistemological projects. Harding's latest
> works, including *Is Science Multicultural?* (1998) and *Sciences from Below* (2008),
> incorporate anti-racist and anti-imperialist analyses into strong objectivity in
> order to conceptualize a more inclusive and democratic understanding of
> knowledge-making.

the "proper" foundation for credible knowledge, is unable to detect
the social biases and androcentric assumptions typically written into
its knowledge-making projects. In contrast, the perspective of strong
objectivity de-links objectivity from impartiality by including scrutiny
of the interests and values of the producers of knowledge. With regard
to the feminist struggle against oppression, then, the trick is to frame
knowledge in terms of values that are inclusive and democratic.

However, like every strategy in the dynamic questioning that con-
stitutes feminist thought, this one has raised yet further queries. Once
again, some critics worry that talk of the inherent subjectivity of knowledge will undermine feminists' ability to speak knowingly at all. Indeed,
a common argument is that any move away from strict ideals of objectivity draws feminist epistemology into irrationalism and/or relativism.
Hence some feminists contend that our ability to create accounts of
the social world that are superior to any competing sexist (or classist,
racist, heterosexist, etc.) versions actually depends on ridding knowledge of subjectivity (see e.g. Antony & Witt 1993). Nonetheless, against
these criticisms, proponents of broader conceptions of objectivity still
continue to uncover the various places in the construction of knowledge where biases contaminate the ideal of neutral objectivity. Such
efforts assume that scrutiny and exposure of the sociopolitical biases
of knowledge, along with recognition of the sociopolitical situations of

knowers, can provide more accountable and responsible knowledge. Other feminist responses to epistemological oppression, however, are more dismissive of attempts to reinvigorate objectivity.

Beyond objectivity: sceptics and postmodernists

For these feminists, the concept of objectivity, like the dominant socio-political order, is far too deeply entwined with (white European) masculine ideals to be worth retrieving. After all, objectivity is not only a symbol of impartiality and neutrality; it is a mark of credibility and authority. Objectivity gives authority to knowledge, and frequently those who have authority are credited as objective knowers. This means that attempts to re-envisage objectivity (such as Harding's strong objectivity proposal) are doomed on either of two counts. First, since groups that do not have epistemological authority perform this re-envisaging, they will be unable to effectively challenge the claims of those who do have such authority. Secondly, and paradoxically, if such groups do gain status, a new, but no less socially contingent, dynamic of domination and subordination dissipates their authority. This effect can be observed, for example, in the way social power gained by feminists championing the knowledge that many women are oppressed by life as a housewife came at the cost of excluding all those women for whom family life is a refuge from terrible employment conditions. The now-familiar insight that every knowledge claim is caught up in a contingent social and historical context (simply because knowledge will always be a human construction) is radicalized here to rule out even the best-intentioned attempts to make the ideal of objectivity as inclusive as possible. This sort of relativist view – often associated with the intellectual movement of postmodernism (which we shall consider in more detail in subsequent chapters) – is taken up in varying ways by several epistemologists.

For example, Haraway's influential paper "Situated Knowledges" (1991b) sets out the tension between "feminist critical empiricisms" (in which she includes Harding's standpoint theory) and "radical constructivism" (referring to the position accepting the radical social contingency of all knowledge claims). As Haraway sees it, what is needed is a strategy that would enable people to make objective knowledge claims while simultaneously accommodating the bind outlined above. Her answer is the articulation of "situated knowledges": "partial, locatable, critical knowledges sustaining the possibility of webs of connections called solidarity in politics and shared conversations in epistemology" (*ibid.*: 191). According to this view, objectivity is not lodged in a single standpoint but in an open practice of mobile and critical positioning, contesting, deconstructing, interpreting, partially connecting, power-sensitive conversation.

This position seems to be transitional between Harding's strong objectivity and more sceptical views that dismiss the concept of objectivity altogether. For instance, both standpoint theory and situated knowledges support the notion of tracking the subjective and perspectival nature of knowledge claims, as well as the multiple relations of domination and subordination that permeate them. To this extent they resonate with (postmodern) criticisms of the possibility of reaching any universal or closed viewpoint, but they are cautious about the radical scepticism and relativism associated with acknowledgements of the subjectivity of knowledge. Nevertheless, Haraway's emphasis on local and partial knowledges is also close to positions that dismiss all aspirations to objectivity in favour of investigations into the different positionings of knowers. After all, Haraway's histories of research in primatology do not attempt to decide between "man the hunter" and "female–infant relations" frameworks. They aim instead to throw light on the complexity and contingency of knowledges in the field.

This sceptical approach to objectivity arises from the claim that frameworks of thought and language that are themselves enmeshed in the contingent situations of their historical creator–participants mediate all of our knowledge of reality. Given the impossibility of stepping outside these frameworks, all there can be are multiple and contradictory knowledges that can never have the coherence entailed in traditional conceptions of objective understanding. However, from this position it is difficult to ascertain just what credible knowledge might be. Consequently, instead of focusing on methodologies of investigation that yield more inclusive knowledge, these responses tend to concentrate on unearthing the exclusionary and oppressive effects of claims to authority. In other words, the problem of epistemological oppression is turned back into mapping the effects of sociopolitical oppression in specific contexts of knowledge claims, and the aim is to bring to light aspects of people's lives that are invisible to conventional approaches to knowledge, while refusing to understand these accounts as providing objective understanding.

This brings us to yet another area of concern: the way contemporary understandings of the world, contemporary knowledges, are affected by the language in which they are expressed. Indeed, from the beginning of the second wave, feminists have worried about the role of linguistic practices in influencing possibilities of understanding and how biases in language have contributed to women's oppression. In the final sections of this chapter, then, we explore feminist strategies aimed at challenging the work of language in the symbolic, discursive and cultural expression of sexual subordination.

Language and oppression

Although the relationship between reality and its linguistic representation is extremely complex, it is clear that language encodes what is important to people and provides the means for them to articulate their understanding of what is significant. It is also obvious, however, that the linguistic categories that people use to do this work both reflect and are reflected by their social positions. Language, then, is normative, and thus an arena of political struggle. Indeed, as many feminists have diagnosed, it is one of the primary means of maintaining women's oppression and exploitation. It is thus no surprise that the feminist "attack on words" shares the stage with feminist challenges to social organization as another of the most obvious and contentious expressions of the contemporary movement (fuelling the backlash against "political correctness" and the denunciation of "language police").

Once again, however, contested understandings of equality and difference frame feminist challenges to the symbolic and linguistic aspects of women's oppression. Early discussions of sexism in English, for instance, emphasized the omission and erasure of women from language through the use of generic masculine pronouns (he, him) and male nouns (man[kind], forefathers, fellows) to denote both males and females. Not only do women become invisible in this system, but such "he/man language" conveys the notion that to be fully human is to be male. Feminists have also drawn attention to the way the use of paired words for males and females – man–woman, master–mistress, husband–wife, bachelor–spinster – systematically encodes female inferiority. More specifically, while the male terms imply power, control and independence, the female terms convey weakness, subservience, dependence and, in the case of "spinster", failure (Nye 1988: 174). This androcentric foregrounding of men as the norm is also evident in the asymmetries coded through the diminutive implications of feminine endings of words such as "actress" and "waitress", and the use of titles for women (Mrs, Miss) that distinguish married (sexually unavailable) women from unmarried women (Cameron 1992: esp. ch. 6; Nye 1988: 176).

Further, women have struggled to express what is significant to them. We have already seen, for example, how Friedan resorted to the phrase "the problem that has no name" to describe women's social condition and how the word "work" implicitly carries the meaning of paid employment, thereby effectively discounting the value of the unpaid labour of women in the private sphere. Again, such terms as "sexual harassment" and "acquaintance rape" only now name phenomena that are important for women but that were inarticulable prior to feminist analyses. Certainly the words "harassment" and "rape" were familiar enough, but women's specific experiences of sexual advances being intimidating, vexatious and unwanted, or the notion that sexual intercourse with an acquaintance could have been forced without consent, lacked independent recognition in the absence of appropriate terms.

Social practices of speaking and writing indicated other difficulties for feminists. Sociolinguistic research on sex differences (e.g. Thorne & Henley 1975; Thorne *et al.* 1983) has indicated that women's speaking styles are less aggressive, less competitive, more tentative, more interruptible and more conservative than men's. While the interpretation of research can always be contested, as noted in the previous discussion of feminist epistemology, evidence showing that males monopolize public speech in churches, parliaments and courts, and that women predominate globally in the ranks of the illiterate (a problem far-reaching enough that the United Nations has several directives aimed explicitly at promoting literacy in women), confirms the intimate links between linguistic and social effects.

The "great he/she battle"

We can see some early feminist responses to these problems, then, as a move towards gaining equality for women in language. The "great he/she battle", as American literary theorist Jane Hedley (1992) puts it (taking the term from Alleen Pace Nilsen [1984]), "is for 'equal opportunity', with an emphasis on the ways in which standard usage interferes with women's efforts to hold their own in public life and in the world of work" (Hedley 1992: 40). The aim was thus to overcome the inequities of the "generic he" and the supposedly neutral nouns that encoded masculinity as normative for humanity and to reinstall a symmetry that would rid language of its sexism. All in all, the idea was that the creation of a new androgynous discourse would allow women to be equally represented, and effect more precision in language use (Miller

& Swift 1980: 8). (As we shall see in Chapter 3, intersexed activists have also called for the revisioning of language – especially pronouns – so that it better represents their experience of the world.)

More radical feminist critics, however, have argued that such strategies are too superficial to address the systematic nature of the biases in language, underestimating the deep work of sexist language in prescribing stereotypes of sexual difference and limiting women's self-expression. The attempt to replace sexist terms with non-sexist ones, they argue, fails to understand that language does not and cannot directly reflect the world it describes. (Like knowledge, language is riddled with subjectivity. Descriptions are far from objective, rather expressing deeply held views and contextual assumptions.) On this view, the whole linguistic system is biased against women, as can be seen, for instance, in the binds that make both feminine and unfeminine terms derogatory for women: "sweet", "pretty" and "gentle" affirm femininity but also confirm weakness and compliance; "ambitious", "bold" and "vigorous" may cast women as strong and autonomous but also condemn them as unwomanly and anomalous.

The dramatic title of Australian scholar Dale Spender's book *Man Made Language* (1980) announces her view that "the English language has been literally man made and that it is still primarily under male control" (*ibid.*: 12), constructing and legitimizing male supremacy. Spender's general idea is that women and men generate different meanings, "that there is more than one perceptual order, but that only the 'perceptions' of the dominant group [men], with their inherently partial nature, are encoded and transmitted" (*ibid.*: 77). As a result, women's voices and their worlds are muted. Lacking the ability to express their experience in male language, they either internalize the male reality or are silenced.

This view raises many questions (some of which we shall pick up again in later chapters), including how men "literally" make language, and how any sense of a different reality is available at all under these conditions of control. But the claim that "equal-opportunity" responses to linguistic oppression fail to express the specificity of women's experience has resonated for several influential feminists, resulting in a struggle to retrieve an authentic and different woman's language. Both Daly and Adrienne Rich, for example, rejected the use of words such as "humanism" and "androgyny" as being too strongly inflected with male meanings to capture the authenticity of female life (see Hedley 1992). Indeed, Daly argued that some of the "neutral" words are more dangerous than overt sexism because they obscure women's existence and mask the conditions of oppression (1978: 24). Further, although their approaches differ, Rich and Daly share a quest for a new language that will allow women to understand and express their gynocentric selves. Daly, for instance, in *Gyn/Ecology* (1978) and *Webster's First Intergalactic Wickedary of the English Language* (with Jane Caputi, 1987), develops and promotes a plethora of surprising metaphors, puns, reconstructions and revivals of old meanings: "Hags", "Harpies", "Crones", "Spinsters", "a-mazing Amazons", "unwooed women", for example, are her heroines, and they "weave" a "hag-ocracy" "crone-logically" in resistance to "stag-nation". For Daly such terms destabilize destructive stereotypes, and can invigorate and empower women in their journey beyond the boundaries of patriarchy:

> The point is to … release the Spring of be-ing. To the inhabitants of Babel this spring of living speech will be unintelligible … So much the better for the Crone's Chorus. Left undisturbed, we are free to find our own concordance, to hear our own harmony, the harmony of the spheres.   (1978: 22)

Linguistic strategies that call up women's difference in this way, however, run many of the risks encountered by difference feminists in both the sociopolitical and epistemological spheres. Critics worry in particular that this sort of "reversal of the hierarchy" response leaves the dominant paradigm intact (see Gatens 1991: 79–84): that it does nothing more than reinforce the special and *subordinate* place already allocated to women in language. That is, although difference linguists assert the strength and value of women's alternative reality, the claim of difference – under the weight of traditional understandings of women – plays straight back into traditionalist and anti-feminist views. Such co-option is especially likely when some of the more specific characteristics claimed for women's language echo those ascribed to women by the tradition. For example, Daly's notion that women's language expresses women's special affinity with nature, and their intense engagement of passions and imaginative capabilities, may appear irrational and incomprehensible to male-identified language-users (as the quotation above perhaps confirms). In addition, as some critics have noted (Lorde 1984b; Morris 1982), this project of liberation leaves out those women who do not see themselves in Daly's "Spinsters" and "Amazons", along with those of other races and cultures.

Once again the "damned if you do, damned if you don't" bind of equality and difference can be seen stalking feminist responses to linguistic oppression. Women have the choice of a superficial erasure of offensive words that fails to capture the extent of the problem or the politically problematic assertion of their distinctiveness. This analysis, however, also oversimplifies the complexities. After all, the outcry against inventing new names and reclaiming archaic meanings suggests that these kinds of changes are indeed disruptive, and many feminists have welcomed the liberatory potential of participation in the ongoing possibilities of meaning-making. Yet even if women could achieve the project of developing a new, non-oppressive woman's language, from a practical perspective the separation from publicly recognized discourse seems to be self-defeating. If the "Crone's Chorus" is to go on "unintelligibly" on its own, it will surely be unable to challenge effectively women's oppression. In order to effect significant change it is necessary to engage intelligibly with the dominant discourse, not simply to refuse it.

Beyond equality and difference

Another influential feminist response to the problem of language starts from an alternative analysis of the way language encodes sexual difference. Challenging early "common-sense" ideas that meaning is attributable to a known relation between word and thing or idea, structuralist linguists argue, following the work of Ferdinand de Saussure (1966), that the relationship between language and reality is not the simple mirroring implicit in the kind of view Spender articulates in *Man Made Language* when she argues that the different realities of different groups generate different languages. Rather, language establishes meaning and the identities of things and people through its network of differentiations and equivalences. (The oppositional relationship between the words "woman" and "man", for instance, is intrinsic to their meanings.) Hence, while a common-sense humanist view understands that individual speakers call up the prior reality of the world and their identities as they speak – this is the kind of assumption that underlies both equality and difference responses to women's linguistic oppression – this structuralist view understands the connection between language and reality as roughly the other way round: it is the (relationships between) words that call reality into meaningfulness. Such thinkers thus contend that although separate items in the vocabulary of a language may be amenable to change, it is impossible to alter the deep structure of oppositional relations that determines, for example, that a "woman" is "not a man".

This is a difficult idea to grasp but the following example may help to clarify it. The adoption of the title "Ms" for women instead of "Miss" or "Mrs" was promoted so that women, like men, would no longer be obliged to reveal their marital status (and sexual availability) through their titles and so this aspect of their identities would no longer take centre stage. However, the structuralist analysis shows that since the web of associations and expectations produced by the connections between words affects their meanings, this move is doomed. While altering one's title, say from "Miss" to "Ms", may superficially hide one's marital status, this single change fails to affect the myriad other social and linguistic relationships that keep the significance of female marital status in place. So the importance of marital status to women's identity remains intact and instead the new title "Ms" brings with it an additional set of associations that link it, for example, with notions of irritating and grandstanding feminists. As a result, women who use "Ms" instead of "Miss" do not dislodge interest in their marital status and they attract scorn for their outmoded political correctness.

What are the implications of these insights for the feminist struggle against women's oppression? First, although the structuralist understanding of the way language works might undermine the notion that language can ever directly represent who individuals are, it also seems to suggest that radical change is impossible. That is, although people's identities are dependent on their positioning within linguistic relations and are to this extent changeable, the overarching hierarchical relationship man–woman – along with associated binaries such as strong–weak, culture–nature, mind–body – that construct woman as the opposite (lack or absence) of man seems just too complex to alter. This sounds like depressing news for feminists. However, some theorists who accept structuralist arguments, most notably French thinkers Julia Kristeva, Hélène Cixous and Luce Irigaray, reject this conclusion. Instead, as we consider again in Chapter 2, they champion (in differing ways) the strategic potential of a female or feminine linguistic practice that can unsettle the grounds of this ubiquitous binary that grounds women's oppression.

These responses rely on a complex body of psychoanalytic and poststructuralist theory that deals with the complicated phenomenon of language acquisition and use, and the mysteries of the relationship between unconscious and conscious processes. It is beyond our scope to go into this work in any detail here, although we shall say more about these developments in Chapters 2 and 3, which deal with the problems raised by bodily existence, sexuality and desire. The gist of their move, however, rests on the view that theorists have underestimated the potential to bring unconscious and repressed processes in language acquisition and use into conscious articulation. Accordingly, while they accept that a male-biased system – that defines positive values by way of contrast to their negative others – structures language and thought, they focus attention on those aspects of language that normally go unnoticed. For example, Kristeva (1982, 1997) highlights those aspects of rhythm, intonation, flow and gaps in rationality that disrupt binary logic, along with the phrasing, patterns of pauses and uses of jargon and obscenities that create loves and hates, feelings of rejection and inclusion. Cixous (1981, 1986) and Irigaray (1985b), in their turn, focus on the elisions, omissions and ambiguities of writing, the spaces between words, on what is not said, and the multiple possibilities of interpretation. The idea is that while male bias cannot simply be refuted in the name of women – a notion championed by difference feminists – an alternative "feminine writing" can not only foreground the unconscious, non-dualistic and repressed dimensions of expressions, but destabilize the entire pattern of asymmetrical oppositional thinking. From this perspective, the label

---

Hélène Cixous (b. 1937)

An immensely prolific writer and the author of well over seventy works – including theoretical works, novels, poetry, plays, essays and articles – Hélène Cixous is known as one of the "French feminists" (despite being born and raised in Algeria). She was the founder of the experimental Université de Paris VIII at Vincennes in 1968, as well as the Centre de Recherches en Etudes Féminines (the first centre of its kind in Europe) in 1974. Along with Luce Irigaray and Julia Kristeva, Cixous is credited with developing a poststructuralist feminist theory inspired by psychoanalysis that focuses on the issue of sexual difference in language. In this vein Cixous is particularly known for her concept of *écriture féminine*, women's writing, which she sees as enabling the positive representation of the feminine (including women's bodies and sexuality) and, thereby, the subversion of masculine symbolic language. Such a possibility is brought to the fore in her well-known essay "The Laugh of the Medusa" (1976), where she deploys a fluid erotic syntax and new images and puns in order to celebrate women's differences and release their bodies and sexuality from the masculine order. Although, as we shall discuss, such views seem to border on essentialism, Cixous herself stresses that men as well as women can access *écriture féminine* (she contends that the work of Jean Genet, for example, is an exemplary instance of *écriture féminine*). Other works translated into English that have been influential for feminist theory include *The Newly Born Woman* (with Catherine Clement, 1986), *Stigmata* (1998), and the selections in the volume *The Hélène Cixous Reader* (1994).

"feminine writing" – "*écriture féminine*", as Cixous calls it or, following Irigaray, "*écriture de la femme*" – is used not to designate language that represents the different or authentic voice of women but is rather a different possibility for positioning individuals (whether male, female or hermaphrodite) with regard to language.

This kind of response to the problem of oppression – aiming to undo the effects of oppression in women's lives by tackling its source in the deep and often unconscious structures of desire, thought and language – while certainly undermining some of the difficulties of equality and difference perspectives, is not without its own difficulties. Some of the criticisms it draws mirror those levelled at the earlier "women's language" strategy and indeed the differences in the two approaches are often elided (see Young 1990). That is, even though the theorists concerned may insist that "feminine" is simply a metaphor for what is repressed, feminine writing still seems to call up some of the same female qualities of its predecessor – for example, radical difference in logic, closeness to nature and bodily existence – that comfortably permit the continuing rationalization of women's marginalization. Other critics worry about the utopian and romantic dimensions of such a radical response: its creation of a substitute world to escape the discomfort and ambiguity in women's lives (Moi 1985; Nye 1988). Perhaps most importantly, however, the complexity and abstractness of the theories on which the strategy relies, and their dependence on analyses of deeply submerged and unacknowledged aspects of women's lives, greatly limit their sociopolitical efficacy.

Further conundrums

This points to a key issue in feminist attempts to counter "the problem that has no name". Specifically, when superficial attempts at reform backfire or are not far-reaching enough, an obvious move has been to search for more encompassing structures of inequality. (This pattern has been played out with regard to challenging women's oppression not just in the social domain but at the level of deep structures in understandings of both knowledge and language.) In the case of language, however, the move to look for its oppressive logic deep in the realm of socio-psychic development has had the tendency of both severing the project from its immediate practical context and drawing it into complexities that make reconnection difficult. Despite the need to develop new ways of writing, speaking and thinking in order to challenge the dominating masculinist order, radical questioning of the global structures of language and consciousness may be too far removed, too long-term and too revolutionary a project in face of the pressing harms of more concrete social inequities (Young 1990). Alternatively, the complexity of such a project may be self-undermining by rendering it unintelligible to the women for whom it has been developed (Cameron 1992).

As a result, feminist thought may seem to have wandered into high-level academic reaches that have little impact on the practical task of reforming the oppressive social conditions that burden women's lives. A reply to this criticism, however, is that no response strategy "is ever adequate to itself" (Colebrook 1999: 139). Radical approaches may over-reach but piecemeal changes do not rethink the grounds of oppression, which reminds us that challenging the grounds of women's oppression entails keeping the possibilities of liberation wide open. Understanding feminism requires, in other words, understanding the limits and opportunities of differing strategic responses, an insight that we shall see demonstrated over and over again in the following chapters as we unpack some of the further dimensions to women's oppression and feminist critique.

Summary of key points

- The equality–difference debate underpins much feminist thinking about social and material oppression. Equality feminists challenge the private–public dichotomy and the sexual division of labour, demanding equal rights and responsibilities in all aspects of social life for women and men. However, "equality" is often defined in masculinist terms.
- In contrast, difference feminists call for a revaluing of the values, interests and practices of women, seeing them as equally valid to those of men. A criticism of this approach is that it affirms women's difference at the expense of adequately challenging their subordination and marginalization.
- Another focus of feminist thinking about oppression has been the male bias of knowledge about women's situations and the world more generally. Some feminists have called for a revisioning of the concept of objective knowledge that takes account of women's experience and perceptions, while others suggest that the biases of those who claim so-called objectivity always taint their claims.

They argue for understandings of knowledge that recognize that objectivity is contextual and mediated by frameworks of thought and language.

- Feminists have therefore examined how language has contributed to the oppression of women through the use of binarized models, the generic "he" and supposedly neutral nouns and adjectives that place masculinity as the norm. More radical approaches have addressed the meanings attached to words, as well as the structural relationship between words. Still others have called for "feminine writing" as a different way of positioning individuals in terms of language.

two

Embodiment

The problem of the body

Having spent Chapter 1 unpacking some of the deep structures at work in the oppression of women and considering how feminists have tried to address these, it is time now to discuss the impact these structures have had on actual embodied women. Hence, although "the problem that has no name" might remain multifaceted, it is clear that it directly affects those with female bodies, albeit in diverse ways. Possessing a woman's body has meant, for instance, not possessing the right or capacity to control everything that happens to or is expected of that body. Women's bodies are, after all, like their lives, affected on all sides by various forms of explicit and implicit social, political, legal, symbolic and discursive control. Women cannot rely, for example, on having the right to decide whether or not to start, continue or terminate a pregnancy, or even whether or not to have sex. They also cannot easily prevent being valued and/or objectified on the basis of their physical appearance and how that appearance matches up with prevailing – and perhaps even impossible – cultural norms and ideals, including those based on colour and race. (The Barbie-doll phenomenon, the jezebels and mammy stereotypes, many people have argued, have a lot to answer for.) Finally, the specificity of women's embodiment (in all its diverse forms) has not always been recognized by social, political and legal institutions, whether with regard to, say, employment or legal representation on issues of sexual harassment or discrimination, or when pregnancy ends up being considered an illness requiring "sick leave" rather than some other kind of special consideration, or when violence against women of colour is seen as somehow mitigated on the basis of their being part of a different culture.

This chapter thus aims to tease out some of the most important ways in which the body has been problematic for feminist thought. To begin with, however, in order to stress the significance of embodiment for feminist thought, we shall briefly outline the longstanding tendency in western thought towards the erasure of the lived significance of bodily existence, an erasure that has been accomplished through a mix of dualistic theories and resultant disciplinary practices. We shall then go on to explore the way these theories and practices have worked socially and culturally to effectively categorize and devalue women's bodies. In particular we shall focus on cultural representations of femininity, reproduction and mothering, and how certain ideals of human nature and beauty (ideals that have also fed the discriminatory practices addressed to those perceived as bodily abnormal, disabled or aged) have affected them. These issues bring us in turn to consider some feminist revisionings of the body inspired by psychoanalytic and poststructuralist ideas, along with a consideration of the way legal and sociocultural discourses have depicted the female body.

The drive to transcend bodily existence

What western philosophers have had to say about the body or about the experience of embodiment has been surprisingly minimal given that everyone experiences the world as an embodied being. Indeed, for many thinkers of the philosophical canon embodiment is simply an unfortunately necessary condition. When they mention it at all, the body is mostly described as something that needs to be overcome or transcended, something that stands in the way of people realizing themselves as properly human. Far from arguing that embodiment suggests a need for individuals to identify themselves with their bodies, the western canon has mostly argued that people would better understand themselves in terms of a soul–body or mind–body distinction or dualism, and further that they should then identify themselves – or that which is most integral to making them themselves – with the soul or mind. After all, many philosophers argue, without the invigorating and informing spark of soul or mind, a person would only be an essentially passive body that would be incapable of anything more than simply occupying space or fulfilling instinctual urges. Hence, despite occasional challenges, the history of the body in the canon primarily depicts a deepening alienation and/or transcendence of the fully human from the body. According to this philosophy, it is the mind or soul that really counts, a point the ancient Greek philosopher Plato has Socrates stress: "[I have spent] all my time going about trying to persuade you, young and old, to make your first and chief concern not for your bodies nor for your possessions, but for the highest welfare of your souls" (1997a: 30a–b).

Overall, then, this dualist tradition has worked to rank minds and bodies hierarchically, and has argued with few exceptions that bodies are either sources of inferior pleasure and achievement, a distraction or even an irrelevance. However, while this tradition spells out a certain distrust of embodiment, it may not necessarily entail a problem for feminist thought and its struggle against women's oppression. While some theorists might argue that the focus of the dualist tradition on the soul or mind does not help the feminist cause against the subordination of women, this tradition does not hinder it either. After all, if human beings should conceive of themselves as being essentially mind or soul, then surely the precise nature of the body that houses this soul is as irrelevant as the body itself. Whether male or female, black or white, abled or disabled, people need to transcend their bodies.

Unfortunately, however, the situation is not so simple, as an argument stating that certain types of bodies actually impede the realization of the highest level of humanity more than others typically accompanies dualist theories of minds and bodies. For example, while Plato argues in several dialogues – in particular in the *Republic* and the *Meno* – that the only real difference between men and women is that women possess weaker bodies, he also suggests that this weaker body, with its engagement in childbirth and child-rearing, means that women find it harder to overcome their body focus. Hence, as he puts it, the worst possible role model for a young man aiming to best refine his soul and reason would be "a woman, young or old or wrangling with her husband, defying heaven, loudly boasting, fortunate in her own conceit, or involved in misfortune or possessed by grief and lamentation – still less a woman that is sick, in love, or in labor" (1997b: 395d–e). Why is such a woman the worst possible role model? Because women are – as a result of their specific embodiment as women – inevitably more challenged than men by the discipline needed to focus on the refinement of their souls and their reason. As such, they are seen in their embodiment to possess all the traits Plato wishes no one to have. Of course this does not mean that no woman could refine her soul and reason in the required manner.

Plato in fact explicitly makes the point in the *Republic* that women may indeed transcend their body focus, but he admits that in order for this to be possible, women would need to have their domestic duties taken from them (*ibid.*: 460d). Although Plato can be seen here to blame not so much women themselves for their body focus – rather blaming their conditions – subsequent thinkers have argued that women's actual embodiment as women entails their inability easily or properly to develop their souls or minds. That is, women are not only thought to have weaker bodies but – by virtue of being women – weaker wills and a stronger sense of their bodies.

Reaping the effects of dualism

This marks the scene of a central issue in this problematic. The dualist tradition not only denigrates bodies but, most importantly for feminist thinkers, it has typically depicted women (and certain groups of men) as being more closely conjoined with and influenced by body than mind. It therefore argues that women are unable to exercise and refine their minds, to be full persons, in the same way that men supposedly can. Indeed, as American philosopher Susan Bordo writes, the "bodily spontaneities – hunger, sexuality, the emotions – seen as needful of containment and control have been culturally constructed and coded as female" (1993: 205–6). This association of women with the body and its "spontaneities" has been enough to depict women as at worst lacking reason, or at best possessing only a limited or complementary, domestically oriented form of it. This latter view is expressed clearly by French philosopher Jean-Jacques Rousseau (the target of Wollstonecraft's critique) in his 1762 educational treatise *Émile*: "A perfect man and a perfect woman should be no more alike in mind than in face" (1911: 321–2); and "The search for abstract and speculative truths, for principles and axioms in science, for all that tends to wide generalization, is beyond a woman's grasp" (*ibid.*: 349).

Despite Wollstonecraft's challenges, and those of later thinkers, this sort of position lasted well into the twentieth century, with a range of theorists arguing that women were biologically incapable of the same development of their minds and reason as men, and that black women were even less capable of such development than white women. Much of the justification for this view is centred on women's sexuality and role in reproduction, with menstruation, pregnancy and lactation all suggesting a body out of control and incapable of being subdued by reason. For instance, even into the twentieth century, western cultures have linked the womb (*hystera* in Greek) with hysteria. Not only, however, are women's bodies perceived to be more bodily than men's – and their minds accordingly weaker – the messy, leaky uncontrollability of their devalued bodies has also been a source of fear and anxiety, a possible risk to selfhood and in some cases global survival. (Think, for instance, of all the ritual prohibitions that menstruating women have been the target of and the forcing of birth control on third-world women in order to stem "unsustainable" population growth; see e.g. Hartmann 1987; Connelly 2008.) Thus while embodiment itself would not seem to lead to the oppression of women – men, after all, have bodies too – the corresponding assumptions regarding the possession of a woman's body have done so.

Feminist thought, then, faces several large challenges arising from these assumptions and theories. For a start, there is the way these theories have come to be understood as ratifying a whole complex of hierarchical binaries where male is to female as mind – or reason – is to body, and so forth. According to this complex, it is only a small shift to see rationality conceived not simply as an overcoming of body, but "as transcendence of the feminine" (Lloyd 1984: 104). This brings us to the situation where mind and reason – as the most important traits and norms of humanity – are traditionally associated with (white) maleness, while embodiment is associated with femaleness, a dynamic that devalues both embodiment and femaleness. Cixous outlines this hierarchical opposition clearly in her influential essay "Sorties":

> Father/Mother
> Head/Heart
> Intelligible/Palpable
> Logos/Pathos
> Form, convex, step, advance, semen, progress.
> Matter, concave, ground – where steps are taken, holding- and
>   dumping-ground.
> <u>Man</u>
> Woman
>
> Always the same metaphor: we follow it, it carries us, beneath all its figures, wherever discourse is organized. If we read or speak, the same thread or double braid is leading us throughout literature, philosophy, criticism, centuries of representation and reflection. (1986: 63)

Not only is this complex deeply entrenched – to the point that some feminists have argued that it is an integral part of western thought itself – but it seems on the surface nearly impossible to change. After all, do we not want to keep reason as one of our most defining and desired traits? Is the capacity to use reason not what it means to be properly human? Hence, the first problem for feminist thought is how to challenge the way women's perceived body focus has categorized and "inferiorized" them. The second associated challenge concerns the systematic devaluation of bodily experience more generally. That is, feminist thought has asked how to give social form and meaning to the contradictions and ambivalences of bodily existence. This last challenge has become even more important as it has been realized that embodiment as female is only one issue and that other bodily markers, such as race, have also been hierarchically understood. As African-American feminist Patricia Hill Collins points out, "race and gender oppression may both revolve around the same axis of disdain for the body" (1990: 171). Additionally, pervasive ableism (unjustified privileging of the abled over the disabled) among both feminists and non-feminists is evidence of the difficulties of coping with bodies that are perceived to be more bodily than others.

As we noted in the Introduction, Beauvoir's *The Second Sex* outlines one extensive and detailed analysis of the use of the conception of woman as body to classify and devalue women. Here, as we saw, Beauvoir based her overall analysis on what she diagnosed as a fundamental problem: the way women have historically been depicted as the exemplary Other, as that against which the mind- and reason-oriented male subject defines himself. However, some feminists have contended (although there is disagreement here) that rather than trying to rethink the female body in a more positive light, Beauvoir ended up arguing for its transcendence. On this view, women want (or rather should want) to take the male path of celebrating mind over body. As we have seen earlier, liberal thinkers dating back to the eighteenth century, including Wollstonecraft and Mill, have also, in varying ways, proposed similar strategies. Women, according to these thinkers, only display such a marked body focus because they have lacked – or been denied – the opportunity properly to cultivate their minds, their reason and their humanity. Such opportunity, these thinkers agree, is the basis for all properly human virtues and dignity. (Note that these early liberal thinkers are not arguing for equality between men and women as such; rather, that women can be better wives and mothers if they transcend at least part of their body focus.) Such a view does not, however, unsettle this hierarchical mind–body dualism. Rather, when transformed into the more recent liberal call for equality, it assumes that differently sexed bodies have no real relevance with regard to who people fundamentally are, to the point that it takes women and men to be essentially the same. The question is whether these assumptions do in fact hold. In other words, is the body being undervalued? Once again in this problematic of embodiment, however, we see the strategic difficulty for women discussed in Chapter 1: should feminists argue that women are essentially the same as men, thereby acceding to understandings that fail to take their bodily particularity seriously, or should they challenge the devaluation of the body and risk reinforcing women's marginalization through their focus on a devalued aspect of existence?

Despite the long history of women's devaluation on account of perceptions of their bodily nature, an early feminist response to this problematic has been a resounding yes to the idea that the body has been inappropriately undervalued. Not only have women and men alike undervalued the body, but a stronger and more positive body focus might be able to provide the resources to challenge the celebration of mind at the expense of body that is so prevalent in western thought, and thereby perhaps develop alternative modes of being and knowing. Specifically, however, it was not until the late 1960s and early 1970s that feminists radicalized the liberal feminist call for equality, citing the need to emphasize the (bodily and psychological) differences between men and women. These feminists – who, as we noted in Chapter 1, have typically been designated as difference, gynocentric, woman-centred or cultural feminists – turned their attention to understanding the body as the locus of women's difference and oppression, developing on this basis a wide array of strategic projects that aimed to rethink the standard mind–body division. In general terms, all of these projects challenged the traditional conceptual disregard for the body. They worked to reinstate and revalue the (female) body, arguing that theoretical abstractions such as disembodied minds are an obstacle to women's liberation. Feminists, they said, needed to deal with embodied and sexed individuals in all their specificity (a point we shall also consider in detail in Chapter 3):

> [T]he fear and hatred of our bodies has often crippled our brains. Some of the most brilliant women of our time are still trying to think from somewhere outside their female bodies – hence they are still merely reproducing old forms of intellection. There is an inexorable connection between every aspect of a woman's being and every other; the scholar reading denies at

her peril the blood on the tampon; the welfare mother accepts at her peril the derogation of her intelligence.

(Rich 1977: 285)

These sorts of insights mark a call to revalue (female) bodily experience: "We must begin, as women, to reclaim our land, and the most concrete place to begin is with our own flesh" (Morgan 1993: 77). In other words, the key feminist response strategy here requires that women learn to see their bodies and themselves differently. As we shall see, this strategy has taken a myriad of different forms.

Revaluing the female body

The step taken by radical difference feminists, such as American Adrienne Rich (and Mary Daly), is both to endorse the differences between woman and man, and to transform and revalue the meaning of such terms as "woman" and "female". Reversing the traditional mind–body valuation, feminists such as Rich celebrated the female body as a site of strength, power, endurance and creativity, particularly with regard to its sexuality and capacity for motherhood. As Rich reminds us, however, this celebration has a prerequisite of "control of our bodies" (1977: 39), and as she notes in her influential essay "Compulsory Heterosexuality and Lesbian Existence" (1984), this control has been and still is contested. Male power, she says, which is typically concerned with controlling reproduction, marriage and motherhood, has historically denied woman control of her body through a wide variety of measures, including:

> clitoridectomy and infibulation; chastity belts; punishment, including death, for female adultery; punishment, including death, for lesbian sexuality; psychoanalytic denial of the clitoris; strictures against masturbation; denial of maternal and post-menopausal sexuality; unnecessary hysterectomy.
>
> (1984: 218)

Although Rich was writing some twenty-five years ago and the specific measures she mentions are largely a thing of the past, in the west at least, it is important to recognize the more general point she is making, which is that historically and cross-culturally women have not had full control over their bodies. And, while it is evidence of a major feminist

intervention that some women in the west can now take the choice to
have comfortable, healthy bodies for granted, many western women still
suffer social constraints – the pressure to be a certain bodily shape, for
example – on account of their ideological relationship to embodiment,
a point we shall consider in some detail later in this chapter. (We shall
also pick this issue up in later chapters, particularly Chapter 6 where
we talk about non-western cultural restraints on women's bodies in
the context of western feminists' political responsibilities.) At the same
time, women's desired control of their own bodies is only the first step
in trying to recuperate the (female) body. In Rich's words, we need
to "touch the unity and resonance of our physicality ... the corporeal
ground of our intelligence" (1977: 39).

Such ideas have also underpinned a range of practical aims. For
instance, women's desire for control over their bodies informed such
projects as the Boston Women's Health Book Collective's publication
of *Our Bodies, Ourselves* in 1973, which saw women fighting against
the entrenched opinion of medical institutions that women knew little
about the workings of their own bodies. Other projects also critiqued
the intrusion of medical technologies into more and more aspects of
reproduction. These projects aimed to re-vision assumptions and practices in the field of women's health by utilizing women's own accounts of

their experiences to empower them in their decision-making regarding their own health. Contemporary feminist criticisms of biotechnological advances that seem to see women as little more than wombs with the potential for successful impregnation also reiterate these aims.

Further attempted recuperations of the female body emerge from some difference feminists' celebrations of maternalism. Here thinkers have drawn on the uniquely female role in procreation and argued that the possibility and/or experience of bearing children and providing nurturance can underpin calls for non-violence, pacifism, ecological sustainability and the development of a better world. (Think, for instance, of the Mothers of the Plaza de Mayo, a group of women – mothers – who, in their peaceful protests regarding the abduction of their children by the then military government of Argentina in what is known as the Dirty War [1976–83], stimulated the movement for democracy in Argentina; see e.g. Femenia 1987; Bouvard 1994.) Maternal thinking, in other words, can suggest a revaluation of both the female body and its significance for the public good. (Related arguments, while not assuming that "mothering" is a strictly female activity, contend that "maternal practice is a 'natural resource' for peace politics" [Ruddick 1989: 157].) Note, however, that such recuperation is problematic in so far as it runs the risk of reaffirming conceptions of women that have been used to oppress women. That is, it ignores the fact that many conceptions of motherhood – those common in African-American communities, for example, such as matriarchs, mammies, hot mommas and so on – may be just as constraining as enabling. In addition to these projects, aims for revaluing the female body and female bodily experience have also inspired a further range of feminist responses, including those revisionings of the body influenced by psychoanalysis and poststructuralism, along with feminist critiques and revisions of the body's legal and social status.

Psychoanalytic and poststructuralist-inspired revisionings of the body

As mentioned in the Introduction, an important and influential contribution to feminist thought has developed under the aegis of psychoanalysis, albeit a comprehensively rethought psychoanalysis compared to that first put forward by Sigmund Freud. Its starting-point, however, is Freudian, expressly Freud's claims that a person's understanding of their self is inevitably entwined with their embodiment. That is, Freud argues that the ego – the I – is produced only through the gradual separation and differentiating of oneself as a separate body from one's primary carer – typically one's mother – and the outside world. More specifically, the I or ego, he insists, is a result of the individual coming to perceive body boundaries and how separate bodies can be in relation to each other. On this basis, regardless of the fact that Freud addresses a very different problem from that considered by many mind–body dualists, it does seem that with this analysis he sets out an understanding of the I that stresses rather than devalues the importance of bodily experiences.

At the same time, Freud still gives a hierarchical account of the difference between women and men, in so far as, for him, this difference rests on one becoming aware of the lack, or the possession, of a penis. Described in terms of the working of the Oedipal complex (as outlined in the Introduction), for Freud this emerging awareness of bodily difference – played out in the child establishing his or her similarity to or difference from the mother – is what eventually produces feminine and masculine subjects. (Freud also argues that these feminine and masculine subjects differ in accordance with their different resolutions of the Oedipal complex. Specifically he contends that women, once aware of their lack, remain not only envious of the penis, and are therefore less just, but are bound up in and reactive to their relations with particular others – father, men, child(ren) – in the family, and are therefore less capable of reasoning impartially.) Such insights have, obviously enough, been controversial to many feminist thinkers. In particular the idea that women are defined via their lack rather than through any positive conception of bodily difference was enough for many feminist thinkers to reject psychoanalysis as inherently patriarchal. Yet other feminists have found psychoanalysis to be a rich source for thinking about the significance of women's bodies. As Jane Flax puts it, "For all its shortcomings psychoanalysis presents the best and most promising theories of how a self that is simultaneously embodied, social, 'fictional, and real', exists and changes" (Flax 1990: 16).

Some of Freud's suggestions concerning psychosocial development have provided feminist thinkers with a basis for describing women's differences from men in positive terms. American theorist Nancy Chodorow's work *The Reproduction of Mothering* (1978) is an important example of this turn, as is developmental psychologist Carol Gilligan's *In a Different Voice* (1982). For both of these authors, the fact that girls resolve the Oedipal complex differently (Freud thinks incompletely) from – and develop what Freud calls a "lesser sense of justice" to – boys is in no way a problem. (The theory contends that through resolution of the Oedipal complex male subjects become independent, active and self-directed, while female subjects are typically more relational and other-directed, even passive.) Indeed, in Chodorow's words, this difference is a positive thing. Unlike boys, for instance, girls develop "a stronger basis for experiencing another's needs or feelings as one's own (or of thinking that one is so experiencing another's needs and feelings)" (1978: 167). This, she argues, means that women possess "a basis for 'empathy'" that has been "built into [their] primary definition of self" (*ibid.*). Gilligan similarly argues that because of their different psychosexual development women have a "greater orientation" than men "toward relationships and inter-dependence" (1982: 22). This constructed capacity for empathy and awareness of interdependence, both Chodorow and Gilligan agree, is a productive capacity, much more so than the abstracted and aggressively autonomous mode of being that men have been socialized into. They propose that it suggests another way of understanding the human condition, a way that is just as "real" and as potentially world-altering as that based on notions of independence and autonomy. In the words of Nancy Hartsock:

> The female construction of self in relation to others leads ... toward opposition to dualisms of any sort, [the] valuation of concrete, everyday life, [and the] sense of a variety of connectedness and continuities both with other persons and with the natural world. (1983: 298)

Such embodied, interdependent and relationally oriented experience is therefore described by Hartsock as the starting-point for a much better way of life than that founded in "abstract masculinity" (*ibid.*). Bodies and embodied relationships, in other words, count. They are fundamental, producing the basis for a healthier, less disconnected social world reconceived in relational terms, a world that does not denigrate everyday embodied life. (We come back to these points in Chapter 5.)

There are, however, other feminist revaluations of female embodiment derived from the psychoanalytic description of human development. One of the most influential of these is that developed by Hélène Cixous and Luce Irigaray, whom we introduced in Chapter 1. Cixous and Irigaray were influenced by French psychoanalyst Jacques Lacan's re-reading of Freud via structuralism, along with the poststructuralist insights of another French theorist, Jacques Derrida. Briefly, both Lacan and Derrida remind us – admittedly in very different ways and

> **Luce Irigaray (b. 1932)**
> Another of the French feminists (although actually born in Belgium) and a
> linguist, philosopher and psychoanalyst, Irigaray sees sexual difference as
> one of the fundamental issues that people need to face and rethink. She has
> been principally concerned with two interrelated projects: first, to show and
> undo the exclusion or suppression of the feminine in both the philosophical
> and psychoanalytic canons that has been brought about by its conceptuali-
> zation as the other or negative of the masculine; and secondly to express that
> feminine in its own positive terms as a substantively different possibility from
> that entrenched in the male-biased hierarchical tradition, a possibility that
> allows masculine and feminine to be genuine peers. These aims inform and
> propel works such as *Speculum of the Other Woman* (1974), *This Sex Which is
> Not One* (1978) and *An Ethics of Sexual Difference* (1984), along with a range
> of other essays and books. Given that much of her focus is on reconceiving
> and expressing a feminine corporeal reality that, she contends, no culture has
> represented in its own positive terms, Irigaray's work develops by necessity
> new and different ways of speaking, new and different discourses. Challeng-
> ing traditional styles of philosophical writing, her work is highly ambigu-
> ous, elliptical, fragmented and poetic, aiming, in fact, to jam the theoretical
> machinery of the canon.

to very different ends – of the role of language or symbolic discourse in
producing (and, of course, disrupting) both meaning and subjectivity,
an issue we began to consider in Chapter 1 and that will be an ongoing
thread in subsequent chapters.

From these admittedly dense insights, French feminists have argued
that the typical role of language and culture has been to produce and
celebrate masculine subjects and male embodiment over feminine
forms. Their response has been to promote the subversion of this linguistic practice, and to champion the development and fostering of a
language that is able to express the specificity of the feminine, including that of female embodiment. (As we discussed back in Chapter 1,
however, this is not the development of a language somehow able to
express some "authentic" voice of women only.) After all, as Irigaray
notes in "Women's Exile":

> The question of language is closely allied to that of feminine
> sexuality. For I do not think that language is universal or neu-
> tral with regard to the difference between the sexes. In the
> face of a language, constructed and maintained by men only, I
> raise the question of the specificity of a feminine language: of

a language that would be adequate for the body, sex, and the imaginary of the woman. A language which presents itself as universal and which is in fact produced by men only, is this not what maintains the alienation and exploitation of women in and by society? (1977: 62)

Such a language would thus need to be able to express the multiple forms of female embodiment and the sexed specificity of corporeality. It is on this basis that Irigaray contrasts the self-touching two lips of female morphology with the unitary penis, contending that, for women, a language expressing their double morphology would be better able to relate to conditions of excess, fluidity and otherness than any language that stresses unity.

The production of such a language that remains continuously disruptive of fixed encodings of asymmetrical roles, however, is by no means a simple matter. Despite the difficulties, *écriture féminine* has been at the forefront of post-Freudian French feminisms, and its production has been based on writing the conventionally excluded bodily experience of female sexuality, an experience summed up by these thinkers, as well as by Kristeva, as *jouissance* (sensual bliss, orgasmic pleasure). *Jouissance* indicates a specifically female bodily energy and experience that exceeds – and thereby problematizes – its conventional negative positioning in the binaries of man–woman, masculine–feminine and mind–body. For Cixous, Irigaray and Kristeva the aim of writing and speaking *jouissance* underpins the whole project of *écriture féminine*, and represents the possibility of writing both a positive embodied female sexuality and a female imaginary. And this, as Irigaray concludes in "Women's Exile", is precisely what women need "to be recognised as bodies with sexual attributes, desiring and uttering, and for men to rediscover the materiality of their own bodies. There should no longer be this separation: sex/language on the one hand; body/matter on the other" (*ibid.*: 76).

As we have seen, then, *écriture féminine* aims to revalue the female body and bodily experience as exemplars of a possible ground for the subversion of conventional discourse and the development of a feminine discourse. Nonetheless the body described in the previous pages is one that theorists have initially understood in terms of the psychoanalytic assumption that there is in fact a basic sexual difference that is able to produce feminine or masculine selves. This assumption, however, is itself open to challenge. In addition, if difference feminists sought to challenge the liberal feminist aim of women joining men in their quest to transcend the body by presenting alternative conceptions of women that actually valorize and celebrate women's bodies and bodily experiences, then these alternative conceptions would seem to be open to charges of essentialism. ("Essentialism" is an important concept in feminist thought and we shall discuss charges of, and debates over, essentialism in more detail in Chapter 4. At this stage, however, it is sufficient to note that the term is used to refer to positions that rest on the belief that there are common characteristics – metaphysical, biological or social – that are universally shared by and define all women.) *Ecriture féminine* and its celebration of women's bodies seem to rest on the (essentialist) belief that there is a specifically female nature shared by all women, a nature entailed by the simple possession of a woman's body. In other words, the charge of essentialism in this case is the charge of a kind of biological reductionism: a female body entails a female nature. This charge is particularly problematic in so far as it suggests that difference-based feminist arguments end up reinstating the very biological determinism that has historically been the central justification of women's oppression.

The challenge to these difference-based conceptions here, then, is whether there can in fact be an expressly masculine or feminine anything, and furthermore whether this masculine or feminine something is the most significant bodily marker for a person. That is, is sex really more significant than race or abledness, for example? In addition, these conceptions have been challenged as to whether (despite common-sense understandings) there can be any bodily given, such as that of sexual difference, at all. That is, is there really such a thing as a woman or, for that matter, a man? Is there really such a thing as a woman's body, or a woman's sexuality? Further, do these positions project a western, nuclear family version of psychosexual development as the universal conditions for male and female embodiment? Such challenges come from (at least) two fronts. There are those raised by women of colour who contend that sex is far from standing alone as the most significant marker in understanding bodies; that rather it intersects with other, just as significant, markers to do with race, ethnicity and so forth. In such a view, any attempt to stress only the sex of a body is itself an unjustifiable, unjust and impossible reduction of a much more complex situation.

There are also challenges made by feminists inspired by the anti-essentialism of poststructuralist thinking, who reiterate Derrida's (and Lacan's) basic claims that any identity – whether feminine or masculine – is nothing more than a precarious and temporary effect of difference, and that difference itself is by no means unproblematic. Indeed Derrida takes great pains in his work to show that so-called absolute binary differences such as mind–body, man–woman or masculine–feminine are by no means so absolute or as obviously demonstrable as might be thought. There is and can be, he stresses, no strict and impassable division between the two sides of a binary. For instance, while it may be thought in common-sense terms that there is an obvious difference between women's and men's bodies, maybe it is not that clear. Maybe the prototypical woman's and man's bodies are the two (albeit common) extremes of a continuum with gradations in between culminating in hermaphrodism and/or androgyny in the middle. It seems clear that simply possessing or lacking such physical characteristics as breasts, vaginas, wombs, penises and so forth does not a woman or man make; nor does having the capacity for menstruation, lactation, gestation or sperm-production. After all, not every woman has periods, becomes pregnant or breastfeeds, just as not every man is capable of sperm production, while some men can in fact lactate.

With regard to these poststructuralist-inspired revisionings – we consider the proposals made by women of colour in depth in Chapter 4, particularly those detailed by African-American feminist thinkers bell hooks and Audre Lorde – anti-essentialist feminist theorists such as Americans Haraway and Butler, along with others such as Australian philosopher Elizabeth Grosz, have aimed to understand the body and embodiment as able to disrupt all essentialist and binarist conceptions of it. That is, they want to propose a notion of the body that does not imply any unchanging essentialist or naturalized identity for sexed, or indeed raced or abled, bodies. Haraway, for instance, in her poststructuralist essay "The Cyborg Manifesto", elaborates a body that can only be understood as blurring all the so-called absolute differences (male–female, nature–culture, human–machine, to name a few): a cyborg. Specifically Haraway insists that the cyborg body undermines all human dreams of true or fixed identity while affirming what she sees as actual lived experience of partiality, ambivalence and hybridity. As she writes in this essay: "a cyborg world might be about lived social and bodily realities in which people are not afraid of their joint kinship with animals and machines, not afraid of permanently partial identities and contradictory standpoints" (2004: 13).

Haraway thus says that cyborg imagery can perhaps "suggest a way out of the maze of dualisms" that has typically been relied on to explain the human experience of being in the world (*ibid.*: 39). That is, she contends that the figure of the cyborg prevents people from seeing the body as an unproblematic wholeness. Bodies and bodily experience, Haraway stresses, simply do not fit into binarized models; they do not have such clear-cut boundaries. Now, it is worth noting here that Haraway is not challenging everyday bodily experience as such. As individuals, we do, after all, know whose fingers were just slammed in the door, and we usually know who is who when it comes to having sex. Haraway's point is rather that a range of technological innovations can both challenge and alter the "natural" body: the body that is either female or male, say. For example, natural bodies might be female or male, but artificial hearts and other prostheses are surely neither. (Even prosthetic breasts and testicles are not female or male as such.) Natural bodies can also not only be resexed through surgery or even performance, but can also have lived experiences online – in avatar form or not – of being the other or even no sex.

Butler sets out a second non-essentialist conception of the body that is inspired by poststructuralist tenets. Critical of the traditional philosophical tendency to "miss the body or worse, write against it" (1993: ix), Butler is also wary – as is Haraway – of how a large proportion of feminist thinking inspired by psychoanalysis assumes a "compulsory heterosexuality". That is, these psychoanalytically inspired descriptions of lived experience seem to see the maintenance and coherence of identity as resting on a normalized fixed opposition of male–female, where the definition of each category depends on the difference between them and the relation of each to the other. More specifically, while Butler accepts that "bodies only appear, only endure, only live within the productive constraints of certain highly gendered regulatory schemas" (*ibid.*: xi), she argues that "there is no gender identity behind the expressions of gender" (1990: 24). On this view, there is no stable pre-cultural bodily given, such as a sexual identity, that provides the basis for the production of feminine or masculine subjects. Rather – like the relationship between reality and language discussed in Chapter 1 – bodies are simultaneously the effect of and condition for norms. Norms script the performance and production of bodies, just as bodies condition normative possibilities. This is a difficult idea to grasp but basically Butler is saying that "pure" bodies – whether our own or those of others – are never encountered directly in the world. A framework of expectations always mediates perceptions of bodies, and while these expectations are to some degree based on the physiology of bodies, cultural values and norms also shape them. This, of course, is why people can be surprised (or perhaps even offended or brought to laughter) to find a body that they see as strongly male or female behaving in ways that do not seem to fit with their expectations. (Films such as *The Crying Game*, *Boys Don't Cry* and *Kinky Boots*, for instance, exploit these ideas when central characters confound taken-for-granted expectations of their bodies.)

Many feminists, however, still see these poststructuralist conceptions of bodies as problematic. In particular, despite their challenge to the oppression of stereotyped bodily differences – of there being distinctively female or male identities and experiences, say – these conceptions seem to make it difficult to talk explicitly of the problems still faced by actual embodied women. For instance, although it is important to recognize that women's experiences and being in the world cannot be simply ascribed to some conception of the uniquely feminine (a point we consider in further detail in later chapters, in particular in our consideration in Chapter 4 of the intersecting of sex with race, ethnicity, class, etc.), it is perhaps even more important to be able to talk of the bodily experiences and abuses that are common to women because of their embodiment as women. That is, surely feminist discussions of women's bodies need to be able to consider effectively such actual experiences as rape and violence against women, without becoming bogged down in issues of cyborgs, ambivalence and irony. As a result, many feminists have claimed that the kinds of anti-essentialist revisionings of the body we have just considered have at best been unable to contribute to, and at worst actually worked against, being able to effectively challenge sex-specific bodily abuses. A further point is that this kind of abstract theorizing not only distracts women from critically examining the difficulties in their lived experience, but may alienate those who might otherwise work for feminist projects. In particular, this criticism is often levelled by protagonists for women of colour, poor women, women of ethnic and cultural minorities, disabled women, third-world women and so forth – all those, for instance, who may not have the luxury of being able to play ironically with their bodily identities, given their pressing need for social justice – against what is seen as the elitism and abstraction of white academic feminisms with their high-flown theories. For these feminists the emphasis should be on improving the actual lived experience of women, along with their social and legal status as women: something they believe that poststructuralist arguments have forgotten or ignored.

Legal and social depictions of women's bodies

> When a woman married [as of 1803], her legal identity merged into that of her husband; she was civilly dead. She couldn't sue, be sued, enter into contracts, make wills, keep her own earnings, control her own property. She could not even protect her own physical integrity – her husband had the right to chastise her (although only with a switch no bigger than his thumb), restrain her freedom, and impose sexual intercourse upon her against her will. (Williams 1997: 72)

As Wendy Williams sets out in her essay "The Equality Crisis" (1997), and as we have discussed in Chapter 1, it is no exaggeration to say that until the twentieth century women were largely invisible in the eyes of (western) law and other sociopolitical discourses. Accordingly, a key focus for many feminists has been to make women's bodies and experiences visible to the law, as it is only then that the law can protect them. This project has seen concerted action to change the legal status of women, to have the law recognize them as autonomous persons with the right to determine what happens in their own lives and to their own bodies in whatever country they may live, and to have adequate protection against violation of their bodies. (We consider these and related issues regarding women's autonomy and human rights in more detail in Chapters 5 and 6.)

As we saw in Chapter 1, this action focused initially on achieving for women the same legal rights as possessed by men: achieving, in other words, full legal equality through the institution of equal rights amendments and anti-discrimination statutes. However, these statutes, while certainly effective in delivering formal rights and visibility to women (at least in western countries), and in promoting justice systems that are apparently neutral with regard to sexual differences, have also given rise to the recognition of a further problematic. Specifically, what do equal rights mean when applied to differently bodied women and men? For example, is it appropriate for pregnant workers to have special workplace rights? Should maternity leave be a right, given that it rests on a sex-specific state of embodiment? After all, under a strict equality of rights vision, maternity leave can be – and in fact has been – seen as constituting an unjustifiable special treatment for women, which can further be seen as discriminatory towards men. Also, what happens when a struggle for women's rights needs to also encompass issues such as race, ethnicity and culture as well as sex? For instance, what would equal rights mean to a Muslim woman who has accepted *purdah* (complete segregation of the sexes in social life) on religious and cultural grounds? Such problems are complex and have led many feminist thinkers to argue that the legal visibility of women must mean the legal visibility of actual embodied women in all their diverse circumstances. This requires, as American legal theorist Catharine MacKinnon contends (e.g. 1993), a new practice and theory that recognizes all the specificity of women's embodied experience.

Such an aim has broader implications. Feminists such as MacKinnon are arguing that the conventional legal understanding of a person with rights is simply too abstracted from concrete reality to be particularly useful, in so far as it has been constructed from the basis of the imaginary disembodied masculine mode of being in the world. Such a person, they say – supposedly a self-sufficient individual who hardly needs to attend to her or his own physical needs, let alone those of others – is a chimera, a dream, an impossible construction of neutral disembodiment. After all, as Grosz has reminded us, there is no "body as such: there are only bodies – male or female, black, brown, white, large or small – and the gradations in between" (1994: 19), and these bodies have physical needs, as do those of the people close to them. Hence the law needs to recognize and uphold people's actual state of being embodied in the world. As MacKinnon puts it, law needs to participate in reality, the "reality of a fist in the face, not [that of] the concept of a fist in the face" (1993: 369). (We consider some of these bodily realities – sexual assault and rape, sex trafficking and violent pornography – in Chapter 3.) Such an argument is, of course, not only relevant for feminists arguing for the legal recognition of women's sex-specific experiences. It has also been at the basis of arguments calling for the law to recognize the experiences and rights of the bodily abnormal, disabled and aged. As British disability theorist Jenny Morris notes, "Disabled people – men and women – have little opportunity to portray our own experiences within the general culture, or within radical political movements. Our experience is isolated, individualized" (1991: 8).

These are important points. That is, feminists have clearly shown through their critiques and proposed revisionings of the legal and social status of women that acts of violence against women, along with instances exemplifying the lack of recognition of women's sex-specific experiences, are not just a matter of individual acts or instances. Rather, they result from systemic oppression and are thereby framed by and dependent on that tenacious view that women are somehow of lesser status than men. This being so, even when the law does participate in reality, when visibility has been achieved for women, it has still been problematic, a point made tellingly in Margaret Atwood's dystopian novel *The Handmaid's Tale*, when the Handmaid Offred, reflecting on the rigid roles set for women in her society – Wives, Econowives, Aunts, Marthas, Handmaids, Jezebels and Un-women – says "Mother, I think … You wanted a women's culture. Well now there is one. It isn't what you meant, but it exists" (1986: 127). That is, while there has certainly been an increase in the legal recognition of real embodied women, it needs to be acknowledged that this very recognition has also led to further modes of oppression, further modes of ordering and constraining women. In this respect, one of the most debated and problematically visible bodies is that of the pregnant woman. Pregnant women – along with the whole issue of reproductive rights – have become the stars in a range of legal, medical (particularly obstetric) and public-health discourses, many of which have actually functioned not to support but to further constrain their autonomy.

To begin with, we mean by reproductive rights both the "power to make informed choices about one's own fertility, child bearing, child rearing, gynecologic health, and sexual activity" and the "resources to carry out such decisions safely and effectively" (Correa & Petchesky 2003: 88). In other words, reproductive rights are a core part of women's right to control their own bodies. Such rights have also been one of the star issues for feminist politics, in so far as the role of women in procreation has been used not only to prevent their full participation in social life (voting, accessing further education and certain kinds of employment, etc.) but also to justify their lack of control over their own bodies and destinies. (We pick up these points again in Chapter 5.) For instance, in the west, if a pregnant woman chooses to engage in certain "high-risk" activities (drinking and drug-taking, say, or ignoring medical advice), she faces probable censure, perhaps even imprisonment. She may find that her foetus seems to carry more weight – and be more visible – than she does – or is – within the legal system. She may also find that others have the power to force her to carry an unwanted pregnancy to term, to decide when and how she gives birth, whether she gets to keep the baby, or even whether she is fit to be a mother or should be sterilized. A case in point regarding these latter issues is that even now in certain jurisdictions not all women are permitted to access reproductive technologies (single women and lesbians have, for instance, typically been unable to access in-vitro fertilization). Women may also face cultural and religious prohibitions (and economic pressures) that limit access to contraception and abortion (at the time of writing there is a move afoot in the United States to redefine the termination of a pregnancy – abortion – so as to include contraception in the definition) or, as we mentioned earlier, they may be subject to coercive birth-control policies and forcibly sterilized on grounds of race or cognitive and physical impairment. Pregnancy and the potential for pregnancy thus place women under continuing scrutiny, and they are fair game for social and legal expressions of disapproval should they overstep what is permitted to them. (In a perverse turn on the sort of social and legal visibility for women's bodies that MacKinnon champions, some body-policing discourses blame feminists for the increased visibility of pregnant women.)

Surveillance of women's bodies is not only the experience of pregnant women; it also affects all women via cultural ideals of proper, perfect or beautiful bodies. For instance, elaborating on the issue considered above, there has been a strong tendency in the past to see the proper adult female body in terms of pregnancy and motherhood. That is, the proper female body is the childbearing and child-rearing body. This is the body, then, that is protected when women are barred from certain jobs: active combat as a soldier, say, or handling certain substances. There is, however, another issue related to this ideal of the proper adult female body that is important here. This relates to the portrayal and reception of the non-maternal or childless female body within society. Since the reference point for adult female identity has traditionally been motherhood, the question arises whether it is actually possible to understand the female body in positive terms apart from its reproductive capacity. This is a pressing issue for contemporary feminisms for several reasons. First, as we have seen, a significant thread in feminist theory from the 1970s explicitly argued for revaluing the female body on the grounds of its reproductive capacities, even though some might see this as an alienating move. Secondly, it is fair to say that women who are not mothers have tended to be either invisible or portrayed as deviant in many theories of female development as well as in many social practices of womanhood. For instance, many conceptions of women in both western and non-western cultures are linked with mothering; for example, the Madonna, the earth-mother, as well as the matriarch and mammy stereotypes that have an impact on African-American women. Finally, at the beginning of the twenty-first century, there is also a growing proportion of women who have either been unable to or have chosen not to have children. This group – women who are childless and/or child-free, depending on their own self-perception – is testimony to the need to rethink contemporary social, cultural and theoretical expectations of female identity and embodiment. After all, as one forty-year-old woman quoted in Mardy Ireland's book *Reconceiving Women* states, "There's nothing in me that has to have a child to feel like a woman" (1993: 132). Given these points, then, the following question needs to be asked: should these women really be portrayed as unbalanced, deficient, selfish, unrepresentative, overly masculine and/or somehow threatening to society? (Think of the characters played by Glenn Close in *Fatal Attraction* or Sharon Stone in *Basic Instinct*, or Lionel Shriver's portrayal of Eva's maternal ambivalence in her novel *We Need to Talk About Kevin*.)

What this shows us is that women's bodies are expected to be not only healthy and well-functioning but to correspond with cultural and social ideals of first maternity, and secondly – in the west at least – youth and beauty. Such ideals, as many feminists argue, are far from innocuous, given that they set in motion and justify practices that order and discipline women's bodies. Importantly, however, these are not necessarily instances of forcible disciplining. Rather, drawing on French historian and theorist Michel Foucault's insights about the operations of power in the contemporary world, the idea here is that cultural ideals regarding beauty circulate throughout society (via, for example, the fashion, cosmetic, music, video, film, celebrity and pornography industries) and through this circulation are affirmed, normalized and internalized, with the result that women engage in practices of self-disciplining. Hence, as Bordo writes:

Through the pursuit of an ever-changing, homogenizing, elu-
sive ideal of femininity – a pursuit without a terminus, requiring
that women constantly attend to minute and often whimsi-
cal changes in fashion – female bodies become docile bodies
– bodies whose forces and energies are habituated to external
regulation, subjection, transformation, "improvement".

(Bordo 1997: 91)

There is a range of implications here. First, as Bordo shows us, such
ideals give rise to sets of "*practical* rules and regulations" (*ibid.*: 103)
through which the (female) body is trained into cultural normalcy. Only
bodies that have been so trained are seen as "normally" feminine and
culturally acceptable. And only bodies that have been so trained are
seen as able to participate successfully in a culture that has come to
understand and represent femininity in terms of a particular bodily
appearance. Indeed, analyses still suggest that the idea that women
whose appearance corresponds to appropriate norms of beauty possess
greater social power than those whose appearance does not so conform
is widely shared.

Correspondingly, it is common to think of the untrained or inadequately trained body as deficient and needing to be "made over", to use
the language of a plethora of television lifestyle programmes, women's
magazines and cosmetic surgery advertisements. Such training, however, as many feminists have pointed out, is so all-encompassing given
its often blatantly unrealistic goals that most women will in fact fail to
fulfil all the requisite criteria. The ideal female body, which is currently
required in the west to be youthful, virtually hairless, toned, healthy-

---

Susan Bordo (b. 1947)
An American feminist and philosopher whose work contributes to feminist,
cultural, literary, gender and body studies, Bordo primarily focuses on exploring the ways theoretical discourses and contemporary culture have had an
impact on and determined the (female) body in particular ways. More specifically, she argues that cultural coding has worked to normalize particular
expectations and evaluations regarding the material body. She suggests not
only that the creation of cultural expectations that associate body shape and
size with both social position and moral rectitude produces self-monitoring
and self-disciplining bodies, but that such expectations can be tied to a
range of social issues related to the body, for example, eating disorders, cosmetic surgery, beauty and the impact of the media. Her main works include
The Flight to Objectivity (1987), *Unbearable Weight* (1993), *Twilight Zones* (1997)
and *The Male Body* (1999).

looking, pre-pubescently slender and smooth-skinned but with ample breasts, and perfectly made up and attired, is itself a dream. It is the body, in effect, of Barbie and her friends, whose bodily dimensions are completely unattainable to many owing to either lack of time and resources or age and body type. Only some can attain such a body, usually at the expense of health (think extensive cosmetic surgery, eating disorders, exercise compulsions, fertility problems, hormonal imbalances and unrelenting self-castigation) and, if they approach achievement of this goal, its maintenance requires ever-increasing effort and discipline. Such effort is evidenced, for example, by Madonna, who, despite her rigorous eating and exercise regimes (she is reported as following a macrobiotic diet and exercising for a minimum of three hours a day), is nonetheless still castigated at the age of fifty for having "unattractive" prominent veins on her arms and hands.

Despite the unrealistic and unhealthy nature of this dream for the majority of women (shown clearly in the 2007 British Channel 4 television documentary *Superskinny Me: The Race to Size Double Zero*, in which two British journalists documented their attempts to reach size zero), such ideals nonetheless seem to be having an impact on more and more women. Of concern, for instance, is the way younger girls and women from non-western cultures internalize western ideals regarding the female body. With regard to girls, feminists such as Bordo (1993) have argued that examples of the impact of these ideals are found in the increase in the development of eating disorders and vitamin and mineral deficiencies in younger and younger children (particularly but not exclusively girls), and the general sexualizing of toddlers' and young girls' fashion (clothing, make-up, hairstyles) matched by the tendency of the fashion industry to promote a pre-pubescent appearance for women. In another twist, with regard to non-western women, feminists have suggested that these ideals are at least one of the factors at work in increases not only in skin and hair modification (typically lightening of both skin and hair, and hair straightening), but also cosmetic facial surgery and breast enhancement. For instance, a range of thinkers have proposed that eyelid, nose and lip cosmetic surgeries are often being performed (in the United States, for example) on no other basis than to make facial features appear more western (see Kaw 2003). More drastic again is the boom in Chinese girls undergoing painful surgeries aimed at lengthening their legs to better match western standards (see Berry 2007).

The dream body – and the all-encompassing body focus – is thus a central problem for feminists and other thinkers concerned with making visible and "normal" all those with bodies that do not meet the ideal. It is owing to this concern that they have critiqued media representations of women (and men) if they consider those representations to be promoting unrealistic and unhealthy bodily ideals. It is also on this basis that they have worked for the amendment of equal rights and anti-discrimination legislation so as to protect the rights of those women and men with non-ideal bodies. Such concerns can also be discerned behind attempts to represent those with non-ideal bodies in a positive light (think, for instance, of such television programmes as ABC's *Ugly Betty* in the United States) and to show the real costs of the pursuit and maintenance of the ideal body.

At the same time, feminists have also striven to understand just how and why such ideals have become so prevalent. Here their analyses have of course varied, but several thinkers have stressed the apparent correlation between the increasing pressure on women to control the shape of their bodies and the development and success of the modern feminist movement. For instance, as American writer Naomi Wolf argues in *The Beauty Myth*, the "more legal and material hindrances women have broken through, the more strictly and heavily and cruelly images of female beauty have come to weigh upon us" (1990: 10; also see Faludi 1991). Here the idea is that although women have gained access to the public sphere, they are required – so as not to be a real threat to men – to engage in time-consuming practices of beautification not expected of their male counterparts in order to get and keep their jobs. Access into the public sphere comes, Wolf says, with the requirement of a "professional beauty qualification". The incorporation of this requirement into what feminist philosopher Sandra Lee Bartky calls the "fashion–beauty complex" (1990: 39) in turn consolidates (and normalizes) it. Bartky indeed suggests that the fashion–beauty complex is analogous to the "military–industrial complex" in that both are "major articulation[s] of capitalist patriarchy ... a vast system of corporations – some of which manufacture products, others services and still others information, images, and ideologies" (*ibid.*).

It is this combination of internalized ideals being fed by a "vast system of corporations" (*ibid.*) that makes challenging these norms so difficult. Certainly radical feminist and lesbian practice and theory called, for a time, for a taboo on feminine display and ornamentation; however, such tactics often drew negative stereotyping and discrimination. For instance, according to Mihailo Markovic in his 1976 defence of the contemporary women's movement, the limitation of feminist thought was its "tendency to reject certain good things only in order to punish men

... There is no reason why a women's liberation activist should not try to look pretty and attractive" (1976: 165). This in turn means that while some feminists and theorists of body studies have accepted the need to resist or transform these cultural ideals as an imperative, there has been overall little agreement on how best to achieve these aims. Conversely, other feminists still embrace traditional norms of female beauty. Chilean author and feminist Isabel Allende, for example, has talked about the empowerment she gained from a facelift and her regret that she had promised her son she would not have another (Allende 2008). So while the aim is clear – an urgent need to "develop a truly liberatory feminist aesthetic of the body" (Bartky 2000: 329) – the solution is much less obvious. Is the best solution simply to work out how to challenge sexist cultural stereotypes and their entanglement within the forces of rampant capitalism? Or is the only real way out of this maze the development of new and quite different theoretical models and practical strategies, such as those produced by poststructuralist feminists?

Finally, the further question arises as to what impact these various proposed solutions have on the desiring and sexually active body, in so far as this focus asks us to move beyond considering the rights of varying bodies to considering what is right with regard to the intimate relations between bodies. This issue of desire and sexuality has been particularly problematic for feminist thinkers. What, after all, is the basis of sexual desire? Is it inherent in some physiologically based sexual difference or is it a matter of sociocultural construction? If the latter, how should sexualities and desires that push people to body modification be accounted for? Given feminist arguments analysing relations between men and women as oppressive towards women, is all heterosexual sexual intercourse constitutively oppressive to women? What about sexualities that desire some form of subordination (ranging from sado-masochistic sexual practices through to "harmless" rape fantasies)? More generally, what is the significance of pleasure and sexual gratification? All in all, it is clear that the interconnection of sexuality with gender inequality marks yet another problematic dimension of the "problem that has no name", and it is this dimension that we turn to in Chapter 3.

Summary of key points

- Under western thinking, human beings have long been encouraged to understand themselves in terms of a mind–body dualism, where the mind is celebrated and the body viewed as something to be transcended. As a result, western dualist thinking has largely ignored the significance of bodily experience and proposed that women's body focus – owing to their role in childbearing and child-rearing – prevents them from becoming "full persons". This has led to a devaluing of women's bodies that structures of oppression reflect.

- Radical feminists, challenging the traditional dualist hierarchy, revalue and celebrate the female body as a site of strength, creativity and sexuality.
- Psychoanalytic understandings of the self as essentially entwined with bodily experience, together with recognition of the role of language in producing meaning, have enabled feminists to re-vision women's bodies in relational, rather than disconnected, terms.
- However, poststructuralist feminists challenge the essentialism of psychoanalytic approaches, claiming that binary conceptions fail to encompass the lived bodily experiences of different women. They highlight the role of norms and cultural values in shaping social expectations about women's and men's bodies.
- Legal and social norms continue to control women's bodies, particularly in relation to notions of reproduction and the "ideal" woman's body. Such norms include the perception that women who fail to meet them are deviant or invisible, or needing to be "made over".

three

Sexuality and desire

What does it mean to be sexed and desiring?

It is no wonder that questions of the meaning and practice of desire and sexuality have vexed many feminist thinkers given the sorts of assumptions regarding women's association with the body we explored in Chapter 2. After all, if women are not clear on the significance of their bodily being, what precisely does it mean to be a sexed and desiring bodily being? Why have people typically been so convinced that particular types of sexed bodies dictate particular types of behaviour and sexuality? Does the possession of XX or XY chromosomes (or any other variation) really have an impact on people's behaviour, let alone on their desiring practices? What about same-sex desire? In addition, how should such desiring and sexually embodied practices as pornography, prostitution and sexual violence be understood? Probably more than any other, questions of sexuality and desire test contemporary theories regarding embodiment.

This chapter thus aims to tease out key feminist arguments concerning some of the presumed interconnections between embodied sex difference, sexuality and desire. More specifically, given both our constitutive sexed embodiment and the common assumption of a causal link between sex (in the sense of sex difference) and sexuality, feminist thinkers have argued that thinking about women's bodily being and their being sexed needs to be tackled in conjunction with thinking about what it is to be a desiring being. Starting then on a critical examination of the problematic of sex difference, we begin by unpacking feminist arguments challenging patriarchal assumptions that sexuality and desire are inevitably heterosexual, male-dominated and causally connected to sex difference (that is, that a certain sex results in a certain sexuality). As we shall show, these challenges to the patriarchal sexual economy – many of which have been presented in the context of debates around pornography and prostitution – arise from a diverse range of approaches that have a further impact on each other. These include the "sex war" debate between radical and libertarian feminists, feminist theories of social constructionism that assume a distinction between sex and gender, queer theory's identification of the constraints of heterosexist understandings of sexuality and gender, and transgender and intersex questionings of binarized sex and gender difference. We then come back again to the question of desire and how a range of feminist thinkers have approached it given the way many of the above projects attribute indefinability and mobility to the categories of sex and gender. Finally, we reflect on how these various explorations of sexuality and desire have shaped and changed feminists' self-understandings and their understandings of the world they yearn for.

Embodiment and sex difference

To begin with, as we have seen in Chapters 1 and 2, which sex you are is understood to be very significant with regard to the life you are expected to live. Understood in terms of the bodily differences between females and males, sex difference matters. Further, when thought of this way, sex difference seems to be fixed. A fundamental biological condition, sex difference has implications for who you can be, and any attempt to challenge it runs, for many, counter not only to common sense, but also to nature. This, however, is perhaps to move too fast. Certainly many feminists have agreed that sex difference is fixed (although, as we shall find, many other feminist thinkers have challenged even this), but, they stress, what this sex difference means for how individuals live their lives is not fixed. It is not necessary to understand simply being either female or male as a recipe or formula for a certain lifestyle, let alone a certain expression of sexual desire and practice; and to argue that it does is to fall into the trap of biological essentialism. Nonetheless it is common to read sex difference as one of the key indicators of how life is to be lived and experienced. Being female has meant a range of things (as has being male), and one of the fundamental implications of this understanding that there is a natural sex difference has been with regard to how human beings understand themselves and each other as sexed and desiring beings. It has, after all, been assumed that being a particular sex entails a particular (hetero)sexuality.

This traditional conception of sex difference underpins the various formulations of patriarchy. That is, it has been on the basis of an assumed natural sex difference that patriarchy has worked to regulate the interactions of females with males in both the private and public realms. Patriarchal assumptions include such notions as: women requiring the protection of men; women being better suited than men to caring professions (for instance, nursing, teaching, care of the aged, etc.) and less suited to high-level high-stress professions (women will not be as reliable or as committed, probably leaving to have children, care for children or other relatives, etc.); mothers naturally wanting to – or being expected to want to – stay at home with young children; and that all women will want to have children (and can be accused of selfishness if they do not). As we know, however, feminist thinkers have systematically challenged the "properness" of these assumptions, arguing on a variety of fronts against patriarchal understandings of women and of how the world should be seen. One issue that is of particular importance, however, and that has also posed an ongoing challenge for feminist thinkers, is that of patriarchal understandings of sexuality and desire. Now there is, of course, a whole range of issues here but they include the following assumptions: women and men are naturally attracted to each other (human beings desire "the opposite sex"); men naturally possess a stronger sex drive than women (or women's sexuality is more repressed than men's), making coercive sexual activity "normal"; sexuality is focused around penetration and male pleasure (anything else is "foreplay"); and "real" sexual stimulation for women is vaginal not clitoral. These assumptions, along with other related ones, have also been analysed by feminist thinkers as endorsing a further range of ideas regarding power, privilege and inequality. And this nexus of assumptions around sexuality and power – making up what could be called a patriarchal sexual economy – has been famously described by radical American feminist Kate Millett as patriarchal "sexual politics" in her influential 1969 book of the same name.

The patriarchal sexual economy

What, then, is this patriarchal sexual economy? Most simply it rests on what feminists and other thinkers have diagnosed as an assump-

Kate Millett (b. 1934)
An artist, writer and activist, Kate Millett is the author of one of the founding theoretical texts of second-wave radical feminism, *Sexual Politics* (1969). Here Millett argued that the assertion of patriarchal power is constitutive for all relationships between females and males. This makes them fundamentally political but, Millett observes, patriarchy has configured this power dynamic – what she calls sexual politics – not only as hierarchical (males dominating females) but as in fact "natural" and therefore not open to challenge or change. According to her analysis, this patriarchal sexual politics has its origins in the institution of the family and promotes itself through its naturalization and endorsement within a culture's fiction, a point she demonstrates through readings of the sexism and misogyny in the work of D. H. Lawrence, Henry Miller and Norman Mailer. Counter to this, Millett contends that this patriarchal sexual politics, far from being natural, is a culturally endorsed mix of ideological control and force. Millett's later autobiographical works, including *Flying* (1974), *Sita* (1977), *The Basement* (1979) and *The Looney-Bin Trip* (1990), continue the feminist project of showing up personal relations as inextricably political.

tion of "compulsory heterosexuality". Used first by Rich in her essay "Compulsory Heterosexuality and Lesbian Existence", which we referred to in Chapter 2, this term describes a system in which heterosexuality – women being sexually attracted to men, and vice versa – is not only accepted as the norm for sexual desire between adults (on the basis that it is the most common form of sexual expression), but is also understood to be innate, inevitable and "natural" (women and men are seen as "made" for each other) to the point that all other orientations and forms of desire are considered deviant and "unnatural". Compulsory heterosexuality, Rich suggests, then, is the main mechanism underlying and maintaining male dominance in a patriarchal sexual economy. After all, Rich continues, if heterosexuality were not presented as or perceived to be the "natural" form of desire and sexual relations, then the erotic choices and identities of both men and women might be very different.

This is not to say, however, that "compulsory heterosexuality" is a claim that all heterosexual practices are coercive, or even that heterosexual activity is simply the result of being compelled by this norm. Indeed, many feminists argue that heterosexual relations can be free, authentic and empowering choices for women. It is nonetheless worth noting that the conception of heterosexuality as the norm also lines up with one of the most influential theorizings of desire and sex difference in the twentieth century: that developed by psychoanalysis. Here the idea is that because women's psychosocial development is marked by what Freud called "penis envy" (girls' socialized envy of the attributes of masculinity), women will naturally come to envy and desire men as possessors of what they lack. Under this model, then, heterosexual desire is both part of and the result of the proper socializing – that is, Oedipalizing – of women and men. (Indeed, for many psychoanalytically influenced therapists – and despite Freud's own comments on the matter – men and women who have not identified as heterosexual have been perceived as immature or sick, needing to be "cured".)

Regardless of its basis, the key point here is that the patriarchal sexual economy privileges heterosexuality. However, as Millett observed, the patriarchal sexual economy rests on and requires another key assumption: that of there being a hierarchical relation between the sexes in which "male" counts more. In its most extreme, although alarmingly pervasive, expression, this patriarchal hierarchy is maintained through violent means. For instance, cross-culturally a variety of practices such as sexual harassment and assault, wife beating, honour killings, female genital mutilation, dowry deaths and preference for sons is used to police females' secondary position in human relations. Such violence-based subordination rests on patriarchal beliefs about male domination; and its shocking prevalence sustains and naturalizes the deep-seated perception that it does not matter that women are seen to be less worthy than men. (For this reason the elimination of violence against women globally is one of the most urgent concerns of feminist activists and United Nations organizations.)

In a less dramatic, although perhaps equally invidious, form, it is possible to conceptualize the heterosexist hierarchical relationship between males and females as a male privilege in sexuality where what matters most is male activity and pleasure, and female pleasure (if considered important) will automatically accompany the above sexual activities. The idea that sexual access and "sexual ownership" (by men, to and of women) are always justifiable one way or the other (Stoltenberg 2004: 402) neatly sums up these attitudes. In the words of radical human rights activist John Stoltenberg (also echoed in the plots of television series such as NBC's *Law and Order: Special Victims Unit*):

> Sexual owners can be heard to offer many justifications for their proprietary sexual proclivity: "It's men's nature … it's women's nature … it's God's will … it's her fault … it's manifest heterosexual destiny … she wants it … I need it … she loves it … she deserves it … whatever turns me on … she's getting paid for it …" (*Ibid.*: 402–3)

This attitude has implications for a wide range of issues. In the past (that is, at least, in western societies) it has played into the assumption that there was no such thing as rape within marriage; husbands legally possessed total sexual rights to their wives regardless of their wives' desires. It has meant that rape that looks like sex has often not been defined or upheld as rape (indeed, in some places rape is only rape – and not sex – when it is accompanied by physical signs of violence), and that if a woman dresses or behaves "provocatively" then she cannot justifiably argue that she has been raped. It has played into the idea that such practices as pornography and prostitution are unproblematic or even potentially empowering for both men and women, despite many feminist analyses having seen them as typically and overwhelmingly oriented to male-privileged sexuality. It has played a role in the legalization of certain forms of prostitution (usually brothels rather than streetwalkers) in some parts of the world, with the effect that many people see prostitution as a legitimate work choice (indeed at the time of writing, reports [see e.g. Reilly 2008] tell of university students within Australia prostituting themselves to pay for their tertiary education). And, again, it has played a role in the development of a multi-billion-dollar global industry trafficking women for the sex trade.

In addition, racist politics further entrench male-privileged sexuality, both normalizing and heightening its effects in so far as the inheritance of colonialism and slavery produces perceptions of black women and women of colour as available for sexual use. Think here of the long history of rape and sexual violence towards women of colour and indigenous women by white men; the stereotypical perceptions of black women as being more highly sexed than white women (and therefore able to "take" more roughing up) and of Asian women being sexually compliant; the way the fashion industry still presents black women as "animalistic" or "wild"; and, of course, the disproportionate number of women of colour in the sex trade.

Although all of these and many other implications of naturalized male sexual privilege within an assumed compulsory heterosexuality have received feminist attention (and the issue of sexual violence against women of colour by white men is one of the most important issues for black women's sexual politics), one of the areas most hotly contested by western feminists in particular has been the cluster of issues around pornography and prostitution. These issues have marked a range of highly contentious divisions between feminists in so far as some women see such practices as coercive while others see them as harmless and in some cases liberating. On the one hand, for example, is the view of radical feminists inspired by the work of American feminist theorists and activists Andrea Dworkin and Catharine MacKinnon – and foreshadowed by Susan Brownmiller in *Against Our Will* (1975) – who have argued vehemently against pornography and prostitution since the early 1980s. These thinkers contend that both pornography and prostitution, far from being "natural" results of healthy sexual impulses, are exploitative, defamatory to and degrading of women, that they encode and promote a pornographic ethic comprising misogynistic and dehumanizing views of women and a permissible sexual violence towards women, and that overall they work to support and naturalize the assumption of male sexual privilege endemic to patriarchy. They contend that pornography and prostitution construct women "as things for sexual use" and their consumers as "desperately" wanting the possession of women (MacKinnon 1997: 167). This is a view that activist and social worker Rus Ervin Funk echoes in his story of coming to oppose pornography and prostitution:

> While looking at pornography, I developed a way of looking at women. I developed, if you will, a pornographic ethics. After looking at pornography, I did not look at women as colleagues, potential friends, or allies, or with any kind of gaze based on justice or caring. I looked at women based on how I compared them to the man-made images of women I saw in the magazines or on the videos. The women I saw on the street, in classes, at meetings, etc. became simply "fuck-able" to varying degrees. I looked at them and thought about the things that I would like to do *to* (not *with*) them sexually – things that I fantasized they would enjoy, but the ultimate focus of which was my own sexual fulfilment.   (Funk 2004: 339)

On this view, then, pornography and prostitution both cause and constitute harm (note that these analyses typically focus on heterosexual models, although they can still be pertinent to queer pornography and prostitution), damaging not only individuals but the chance of developing truly just and equal relations between the sexes in the realms of sexuality and desire. That is, Dworkin and MacKinnon and others (male as well as female) argue that pornography and prostitution effect the reduction of sexuality and desire to simply "fucking", and a "fucking" that privileges men's desires and subordinates, if not silences, the legitimacy and even the possibility of women's desires. In other words, pornography and prostitution privilege a model of sexual dominance and perceived ownership of others' bodies that comes to be seen as normal, justifiable, even harmless (a model that even comes to stand for sexuality as a whole, thus explaining the backlash against Dworkin and MacKinnon, who were misread by some as saying that all sexual intercourse is harmful, the equivalent of rape). Such norms, radical feminists argue, need to be challenged and resisted. This means recognizing that both pornography and prostitution are in fact harms in themselves as well as causing real harm – that they do more than offend sexually repressed prudes – and that the sexual ethic of ownership and male-privileged "fucking", exemplified in most pornography and prostitution, need not be accepted either as an inevitable part or the whole of human sexuality.

This, however, has not been the only response to pornography and prostitution by feminist thinkers. Some "pro-sex" protagonists, in response to what they see as the "kill-joy", "anti-sex" or, derogatorily, "vanilla sex" views of radical feminists such as Dworkin and MacKinnon

---

Andrea Dworkin (1946–2005) and Catharine MacKinnon (b. 1946)
An influential radical feminist writer and activist, Andrea Dworkin was a passionate critic of male power and sexual privilege. She is most famous for her work on pornography and institutionalized inequalities in heterosexual practices, arguing that male sexual privilege was at the root of pornography, rape and other forms of violence against women. Such attitudes to women, she contended, enabled what she called a "gynocide": a cultural holocaust against women. Dworkin presented these views in a variety of books and essays, including *Woman Hating* (1974), *Pornography – Men Possessing Women* (1981), *Intercourse* (1987), *Pornography and Civil Rights* (1988) and *Life and Death* (1997). In the early 1980s (hired by the Minneapolis city government) she teamed up with American lawyer and radical feminist Catharine MacKinnon to draft the Antipornography Civil Rights Ordinance, which defined pornography as a violation of women's civil and human rights. MacKinnon's view that in a male-dominated society sexual relations between women and men amount to the sexualization of dominance and subordination also underpinned her internationally recognized work on sexual harassment, *Sexual Harassment of Working Women* (1979), which influenced US legislation prohibiting sexual harassment on the grounds of discrimination. Her later analysis of pornography is published in *Pornography and Civil Rights* (1988), and she has also written more generally on feminist politics in *Feminism Unmodified* (1987) and *Toward a Feminist Theory of the State* (1989). Dworkin and MacKinnon's anti-pornography ordinances were ultimately defeated in the Supreme Court of the United States in 1986, but their uncompromising position has drawn public attention to a range of issues regarding sexuality and desire, and polarized feminist debate concerning such issues.

have argued that such views amount to censorship of the full array of human sexual expressions and desiring practices. This "pro-sex" or libertarian position argues for taking all varieties of desire and sexual pleasure as legitimate expressions of sexuality, and practising whatever gives people pleasure and satisfaction. Such thinkers propose that, as long as they are consensual, pornography and prostitution can be embraced as possible "sites of freedom, adventure, and rebellion" (Stark 2004: 278), and that prostitutes (and female stars in pornography) may be independent professionals (like self-proclaimed whore, porn star and sex guru Annie Sprinkle) who not only work for a living by engaging in consensual sex but free up conventional ideas regarding sexuality. They suggest that the Annie Sprinkles of the world remind women that they need not be the passive tools or recipients of a male-oriented sexuality. Celebrating sexual freedom, experimentation and transgression (including consensual forays into sado-masochistic practices), pro-sex feminists argue in support of free choice in sexual practices and the removal of censorship from the domain of sexuality. Or, to put it otherwise, they contend that feminist attempts to regulate sexuality actually work to support patriarchal assumptions of female sexual passivity.

In their response to the pro-sex contingent – and this is very much an ongoing debate – radical feminists have argued that the notion of "choice" here is highly problematic. Specifically, they contend that it is not at all clear whether all sex-workers have in fact made a free choice to enter the industry or whether their choice has been informed by such factors as poverty, racism or classism; or whether they were somehow tricked or misled. (For instance, one of the commonest stories regarding the entry of girls into the sex trade is that they were promised some kind of "better" life. This might be the promise of escaping domestic violence, of being able to earn enough money to send some back home to support a family, of having a life in the first world, of finding a husband, or even that of simply attaining the necessities for life.) In this vein they would question whether those students, say, who support themselves via prostitution or exotic dancing – and who claim that they made free choices based on economic factors (making the most money in the least time) – really made authentically free choices or were coerced. For radical feminists, then, coercion and commodification in the pornographic and prostitution industries are major concerns and they see them as issues that the pro-sex lobby has overlooked or minimized.

Of course not all pro-sex thinkers are as uncompromising as radical feminists might suggest, and many thinkers from both sides recognize that there are far more views available than to see women as simply either victims of patriarchal sexual control or free to express their sexuality in any way they please. For instance, some thinkers who are cognizant of the history of prohibitions of certain sexual practices (see Vance 1984; Snitow *et al.* 1984) have suggested that it is easy to subvert perspectives that see sexuality solely in terms of the expression of men's dominance over women into a stance that demonizes sexuality as the source of all social problems. The history of outlawing all but heterosexual sexuality in modern western societies, they argue, suggests that censorship of freely consented-to sexual practices (such as participation in prostitution and the production of pornography) runs the risk of being co-opted by conservative right-wing movements to promote traditional (patriarchal) values and to censor feminist opinion. (Lisa Duggan and Nan Hunter's *Sex Wars* [1995] documents Dworkin and MacKinnon's uneasy alliance with the moral right.) All (non-traditional) sexual practices of subordination (regardless of whether they are freely consented to and pleasurably experienced), as well as all same-sex practices, are vulnerable to this move. Even the provision of information concerning sexuality, reproductive control or lesbianism is a likely target.

Despite these dangers, anti-anti-porn positions also recognize the tension regarding where individual freedoms should and can legitimately be restricted in favour of other values such as a broader community good. Such thinkers thus make a distinction between what in "Sex War" (1984) American feminist philosopher Ann Ferguson has called "risky" and "forbidden" sexual practices. As Ferguson sees it, risky sexual practices are those that *may* lead to a dominant–subordinate relationship, while forbidden practices, conversely, *will* lead to such a relationship. Hence, on the basis of this difference, Ferguson contends that feminists should become more tolerant of risky sexual practices:

> Sadomasochism, capitalist-produced pornography, prostitution, and nuclear family relations between male breadwinners and female housewives are all risky practices from a feminist point of view. This does not mean that feminists do not have the right to engage in these practices. (1984: 112)

Nonetheless, regardless of what stance people take in these sex wars, what the debates show is that what is at stake is just what expressions of sexuality and desire are counted as legitimate. Further, despite their profound disagreement over this issue, it is fair to say that both radical and "pro-sex" feminists are looking for desiring practices and expressions of sexuality that transgress formulations founded on and restricted by patriarchal assumptions of male dominance or privilege. This, of course, is a much broader issue than the legitimacy or not of practices of pornography and prostitution (despite the significance of the latter in contemporary societies and in popular understandings of what feminism is all about). Indeed, it is an issue that takes us back to our starting-point in this chapter concerning just how natural sex difference really is. That is, can sex difference really stand as the basis of arguments for men "naturally" possessing a proprietary sexuality?

One feminist response to this broader question has been to suggest that even if sex difference is fixed, and people can all be assigned without question into one sex or the other, it is problematic to use this simple fact of people's bodily femaleness or maleness as the basis and justification for "properly" feminine or masculine behaviour in the realm of sexuality and desire (or anything else). Ideas regarding proper feminine and masculine behaviour, after all, have varied considerably over time and between different cultures. And it is this realization that has sparked what has probably been one of the most influential distinctions made by feminists: that between "sex" and "gender". More specifically, it is this distinction that has enabled many feminists to accept the fixity and facticity of sex difference, yet at the same time challenge the common-sense assumption that sex difference by itself entails and justifies certain behaviours. According to this distinction, there are two types of sexed body – female and male – that are then inscribed with and described in terms of social expectations. As British sociologist and writer Ann Oakley puts it in *Sex, Gender and Society*:

> "Sex" is a word that refers to the biological differences between male and female: the visible difference in genitalia, the related difference in procreative function. "Gender", however, is a matter of culture: it refers to the social classification into "masculine" and "feminine".   (1985: 16)

Here, then, "sex" relates to bodily differences, while "gender" is understood as covering everything about conduct, disposition and expressions of desire and sexuality. Everything, that is, that has proved to be variable across time and culture, where variability in what counts as proper feminine and masculine behaviour acts as the proof for gender being socially determined.

Social constructionism: separating gender from sex

A form of social constructionism, this view has been profoundly influential for many feminists. For instance, social constructionism allows feminists to argue that the differences in attitudes, worldview and behaviour between women and men do not arise from biological facts of nature but from deeply embedded social practices and traditions. That is, one's understanding of what it is to be and behave as a woman or a man is "not something innate or unchangeable, but rather something that is created by social and historical forces" (Gilbert 2001: 42). And it is on this basis that social constructionism has allowed feminist thinkers to envisage a non-patriarchal future for women and men, a future that has been variously described as androgynous, loving, plural, cyborg and as fully realizing and esteeming principles of equality, justice and human rights.

This idea that one's gender identity and performance – one's identification with and practice of norms of femininity or masculinity – is the result of social and historical forces has had an important role in recent feminist theory. For a start, it reminds us that expectations regarding behaviour are open to challenge and modification. For example, contemporary western social expectations for appropriate gender behaviour for both women and men are considerably different from even those of the 1950s. Western societies no longer consider it inappropriate or unnecessary for girls to gain a high level of education. It is no longer unthinkable or politically transgressive for women and men to share household chores of cooking and cleaning. It is no longer considered socially shocking or selfish for girls and women to work for their own independence and satisfaction rather than for that of their male partners; or for females to "kick ass" just as much as males (think of female action stars in both television and film: Buffy the Vampire Slayer, Charlie's Angels, Lara Croft and G. I. Jane; although there is of course the added "need" for "girls" who "kick ass" to still look feminine and attractive). It is also no longer considered as socially shocking (or deviant) for women to express sexual aggression, although this can still be a very fraught issue. The point is that gender and gendered behaviour is never cut and dried, a point famously made by Judith Butler in her 1990 classic *Gender Trouble*:

> Gender is a complexity whose totality is permanently deferred, never fully what it is at any given juncture in time. An open coalition, then, will affirm identities that are alternately insti-

tuted and relinquished according to the purposes at hand; it will be an open assemblage that permits of multiple convergences and divergences without obedience to a normative *telos* of definitional closure. (1990: 16)

What Butler is saying here is that gender identity can only ever be provisional. Not only is it reliant on sociocultural assumptions but people can and do take on gender identities and behaviours to suit their own purposes. For instance, they might utilize a range of different gendered behaviours depending on whether they are working, flirting, spending time with friends, caught up in a crisis of some kind, and so forth. Such an understanding of gender has also been of use for thinking about some queer and transgender issues. That is, if gender is the result of socialized rather than innate behaviour, whatever norms or rules it has can be broken (a point also recognized by pro-sex feminists when they argue in support of erotic transgressions). Women do not have to behave femininely, and men do not have to be masculine. Gender can rather be transgressed and/or mimicked, a possibility that can be seen in practices of tomboyism (and tomgirlism), cross-dressing, drag and, of course, by transsexuals and queers (gays, lesbians and bisexuals), all of whom demonstrate the potential for a multiplicity of ways of doing or performing femininity or masculinity or perhaps even genderlessness. (This last is a possibility championed by male to female transsexual and self-proclaimed "gender outlaw" Kate Bornstein in her classic book, *Gender Outlaw* [1994].)

Nonetheless there is an issue here that various feminist, queer and transgender thinkers have raised: is the doing or performing of a gender or genderlessness as easy as simply choosing to do so? After all, while it seems clear that the form of gender socialization individuals receive is contingent – based on when and where they are brought up – the fact that they are socialized in accordance with those factors is not. That is, people cannot fully choose their socialization given that it all starts well before the age they could conceivably make a choice. Hence any gender-crossing that people might do – that is, where performance of a gender is not matched by an individual's sex (and presumably also not matched by the gender they would have been initially socialized into) – is necessarily going to be problematic in so far as they would have probably missed out on some of "the subtleties and nuances of what is right, what is wrong, how to behave" within that gender (Gilbert 2001: 46). Of course, to take this argument too far is to fall back into the position that there is properly only one way to perform (or be) feminine or masculine, which – according to the basic notion of gender being socialized behaviour – is manifestly untrue. However, if we do not push it to extremes, there is an important point here. That is, what if, instead of seeing gender-crossing as a queer's or transperson's performance of a gender that is already socially known, and evaluating that performance for fit, we could rather see it as the performance of something not yet known? An example is if we see a male-to-female transsexual not as attempting a performance of femininity as such, but as attempting the performance of something that might suggest some *notions* of femininity but is not supposed to *be* femininity.

Is sex really separate from gender?

This idea points us to another problem, which is that even when it is recognized via the sex–gender distinction that much of what gets counted as feminine and masculine is to do with cultural context and socialization rather than biology, it still seems that gender is typically thought of in terms of sex. That is, gender is understood as a "social dichotomy determined by a natural dichotomy" (Delphy 2003: 60), meaning that gender is understood as the socially approved behaviour of specified sexes. Why, however, should sex determine gender? Why should gender be dichotomized just because sex is? Could gender be more complexly connected to sex than a simple causal relation suggests, perhaps even completely independent from sex? Finally, given the assumption that gender is socially constructed and variable, are we really justified in thinking that sex is fixed? These questions are of course specifically anti-essentialist in so far as they challenge the idea that there are some essential and recognizable features that determine gender (or sex). They are also pressing questions in so far as some feminist and queer thinkers have argued that the sex–gender distinction and the associated understanding of the social constructedness of gender are not actually radical enough to challenge patriarchal formulations.

These are issues that Butler in particular takes up. Well known for her description of gender as social and performative, Butler also, more radically, problematizes the very notion that it is possible properly to understand sexual difference (indeed the sexed body itself) in terms of natural and therefore fixed categories. Specifically, as we introduced in Chapter 2, Butler argues that there is no pure biological substratum of sex underneath and determining a socioculturally constructed gender. There is, she stresses, no notion of sex difference independent

> **Judith Butler (b. 1956)**
> A feminist poststructuralist and philosopher, Judith Butler is one of the fore-
> most theorists in gender studies and has inspired a range of arguments in
> queer theory. More precisely, Butler interrogates – or in her words, troubles
> – gender, the categories of biological sex and sex difference, arguing not
> only that none of these can provide a "natural" ground for individual iden-
> tity, but that assumptions that they can and that there should be a match
> between sex and gender are simply the result of a deeply embedded social
> construction of compulsory heterosexuality (what she calls "heteronormativ-
> ity"). These ideas are explored through several texts including *Gender Trouble*
> (1990), *Bodies that Matter* (1993), *Excitable Speech* (1997), *Undoing Gender*
> (2004) and *Giving an Account of Oneself* (2005). Butler's main ideas include:
> that gender is performative; that the assumed unity of biological sex, gender
> identity and performance, and heterosexuality is illusory; that understand-
> ings of the biological or "natural" are always and already mediated by social
> and cultural assumptions (of there being only two sexes, female and male,
> say); and overall that there is no distinction that can coherently be made
> between socialized performance and understandings, and some supposedly
> un-mediated pre-cultural notion of the real or the natural.

of and uncontaminated by society, in so far as sex difference seems
only to become relevant – to mean something – with regard to social
understandings and expectations of gender performance. For instance,
even when it might be argued that sex difference can be seen purely
in terms of biological reproduction and hence as independent of any
social meanings and expectations – after all, reproduction could not
happen without some actual sex difference – Butler would respond that
reproduction is actually thought of from the context of a whole range
of social assumptions. To put this otherwise, it could be said that social
and cultural assumptions around sex difference are what make people
not even notice some gender performances as performances – they
see them as "normal" – and to see others as somehow transgressive or
shocking or even as a mockery.

There is another issue that Butler points us to, which is the question
as to why human beings have so persistently categorized sex differences and socialized gendered attitudes and behaviours into just two
categories: female and male or feminine and masculine. Why have they
invested so much into a strictly dichotomized – dimorphous – model?
Why have they policed the binarism and match of sex and gender so
fiercely, to the point that many people have accepted the need to rebuke,
humiliate and brutalize "gender offenders" (Gilbert 2001: 46)?

Challenging the binaries

These issues, in turn, suggest several options for feminist, queer and transgender thinkers. First, it could be argued that there are in fact more than just two sexes: for instance, that hermaphrodites and other intersexed people make a third sex. Or, secondly, it could be argued that maybe it is time to stop working with such categories as sex (and gender, and male and female, etc.). Now these are challenging issues for many feminist thinkers in so far as they seem to shake feminism's very starting-point, which is to change for the better the position of a specific group – females – in society. After all, what happens if it is not possible to appeal to "women" or "females" as a coherent category? A range of thinkers have taken up these complex issues within not only feminist theories but also queer and transgender studies, all of which have vested interests in how categories of sex, gender and sexuality are perceived, and all of which work to continue and promote debate about sex and gender norms.

The first challenge to the assumption of the binary we shall consider here is that raised by hermaphrodites and other intersexed people. More specifically, such individuals remind us that the spectrum of sexed bodies simply does not fit neatly into the binarized model of female versus male bodies. That is, far from everyone being, through their chromosomes, either biologically XX (female) or XY (male), individuals can be chromosomally intersexed and XO, XXY, XXXY, XXYY, XXXXY, XXXYY, or XX or XY but with ambiguous genitalia. This is also not statistically improbable. Estimates vary, but the Intersex Society of North America contends that one in every two thousand babies is born with some form of intersexuality (from approximately fourteen different causes) (Nataf 1998). Under a model of compulsory binarism – at least in the modern western world – medical and social practices have forced these anomalies into conformity with the norm. Newborn babies have been surgically "fixed" (via sex reassignment surgery) so that they possess unambiguous genitalia, a process that typically continues on into adolescence with hormone therapy. The argument here is that being clearly either female or male is essential for the child's psychosexual development and well-being. As ethnomethodologist Harold Garfinkel puts it, the "normally sexed" person possesses either a vagina or a penis, and if nature "errs", then human-made vaginas and penises will need to be provided (1967: 126, 127). On this view, then, ambiguous genitalia mark not just a birth defect but one that will be an obstacle to "normal" development. The question, however, is whether this is too reductive: whether the either/or of unambiguous genitalia is in fact "normal". After all, human beings do come in forms other than unambiguous females and males, and on what basis can anyone really say that these other forms are "abnormal"? Such an argument has led to the previously accepted "need" for early sex reassignment surgery to now be contested, with groups within the "growing political intersexual community" lobbying to "abolish all unnecessary surgery and ensure that what surgery is performed is with the full understanding and consent of the intersexual individual involved" (Hird 2000: 352).

We need to remember that gender identity and performance are also at stake here. After all, surgically reassigned intersexuals (especially those who underwent surgery as babies or young children) may find themselves with sexed bodies that do not match their sense of gender identity. (A particularly famous case is that of John/Joan, whose bungled circumcision led to him being reassigned as female, but who later chose to be reassigned again as male; see e.g. Colapinto 2000.) Transsexuals who – regardless of whether they are seeking sex reassignment surgery or not – effectively privilege gender identity over the sexed body further problematize these issues. Many transsexual narratives, for example, talk of the feeling of being "trapped in the wrong body", a condition known as gender dysphoria. Some intersexuals and otherwise transgendered people, however, have wondered why, if their sexed bodies are not unambiguously either female or male (but both, say), they should be expected to identify and/or perform as either feminine or masculine. Perhaps they could identify or perform as a third sex and/or gender or androgyne or gender outlaw:

> You accept yourself as then not totally male or female … in some ways I'm not a man, [but] whatever that makes me, it doesn't make me a woman. I wouldn't like the idea of saying that I'm a woman. I don't think I would go that far, but I would go as far as to say that I'm in between, or I'm neither or both or third sex or something like that.
> (Simon Dessloch, cited in Monro 2001: 158)

In such a view, some intersexuals have refused female or male gendered pronouns, citing their inapplicability, and use "ze" or "xie" (s/he) and "hir" (her/his).

This, of course, is also similar to the position put forward in queer theory, which argues – albeit from a very different basis – that female–male and feminine–masculine dichotomies are simply too limited and rigid to encompass the lived sexed and gendered experiences of many queers (gays, lesbians and bisexuals). More specifically, the argument here is that in so far as "queer" stands for "*whatever* is at odds with the normal, the legitimate, the dominant", it is an "identity without an essence" (Halperin 1995: 62). The point, then, is to not present oneself as accountable to any dichotomies, to realize that sex and gender and sexuality are all intrinsically in flux, and that rigid female–male, feminine–masculine and even queer–straight binarisms are not inevitable structures with regard to how individuals understand themselves.

Some implications for feminist projects

Such aims, however, as mentioned earlier, have been seen as problematic by some feminists in so far as they seem to make trouble for feminist projects on account of the underlying assumption that there is an identifiable group – women – whose position within society needs to be and can be improved. Hence, as British feminist philosopher Margrit Shildrick puts it, even though she might write of a "posthumanism", she has "no wish to fully abandon the concept of the feminine". Certainly, she continues, the boundaries and categories used in current thinking and practices might well be much more "fluid and permeable" than is often thought, but they should not be seen to "cease altogether" (1996: 9–10). Nonetheless, despite such wishes, it does seem clear that the questions surrounding and inspired by queer theory, intersexuality and transgenderism do trouble conventional patriarchal and feminist understandings of sex, gender and sexuality, especially when they demonstrate the open-endedness, indefinability and mobility of our ideas of sex, gender and sexuality. As a result, despite the fact that many queer and transgendered people regularly undergo harassment and discrimination regarding the challenges they issue to sex and gender dichotomies – the sorts of issues that, of course, actually kick-started feminist projects – the queer and transgender movements are often seen in opposition to some feminist positions.

Some feminists have seen issues of transgenderism – especially those surrounding male-to-female transsexuals – as particularly problematic. Such a view is exemplified by the 1979 text by American lesbian feminist Janice Raymond, *The Transsexual Empire*, where she argues that transsexual women "are not women … [but] deviant males" (1979: 183). Raymond's view overall – essentialist, of course – is that male-to-female transsexuals, because they are not women born as women, are not "authentic" women; that, because they have been born and initially socialized as male, they can never truly be female, and are therefore undeserving of support by feminist projects. This view also underpins a further feminist critique of male-to-female transsexuals (and cross-dressers), which is that they – knowingly or unknowingly – collude with patriarchy and sustain misogynistic views of women by presenting them-selves – passing – as stereotypically feminine. As British lesbian femin-ist Sheila Jeffreys has put it in *Anticlimax*, "transsexual males want to become their image of what women should be, not a liberated or feminist version" (1990: 178). This, of course, is particularly problematic for fem-inists in so far as they are fighting for the liberation of women from patri-archal expectations. Conversely, female-to-male transsexuals have been criticized by some lesbians with regard to their desire to exchange what was perceived as a transgressive butch lesbian female identity for a more stereotypically normal, even heterosexual, male identity. Such a move has been seen by some as going over to the enemy: even as heresy.

These sorts of responses, however, are from versions of feminism (and lesbianism) that are still invested heavily in binarism and are thereby unwilling to see concepts of sex difference, sexuality and gender as ques-tions rather than as answers. They are from feminisms that have not yet come to terms with Irigaray's challenge – presented, for instance, in *Speculum of the Other Woman* (1985a) – to imagine "woman" outside of the "logic of the same"; that is, the need to imagine "woman" outside of any vestiges of a heterosexual binarism. This is also a challenge that some third-world feminists, radical women of colour and queer theorists have set when they urge people to find another path beyond the tendency towards comfort in clear-cut categorization. With such an aim they sug-gest a path of hybridization, of the uncomfortable being in the world of the queer and *la mestiza* (the boundary-crosser), where a struggle against overly constraining and strict categorization is a central feature of life.

Having said that, some feminists still perceive a problem in these "queer" desires to challenge or escape categorization. Specifically, they contend that a "queer" desire to escape limitation marks a refusal to rec-ognize the differences between women, between lesbianism and gayness and bisexuality, between transsexualism and cross-dressing and drag and the intersexed. They also stress that it ignores differences of race, class, age, cultural background and location, and so forth. In the words of Chicana feminist Gloria Anzaldúa:

> Queer is used as a false unifying umbrella which all "queers" of
> all races, ethnicities and classes are shoved under. At times we

need this umbrella to solidify our ranks against outsiders. But even when we seek shelter under it we must not forget that it homogenizes, erases our differences. (1991: 250)

In response to Anzaldúa's first and last points above, some critics of queer theory argue that queer theory needs to take a lesson from earlier feminist debates and develop a much more nuanced understanding of how "numerous systems of oppression interact to regulate ... the lives of most people" (Cohen 1997: 441). (We explore these points in further detail in Chapter 4.)

But there is another important point here that concerns the ongoing tension between more practically and activist-oriented and more idealistically and theoretically oriented feminisms. Briefly, as we have already seen in Chapters 1 and 2, the more practically oriented feminisms have often criticized idealistic or complex theoretical movements for their seeming lack of relevance for the vast majority of women who are struggling with subordination, exploitation and violation in the real world. That is, feminists concerned with "real-world" issues typically argue that the radicalizing and refinement of theoretical understanding is not only far too obscure to be of any practical use but has in fact got in the way of, or distracted attention from, the important business of trying to change policy and practice on the ground. For instance, many feminists have felt that to focus attention on such theoretical ideals as reconceptualizing sexual difference is misguided, even unethical, given the very real inequalities that women still suffer from. Refining theory, they suggest, is a luxury that feminists might indulge only after they have dealt with the actual social problems facing women. While there is no doubt that sexual violence and rape, sex trafficking and exploitation are enormous problems for women, there is also a counter-argument here, which is that unless theoretical understandings and categorizations are refined, it may not be possible to tackle and solve some problems. One example of this is the idea that certain practices – such as those incorporated in male-privileged sexuality, say – are tied to certain understandings of sexual difference and sexuality, which means that the only way to change such practices is to change the understandings.

Given these kinds of issues, then, the challenge is to build and promote some sense of solidarity across the various practical and theoretical feminist, queer and transgender movements, while also recognizing that the experiences of many women, queers and transgendered and intersexed people reveal the limitations of these movements. For example, queer individuals of colour have noted the intolerance of their own communities to same-sex or otherwise non-heteronormative relation-ships, and detailed their struggles of fitting transgressive identities and relationships in and around traditional cultural expectations. And again, returning to the investment in the sex–gender distinction made and upheld by many feminist and queer thinkers, the transsexual's claim that there is a "realness" and authenticity to hir gender identity – a "realness" able to justify a sex change – is constitutively in tension with the idea of gender being no more than a social construction. It also problematizes a range of feminist and queer assumptions as to what really matters in notions of identity, identification and belonging.

Transgressing compulsory heterosexuality

There is, however, still another layer to this problematic that we have so far elided, which is the relation between sex, gender and sexuality, on the one hand, and desire, on the other. More specifically, this question is to do with the way we can understand the various issues discussed so far as transgressing (or not) what theorists have variously called patriarchal sexual politics or compulsory heterosexuality.

Compulsory heterosexuality has not only underpinned the patriar-chal assumption of male sexual privilege discussed earlier in this chapter, but has also underpinned the assumptions that sexual desire is naturally heterosexual desire (desire for the "opposite" sex) and that all other forms of desire mark a pathology. Such a model, Rich contends, is constructed as the paradigm not only for people's senses of identity but for all of their relationships, whether social or sexual. And this, she stresses, has worked to effectively erase – or make seem deviant – the possibility of lesbian or woman-centred relationships. The result, in Rich's eyes, is that one of the most urgent tasks for feminism, given its avowed challenge to patriarchy, is the recuperation of those relationships that stretch along what she calls a "lesbian continuum" (in which she includes woman-centred or woman-connected friendship, support and collective action, as well as specifically lesbian erotic and sexual relationships). The task of recuper-ating non-normative heterosexuality, those heterosexual relationships that are not compelled by the normative understandings of compulsory heterosexuality, of course, also accompanies this goal.

Anti-essentialist feminist, queer, transgender and intersex the-orists have also questioned the very starting-points of binarized sex, gender and sexuality, and they have destabilized this strictly naturalized heterosexual desire in several ways. First, as we have already discussed, having discerned the structures of compulsory heterosexuality, feminists and other activists argued that it not only promotes and naturalizes a male sexual privilege, but works to shape female (and of course male) sexual desire in specific ways. For instance, not only are people supposed to desire the opposite sex, but they should desire that which gives males pleasure, and they should see all other sexual pleasures and practices as deviant. However, feminists argue that, as particular sociocultural constructions, these models of sexuality and desire are open to change. Some argue, for instance, that there must be a possibility of developing desiring practices "rooted in an egalitarian ethic of mutuality and respect", as to think otherwise is actually to "forgo part of our humanity" (Jensen 2004: 33).

For heterosexual women (and men) who desire to construct non-heteronormative meanings in their sexual relationships, however, this task presents a range of difficulties, in so far as their desire lines up so closely with many, although of course not all, of the assumptions of what is sometimes called heteropatriarchy. This being so, some thinkers have argued that what is key is to separate the notion of heterosexuality *per se* from its institutionalized privileging of the male and subordinating of the female: to develop, in other words, the concept of a feminist heterosexual relationship that expresses "mutuality and respect". This would require the challenging of all patriarchal assumptions regarding the differential status of men and women, along with many of the prevailing social and cultural constructions regarding both masculinity and femininity. More specifically, it would entail:

> An equitable power distribution in terms of economic independence, where the woman does not engage in domestic, sexual and emotional servicing; a relationship in which sex or intercourse is not the primary way of relating, but merely part of the relationship alongside other important dimensions, such as friendship and companionship. It would include a respect for the independence of the working lives of each partner; and it would include a recognition and respect for other networks of intimacy and closeness, particularly woman to woman relationships, which enable the woman to retain a sense of separateness, an intimacy companionably outside the heterosexual partnership.   (Rowland 1996: 82)

What is fundamental, then, for feminist desiring practices is that each partner is able to possess integrity, self-respect and a sense of self-empowerment, and that these attributes are not gained at the cost of the other.

Such desiring practices, some feminists have thought, might also be developed from lesbianism. In this vein, theorists attempting to undermine patriarchal assumptions about sexuality and desire have drawn on models of lesbian same-sex desire in a range of ways. In particular, some theorists have portrayed lesbianism as a model for a cultural revolution in interpersonal relations. In the 1970s and 1980s this model was typically a separatist one, as exemplified in the 1970 manifesto of the group Radicalesbians – "our energies must flow toward our sisters and not backward toward our oppressors" (1997: 156) – but it can also be read as the projection of a potentially different set of interpersonal relations from that normalized in heteropatriarchy. Such relations, the proponents of this form of lesbianism contended, would be based on a lack of oppressive practices and the promotion of friendship and emotional support. This view did not, however, achieve unconditional support. Some lesbians saw lesbianism as being co-opted into a political stance that placed little if any emphasis on same-sex desire and sexuality. According to them, feminists promoting a lesbianism without sexuality actually worked alongside patriarchy to stress the unimportance and invalidity of female same-sex desire and sexuality. Additionally, and much more importantly when it came to gaining wider endorsement, many women who identified as heterosexual did not support a movement that seemed to de-emphasize and invalidate their desires. Despite these issues, however, it still seems fair to argue that lesbian desire and sexuality do challenge heteropatriarchy in so far as they demonstrate the possibility for a female sexual desire that is not tied to compulsory heterosexuality. That is, lesbianism presents a model in which women can actively construct non-heteronormative sexual meanings and affirm desires of their own making.

Several other positions have also used this latter argument against the pathologizing of same-sex desire. These range from the essentialist assumption that there is a "gay gene" or some other biological imperative (making same-sex desire an inevitable and "natural" part of life for those possessing the gene), to the argument that same-sex sexuality has been a legitimate – even esteemed – part of a wide range of cultures, and the argument that same-sex desire is a "natural" extension of the familiarity individuals feel with their own bodies. In all of these cases the aim has been to normalize same-sex desire, and thereby show that sexuality and desire do not come only in heterosexual forms. (Such attempts to normalize same-sex desire also underpin aims such as legislating for the recognition of gay marriage.)

Finally, however, as considered earlier, some feminist, queer, transgender and intersex thinkers have contended that it is possible – and desirable – to conceptualize desire outside of all binarisms of sex and gender. Or, better, that it is possible to conceptualize it differently from the way that these binaries usually frame it (after all, it is impossible to ever completely escape or get outside all of our norms). Or, better again, that binarized norms simply cannot constrain desire. After all, these thinkers have all argued that desire cannot be limited to the idea of it that is assumed in the binarisms of compulsory heterosexuality and patriarchy or the notion that desire is either same-sex or heterosexual. Instead, such thinkers contend, desire is unregulatable: it escapes or exceeds all the conditions constructed around it. This, however, is something that makes proponents of the need to regulate desire very uncomfortable, as we saw played out in the sex wars around "risky" sexual practices. If desire is unregulatable, then can there even be a specifically queer community, let alone a heterosexual one? More generally, could there even be such a thing as an identity based on desire and sexual orientation?

These issues bring us back to the question of desire itself, which in turn brings us back to the question of just what it means to be a desiring being. Do people have to understand their feelings of desire on the basis of supposedly natural or recognizably social categories and discourses? Could it be seriously considered that desire is somehow separable from such categories and discourses? Or that human beings could somehow experience a non-discursively constructed desire? These are questions that feminists are still struggling with in so far as they cut to the core of feminist projects. That is, they require people to think about what the criteria are for being a woman, as well as to speculate on what a non-patriarchal future could look like. Could society, as the *Questions Féministes* collective speculated back in 1977, ever reach a point where there is no social or moral weight given to whether someone is female or male, straight or queer: where "individuals will meet as singular individuals with their own specific history and not on the basis of their sexual identity" (1981: 215)?

The answers to these questions are still unclear (although reproduction, of course, still requires differently sexed individuals or at least different gametes). Further, even if society could reach such a point, surely people would still need to struggle to ensure that such a world is and remains liberating and just? (After all, as Chapter 4 will stress in particular, challenging one "-ism" – sexism – is no guarantee that any others are also challenged.) In addition, it would be important to remember that feminist responses to the questions and challenges that keep on arising through the gradual recognition of the impact of social, cultural and conceptual contexts on sexual and desiring practices are not unified. None have unconditional support. There are, however, two pragmatic points to make in the face of this problematic. The first is that perhaps what matters most is that feminist thinkers – as they respond to the changing material conditions of their lives and to the challenges set them by queer, transgender and intersex studies – continue to pursue a practice of questioning that refuses to rest on the laurels of any particular answer or resolution. The second point is the realization that, despite the continuation of questioning, a particular answer or resolution can still be strategically helpful in a particular context. For instance, while those working to get rid of the sex trade in refugee camps are probably going to be impatient with concepts such as "gender performativity" or "moving beyond binarisms" because the immediate context makes such concepts well-nigh irrelevant, queers who are marginalized may nonetheless find these concepts highly useful. These insights in turn point us to a more general issue that we shall be considering in detail in Chapter 4: the tension between the aim of struggling against women's oppression in general, and the danger of assuming that there is some coherent collective of women to speak on behalf of.

Summary of key points

- Feminists argue that sex differences, conceived as "natural" and fixed, have underpinned a patriarchal sexual economy that privileges males and "compulsory heterosexuality". This system has implications for how we understand desire and sexuality and for sexual practices such as pornography and prostitution.
- Using social constructionism, feminists have argued that differences in attitudes and behaviour between men and women do not arise from biological facts of nature but from deeply embedded social practices and traditions.
- The western tradition has viewed both sex difference and gender as binarized models: male–female, masculine–feminine. Queer, transgender and intersex theorists have challenged these binaries as failing to recognize the many ways in which people understand themselves sexually. Poststructuralist theorists have also challenged the distinction between the biological and the social.
- Anti-binarized views of sexuality have proved problematic for

many feminists, challenging traditional understandings of what it means to be a woman and whether in fact it is possible to consider women as an identifiable group.

- Debates around sex and gender also raise questions about the nature of desire, what being a desiring individual means and ways in which "compulsory heterosexuality" may be transgressed (such as through heterosexual or same-sex relationships based on mutuality and respect, or through a notion of "unregulatable" desire).

four

Differences among and within women

Ain't I a woman?

Ain't I a Woman, the title of bell hooks's 1981 exploration of "black women and feminism", symbolizes one of the most urgent and worrisome problems that has shaped contemporary feminist thinking, and a problem that we have seen arise in various ways in previous chapters. This title, echoing the words of nineteenth-century black slave Sojourner Truth, hailed both white and black women: white feminists for their silence about the lives of black women, and black women for their complicity with black men's accounts of racism. More generally, hooks makes the point that although feminist attention to the problems of oppression and embodiment has revolutionized analyses of gender roles, knowledge and understanding by showing up the biases of mainstream thinking, it has also often been misguided and exclusionary in its own right by neglecting the impact of the many differences – race, class, sexuality and ethnicity, and so on – among women. Talk about oppression and subordination, about the gendered divisions in labour, sexist language, bodily consciousness and assumptions about desire and sexuality, while taking the false generalizations of dominant masculinist understandings to task, has too often involved homogeneous conceptions of women and femininity. Unsurprisingly these conceptions have reflected the situations of privileged white women: those with the power to have their voices heard.

We have seen in Chapter 1, for instance, how some feminist challenges to the problems of oppression in terms of the exclusion of women from work in the public sphere extrapolated from the situation of some middle-class white women to make their claims. However, for lower-class women and many women of colour these terms utterly failed to capture the nature of their oppression. Similarly, visions of women's nature taken up by gynocentric and cultural feminists have often relied on heterosexual descriptions of sexual difference. In addition, feminist critiques of the undue significance of motherhood as central to women's identities and activism for abortion rights have also frequently over-looked the importance of motherhood in the lives of many postcolonial and indigenous people, their struggles against forced sterilization and the loss of children to welfare agencies.

These difficulties of differences among women seem straightforward and obvious enough. Of course different women have different values and aspirations, needs and desires. Are there not always struggles and conflicts in any social movement? And are tolerance and compromise not the tried and tested means for managing these tensions? At first sight this might seem like well-trodden terrain, but the emergence of the problem of differences among women and the responses to it have had a radical effect on the nature of feminist thought and action, taking it into new reaches of understanding. The problem is complex, in the first instance because it cuts across several different strands of fem-inist work, each with their own aims and purposes. As a result it is multifaceted because the diverse exclusions that form it have manifold implications for the practical and conceptual projects of feminisms. But most importantly, like the other problems we take up in this book, it has become a pervasive aspect of feminist thinking itself, part of what shapes feminists' understandings of the world and their aspirations for change. In this chapter, then, we shall trace its development in the inter-section of the practical challenges levelled by women of colour, socialist, lesbian, disabled and postcolonial feminists with the conceptual work of poststructuralist theorists, culminating in what feminists and other theorists call the essentialist debate (a debate we have touched on briefly in previous chapters). Finally, we shall show how different approaches and responses to this issue have thrown up new directions and new problematics for feminist thought.

False generalizations and structured differences

Differences among women were recognized in a variety of contexts during the revival of feminist ideas in the second half of the twentieth century. As we have already mentioned, it became obvious very early on that Friedan's analysis of the oppression of women like herself had little resonance for women in different socioeconomic situations for whom paid work was a deadening necessity for survival and more opportunities to participate in the nurturing activities of domesticity a far-off dream. In their turn, feminists influenced by Marxism and socialism drew attention to the ways women's social possibilities depended on their positioning in the class structure of society and how this was subject to historical change. In addition, the writings of African-American scholars in the United States strongly pressed the need to acknowledge race, along with gender and class, in feminist thinking. Of these, the Combahee River Collective's (1977) assertion of the irreducible specificity of black women's oppression and the crucial requirement for the input of black women to the movement was one of the most forceful statements. (Importantly, this statement of the significance of race with regard to oppression also noted the significance of economic status – these women being mainly poor – and involved both lesbian and heterosexual views.) Women from other marginalized ethnic groups – Hispanics, Latinos, Chinese, Korean, Native American and indigenous women, as well as third-world women – joined the fray, highlighting the racism and ethnocentrism of white feminism's call to sisterhood (a term that originated in black culture) while claiming a place for their own voices.

Lesbian feminists also challenged the assumptions of heterosexuality that dominant feminist accounts had written into their understandings

---

bell hooks (b. 1952)

An African American, born Gloria Jean Watkins, bell hooks adopted the uncapitalized name of one of her great-grandmothers for her public-speaking and writing voice. Her first book, *Ain't I a Woman* (1981), was motivated by her inability to find writings in which the multi-layered complexities of oppression in black women's lives were accurately expressed. Her writing is determinedly free of academic jargon and aims towards understanding the impact of the intersecting oppressions of race, class and gender under the system she calls "white supremacist capitalist patriarchy". She is outspoken in her criticism of white feminists' false and corrupt idea of a common gender oppression with its failure to comprehend the varied and complex nature of different women's (and men's) lives. Her prolific and diverse writings encompass feminist theory, cultural criticism and autobiography, and include *Feminist Theory* (1984), *Talking Back* (1989), *Bone Black* (1996), *Wounds of Passion* (1997) and *Feminism Is For Everybody* (2000).

of women's lives. Sexuality, like class, race and ethnicity, created another significant difference in the forms of gender oppression that women faced.

By the 1980s, many feminists noted that there were significant differences among women and included statements to this effect in their writings. They often handled the problem of inclusiveness and accuracy in the representation of diverse women's experience with aspirational statements for inclusivity and/or confessions on the part of particular theorists concerning the sociohistorical biases of their vision. However, as feminist scholarship gained ground and intensity in the academy, it became clear that the problem was deeper than these tactics suggested. Anglo-American feminists continued to explore what they understood as the commonalities of women's experience, as if this would yield the fundamental basis for understanding oppression and as if their perceptions of these commonalities were universal. Sweeping generalizations about the causes of oppression, the nature of psychosocial development and conceptions of woman and femininity (some of which we have explored in the preceding chapters) falsely presumed their relevance and applicability to all women in all circumstances. In response, critics redoubled their efforts to demonstrate the ways in which false understandings of a common essence of womanhood underpinned these theories. Most importantly, failure to build difference and diversity into the central structure of feminist theories not only excluded those who did not share these characteristics but resulted in the presumed essences becoming a *de facto* norm.

French author and feminist theorist Monique Wittig's paper "One is not Born a Woman" (1992), which argued that the category of "woman" functions normatively to exclude the possibility that a lesbian can be a genuine woman, illustrates this sort of critique. Using Beauvoir's *The Second Sex* as her target, Wittig shows how the focus of Beauvoir's conception of woman, usually regarded as a biologically based category, is thoroughly heterosexual. For instance, while it is true that Beauvoir included a chapter on lesbians in her book and that this may give the impression of inclusivity, Wittig explains how such an impression is mistaken. This is because, throughout the work, Beauvoir takes heterosexual unity with man as a primordial base for understanding the nature of woman. As a result, an authentic lesbian orientation is impossible. From this perspective, the concept of "woman" functions normatively (if unintentionally) in Beauvoir's book in the service of a compulsory heterosexuality, and liberation from this norm, for lesbians, requires what looks like a self-contradictory move: the refusal to be a woman.

This paradoxical implication highlights the difficulties that differences in sexuality, and differences among women more generally, pose for understanding how to theorize individual selves and collective feminist projects. Are lesbians not real women? Or is something wrong with the category "woman"? If something is wrong with the category, what is it that unites feminist aspirations? (These issues are at the heart of Chapters 5 and 6.) In addition, from Wittig's analysis we can see how the notion of difference, in this case homosexual difference from heterosexuality, operates to mark particular individuals in relation to an apparently neutral norm. Heterosexuality is not different, homosexuality is; heterosexuality does not require explanation, homosexuality does. As Chapter 3 showed, this dynamic readily becomes transformed into a hierarchy of values that sets those who comply with the "neutral norm" in a position of domination with respect to those who are "different". (In Chapter 3 this supposed normativity, of course, provided the basis for queer, transgender and intersex challenges.)

Some of the most potent criticisms of white feminists' false generalizations about women, however, have come from women of colour: African-American feminists such as hooks, Audre Lorde, Patricia Hill Collins and Patricia Williams; Chicana feminists Gloria Anzaldúa and Cherrie Morago; and Latina feminist Maria Lugones. One of Lorde's pieces, "An Open Letter to Mary Daly" (1984b), has been particularly significant in raising consciousness of racial bias in feminist thinking owing to Daly's high profile as a radical feminist. Lorde takes Daly to task for the complete neglect of the vision, culture and myths of black women in Daly's call to all "true" feminists, *Gyn/Ecology* (1978). More specifically, Daly's vision of feminist authenticity employs understandings of female strengths and values inspired by western myths as if they provide universal inspiration for feminists everywhere, and it is indifferent to alternative sources of value in African cultures and their power for women in those cultures. Lorde points out that Daly's error is not a matter of simple omission that she can correct by the addition of missing information. More profoundly, Daly's stance blocks the possibility of productive dialogue with "noneuropean" women and works to entrench "the destructive forces of racism and separation between women – the assumption that the herstory and myth of white women is the legitimate and sole herstory and myth of all women to call upon for power and background" (Lorde 1984b: 69).

Lorde is not making a plea for acceptance or toleration of differences among women (racial differences in this case). Her important message is that white feminists' privilege and their visions of commonalities among women are built on the backs of those seen as different: that the differences among women's lives are structurally connected and shaped in relation to each other. After all, white western women have historically collaborated in the exploitation of women and men of other races and ethnicities that has been a constitutive part of their western culture. They have used and abused the labour of third-world and indigenous women and women of colour in their homes. Furthermore, the goods that they purchase and their social standing more generally have benefited from the subordination and dispossession of these women, and the plunder of their land and resources. Accordingly, racial oppression is not an individual person's problem, or more generally a colour problem, or even a matter for white guilt. It is both individual and structural, and relies on a binary "us and them" relation in which whiteness is the unmarked but dominant term. Failure to question white privilege – what is included as common and what is left out as different – leaves that relationship intact. As Lorde explains in another essay, "as white women ignore their built-in privilege of whiteness and define woman in terms of their experience alone, then women of Color become 'other', the outsiders whose experience and tradition is too 'alien' to comprehend" (1984a: 117).

More recently, disability theorists have also joined in the criticisms that feminist thinking has been structurally exclusive and biased towards the values and aspirations of a specific group of relatively privileged women. These challenges are especially confronting in so far as norms concerning physical and mental capabilities are pervasive and deeply embedded in most "normally" abled women's understandings of the world and its possibilities. Yet the severe limitations of disability are inescapable. Canadian disability theorist Susan Wendell (1996) has suggested that the dominant culture in general is unable to take the aspirations of people with disabilities seriously because fear of the loss of control and the suffering that disability brings blocks genuine engagement and understanding. (Many films portray this tension, including, for example, *Dancer in the Dark*, *Coming Home*, *Dance Me to My Song*, *The Quiet Room* and *Le Huitième Jour*.)

As a result, many feminist theories that draw attention to women's oppression and subordination have neglected the situations of women with disabilities and in this way have played into the consolidation of disability oppression. For example, the sorts of feminist positions promoting the significance of embodiment in the face of patriarchal objectification and denigration of female bodily existence that we discussed in Chapter 2 often presume smooth functioning, pleasurable bodies, as if these qualities were part of the essence of bodily existence. Indeed, as we also noted in Chapter 2, theorists of embodiment rarely address the pain and suffering of bodily experience, let alone the distancing from bodily existence that is required to get on with life while one's body exacts ongoing attention to itself in the performance of everyday tasks. Other feminists rely on generalizations of women's social roles as nurturers and carers as sources either of exploitation or of revaluations of women's significance, building in a bias against those who are incapable of fulfilling these roles and/or are dependent on the care of others. Once again the familiar logic of false generalization at the expense of the subordination and exclusion of a "deviant" other is evident.

Multiple identities and intersectionality

Talk about differences among women and the complexities of identity also readily becomes embroiled in analyses of the cross-cutting effects of different forms of oppression. Lorde's writings, for example, challenge white feminisms on the basis of their exclusion of black women from their terms, but at the same time she draws attention to the multiple sources of her identity and difference – woman, black, lesbian, mother, middle-aged, member of an interracial couple, poet – to give voice to the complexity at stake when differences are taken seriously. She repeatedly asserts her own multiple "differences" to defy the implicit and taken-for-granted commonalities of experience, desires, values and

---

Audre Lorde (1934–92)
The daughter of a West Indian immigrant family to the United States, Audre Lorde was a passionate and visionary protagonist for social justice for women, blacks, lesbians and gays. She was pre-eminently a poet and published numerous award-winning volumes of poetry. Her prose publications include the influential collection of essays and speeches *Sister Outsider* (1984), and the quasi-biographical work *Zami* (1982). Her writings are notable for the way she uses her personal experience to draw together personal, political and spiritual themes in the struggle against oppression. Her assertions of the cross-cutting forces in her own life – as black, feminist, woman, lesbian, activist, poet, mother – are mobilized to express a vital sense of the power of differences to transform the practical and theoretical projects of equality and justice. In the later part of her life she also made international connections between black and indigenous women in the United States, South Africa, Europe, Australia and the Caribbean.

aspirations that are the basis for many feminists' understandings of womanhood and femininity. Her lived experience, she insists, is one of simultaneously contradictory and shifting identities on the edges and at odds with dominant standards of femininity. This continuous negotiation and renegotiation of subjectivity between plural and intersecting social forces makes any attempt to set down the essence of womanhood or gender an impossible task. It also shows up the way different patterns of oppression interact, creating multi-dimensional identities – a condition known as "intersectionality" – that are different from the sum of their parts.

The voices of other "others" – of race, ethnicity, postcoloniality, disability, queer sexualities and so on – who inhabit the in-between lands of criss-crossing lines of disadvantage confirm the reality of this experience. Not only do such accounts discredit the generalizing projects of feminisms, but they demonstrate the impossibility of creating a more inclusive understanding of the movement by simply extending its boundaries to incorporate the experiences and values of the marginalized. (A parallel criticism emerged in the more specific context of queer theory in Chapter 3, where we mentioned Anzaldúa's charge against theorists who use the term "queer" as a "false universalising umbrella".) For feminists to include the experience and aspirations of black lesbian mothers, for example, in their understanding of their projects requires changing the aspirations of white heterosexual mothers, in so far as they conceive of whiteness and motherhood in opposition to blackness and lesbian child-rearing. The relations of dominance and subordination between different identities demand transformations of both the dominant and the subordinate in order to accommodate successfully everyone in a shared vision. In other words, it is necessary to work creatively across differences to undo the hierarchies of privilege and disadvantage that these differences create if feminists are to overcome the exclusions and oppression that mainstream feminisms involve. This, of course, is a message that feminists should already have absorbed in their attempts to overcome the problem of women's oppression in relation to men. After all, we saw in Chapter 1 how attempts by liberal feminists to extend male values of equality to include women have required attention to the way that western male privilege is structurally dependent on female subordination through the social ordering of the public–private split. This struggle shows that changes to the situation of women require changes to the structure of the public–private dichotomy, and thereby changes to the situation of men. Genuine inclusion thus requires undoing the very bases of privilege and oppression. But for the privileged this is a very difficult lesson to learn, especially when, as in the case of white western women, tackling their privilege may seem to come at the expense of challenging their oppression, or they may see tackling their privilege as too indirectly connected with the immediacy of their oppression.

The lesson is further complicated by the insight that just as different groups with different identities cannot be simply added together, nor can different oppressions within any particular group. In other words, it is impossible to assess the effects of racism, sexism and heterosexism, for example, by adding accounts of each form of oppression to the others. In her book *Inessential Woman* (1988), American philosopher Elizabeth Spelman has memorably dubbed this strategy the "pop-bead" approach, referring to necklaces made from plastic beads that are joined together by "popping" each one into another. Pop-bead approaches do not work because analyses of the separate dynamics of sexism, racism and so on are inevitably inflected by understandings of the dominant groups to which they refer. Sexism, for instance, is based on the paradigm of white women's oppression; racism, on the paradigm of black men's oppression. When they occur together, the two axes interact to create a new relational composite that the terms of its single-axis constituents cannot fully capture.

Kimberle Crenshaw has provided potent evidence of this insight in her discussions in "Demarginalizing the Intersection of Race and Sex" (1989) of legal cases in the United States relating to employment discrimination against black women. In her analysis, courts in the United States repeatedly fail to consider black women as victims of discrimination because these women are unable to disaggregate the racial and sexual dimensions of their oppression. Black women are unable to gain redress for injustice either in terms of discrimination against women (because the norms for gender discrimination are based on the situation of white women), or in terms of discrimination against blacks (because the norms for racial discrimination are based on the situation of black men). The established forms of oppression fail to recognize the intersectional experience of black women and the distinctive intersectional oppression they suffer. It would seem that the more the problem of differences among women is investigated and analysed, the more complex it becomes.

Identity politics and separatism

The struggle and failures of various mainstream feminisms to acknowledge differences among women raise two interrelated difficulties. First, it seems clear that the social and political agendas of these feminist projects cannot serve the interests of all women. Secondly, many women's lived experience and self-understandings of their womanhood are inadequately recognized. More precisely, when mainstream feminisms do not recognize the links between differences among women and patterns of domination and subordination – race, class, heteronormativity and so on – in effect they collude in sustaining these inequitable relations. In this situation, for those who are disadvantaged a refined form of identity politics seems to offer a ready solution, where the aim would be to tie different political agendas directly to different identities. Hence, if we understand feminism as a whole to be a movement based on its members' identification with a set of political claims that are significant for all women, the problem of differences among women suggests that multiple political agendas based on multiple different group understandings of women's aspirations are required. Indeed the Combahee River Collective's (1977) declaration that the politics that could serve them best could only come directly out of their own experience of the oppression of racism, sexism, heteronormativity and poverty exemplifies this kind of response to the problem of differences among women. In this instance, the women of the collective reasoned that white feminists' inability to understand the impact of racism invalidated feminist politics from the perspective of the collective; only black women could provide the support and commitment required to realize black women's aims. Along with a sense of solidarity and support, then, this form of identity politics also offers a positive identity to members of marginalized groups, and with this a means to resist the identities imposed on them by dominant sexist, racist and heterosexist cultures. Lesbians, women of colour, third-world women and women with disabilities have all mobilized in these terms to reshape feminist representations of women.

Nonetheless, while identity-based politics implies a degree of separation of marginalized groups from the dominant movement, it jostles together with other political agendas in the same political arena. Struggles forged in the name of particular identities might challenge the exclusions and oversights of more generalized movements, but a more thoroughgoing separatist response is to try to change the rules of political interaction so that the assumptions on which hierarchies of power and disadvantage are based become meaningless. For example, some lesbian feminists have looked to separatism to address the intersecting effects of sexism and heteronormativity in the mainstream culture, sexism in the gay movement and heteronormativity in the feminist movement (see, for instance, the Radicalesbian manifesto [1997]). Obviously it is well-nigh impossible for any group to separate itself from the rest of society but this is not the point of separatism in this context. In this instance, rather than trying to segregate themselves from oppressive cultures, lesbian separatists endeavour to withdraw from relationships that are premised on heterosexist values: the sexual accessibility of females to males, and the identification of womanhood with male predation and protection. They do not refuse to interact with sexists or heterosexists, but they struggle to shape their interactions through values that dissolve the significance of male sexual access to women.

Some lesbians have also challenged the institution of marriage on these terms, arguing that marriage legalizes men's sexual access to women, especially in contexts where domestic violence, rape and sexual abuse of women by men are common and often remain unpoliced. Their aim is to create spaces in which women-identified women, and their activities and institutions, render male-defined and heterosexist practices meaningless. (Other lesbians, conversely, have championed lesbian access to marriage because of the various privileges given to married couples in western societies. Such division illustrates the double binds imposed on the oppressed by hierarchically structured societies and the distinction between "pop-bead" and transformative structural approaches to change. In this instance, extending marriage to include the partnerships of lesbians and gays affirms the inclusion of homosexuals in heterosexual institutions, but at the expense of leaving the normative relations of men's sexual access to women in place.)

Identity politics and separatism can certainly play a positive role in allowing specific groups of women to contest their invisibility and oppression by giving voice to their presence, their needs and their values and, in the case of separatism, creating a space of alternative possibilities. (We shall come back to this understanding of separatism as a strategy for women's agency in Chapter 5.) However, these strategies raise new difficulties of their own, or, rather, they tend to repeat the problem of differences among women at another level. That is, the fragmentation of agendas significantly undermines opportunities to forge a broad-based feminist movement, and there are serious risks of reinforcing marginality and creating new exclusions as each group reinstates its own fixed understandings of identity. Marginal groups that draw attention to the specificity of their experience risk losing the power of collective action, confirming damaging stereotypes and producing still more nuanced forms of exclusion. The Combahee River Collective, for example, expressed their solidarity with progressive black men against mainstream feminisms but also their concern about fractionalization, while lesbian "women-identified women" identities, as we saw in Chapter 3, have been censured for the exclusion of bisexual women, female-to-male and male-to-female transsexuals, and so on. In addition, the kinds of complexity in identity pointed out by those burdened by intersecting lines of oppression suggest that identity itself is a work in progress, forged by acknowledgement, negotiation and resistance in response to shifting strands of the multiple, personal and institutional relationships in which individuals participate. On these terms, identity politics also becomes a fragile work in progress, rather than a robust movement for change. As discussions of difference developed through the 1980s and 1990s, then, the possibility and the value of pinning down any identity at all became more and more problematic.

Poststructuralist resonances

The resonance of these practico-political difficulties for feminist projects with the conceptual work of poststructuralist theorists interested in the nature of language has deepened their import. As we have mentioned in the preceding chapters, the basic idea underlying structuralist approaches to language is that rather than transparently representing the objects in the world that it names in something like a one-to-one relationship, language is a system of signs that brings meaning (the meaning of every aspect of human lives) into existence through the relationships between elements of its system. So, revisiting the examples used in Chapter 1, the oppositional relationship between the word "woman" and the word "man" necessarily affects the meaning of "woman", and the oppositional relationships between the title "Ms" and the titles "Miss" and "Mrs" inevitably colours the meaning of "Ms".

Where structuralists claim that the linguistic system of relationships largely determines meaning, poststructuralists develop this understanding by showing how meanings shift and change in relation to the sociohistorical context in which language is used. In non-indigenous Australia, for example, the term "woman" may call up meanings and expectations connected with equal opportunity, whereas in many Aboriginal circles "woman" identifies those whose opportunities are severely limited by a history of disinheritance and struggles against white sexual predation, sterilization, stolen children, domestic violence and so forth. That is, the meanings of the term alter as its relationship with the meanings of other expressions changes (in this case, these would include locally specific meanings concerning the nature of social order, autonomy, dependency and so on). From this perspective, it is also evident that language is not some abstract system that floats above the world to which it refers. On the contrary, it is embedded in the world, simultaneously the product and the producer of social and political institutions and processes, and the ideologies of power that drive them. The different meanings of "woman" in indigenous and non-indigenous Australia show up this insight in stark relief.

Since, as we stressed in Chapter 1, language and linguistic expression are central to our understandings of who we are and our relations to the world – that is, to our subjectivity – and since the meanings constituted in language are not fixed, subjectivity is also vulnerable to changes in meanings and is often the site of contradictory meanings. Being identified as an Aboriginal woman in Australia, for example, can simultaneously signify disinheritance, disrespect and devaluation, as well as higher levels of community-building responsibilities than those expected of white women. Individual women in Australia juggle, affirm and resist these tensions in their specific sense of self or subjectivity, in a dynamic and continuing process of interaction between pre-existing meanings and their uptake of them. In other words, poststructuralism confirms that who one is cannot be pinned down once and for all, or wholly by any individual. Rather, subjectivity is part of a web of shifting meanings produced by the linguistic practices, or discourses, within which people interact. People are born into specific sociohistorical contexts of linguistically constituted meanings and their subjectivity changes as these contexts and their relationships to them change.

As we have already seen, feminist poststructuralists – such as Julia Kristeva, Luce Irigaray and Judith Butler – are critical of overarching "grand narratives" and generalizations about womanhood and femininity on the basis of these sorts of conceptual analyses. In different ways they argue that the terms "woman" or "women" can never accurately represent women's lived experiences of their subjectivities. On these accounts, further influenced by psychoanalysis, some theorists reject the very term "identity" for its associations with fixity and self-presence, its sense of transparent identification with, and of, oneself, which is closed to the complexity and opacity of the multiple forces that make individuals who they are. Subjectivity, their preferred concept for an individual's discursively produced sense of self, is always unstable and in process, since it is constituted in the shifting sands of language and the sociopolitical institutions through which language is mediated. In this line Kristeva explains that in so far as patriarchal cultures constitute women as marginal subjects, women are actually continuously engaged (consciously and unconsciously) in a process of refusing the meanings of the term "woman". They are always more than, and thus omitted by, the term, which consequently designates "a lack", something that remains outside linguistic names. As she puts it in the aptly titled interview "Woman is Never What We Say", "'woman' is something that cannot be presented or verbalised; 'woman' remains outside the realm of classification" (1996: 98).

Poststructuralist accounts such as Kristeva's confirm the profound logic that underpins feminists' troubles in coping with the differences among and within women. They demonstrate how all attempts to categorize and generalize about the nature of women or the female subject – imprisoned as they are within the limits of linguistic meaning-making – inevitably fall prey to a false opposition between all those who are included in the category and all those who are excluded, all

---

Julia Kristeva (b. 1941)

Originally from Bulgaria, Julia Kristeva came to prominence through her work in linguistic analysis while she was studying in Paris. She has subsequently become one of the most prolific theorists in France, taking up questions in linguistics, literature, art, philosophy, politics and psychoanalysis, along with writing several works of fiction. Among her most famous theoretical works are *Desire in Language* (1980), *Revolution in Poetic Language* (1984) and *New Maladies of the Soul* (1995), the last including her controversial essay "Women's Time". *About Chinese Women* (1977) is based on her travels in China in the 1970s. Kristeva's work is notable for its incorporation of psychoanalytic insights into the understanding of signifying processes and subjectivity. She argues that the subject is always unstable and internally conflicted by the disruptive challenges of unconscious pre-subjective drives – the "feminine" semiotic order – to the more stable forces of conscious meaning-making in the "masculine" symbolic order. Although Kristeva takes seriously the notion of sexual difference and gives special transformatory status to the experience of pregnancy, she resists the idea of any essential bodily or cultural differences between the sexes. Instead feminists can use the force of the semiotic (and the maternal) to re-evaluate their positions on what it is to be feminine or masculine, and to signify a sexual difference in which women can freely express their individual particularity, contingency and sexuality.

---

those who are identical and all those who are different. Such identity categories endow their members with the power and status of exemplars while derogating the status of those excluded. Reflecting again on the example of "woman" and the differences between indigenous and non-indigenous women, it can be seen that whatever meanings are associated with "woman" – equal opportunity, sexual predation, childcare responsibilities, stolen children, for example – by fixing "woman" according to these meanings, the category will exclude and marginalize different experiences of female subjectivity, as well as the experiences of individual subjects whose lives take them across its boundaries. This is the logic of categorization and the logic that comes into play, it is claimed, whenever feminisms invoke generic or universal understandings of womanhood and femininity.

Debating essentialism

What we have seen in these previous sections are, of course, differing rehearsals of the debate concerning essentialism that cuts across all of the feminist challenges to women's subordination. More specifically, as we have already noted, feminists have used the term "essentialism" to label all those approaches that have tried, in one way or another, to categorize and universalize the meaning of the term "woman". In other words, they have employed the term "essentialism" to describe (and usually discredit) those positions that call on properties that are seen as essential and universal to all women. Early on, for instance, feminists criticized theories that presumed that some real biological or metaphysical essence, or some common properties, defined the sexes, and specifically females, as essentialist (and universalist). The beliefs that women are women in virtue of having wombs or being able to bear children exemplify this form of essentialism. Understandably, feminists have been particularly anxious about the way assertions of essential differences such as this, even when they are invoked to revalue neglected aspects of women's lives, have been used to confine and subordinate women. Beauvoir's position, as unravelled by Wittig – that heterosexuality is essential to "woman" – might attract this criticism too (if heterosexuality is taken as a metaphysical or biological property). More recently, as we discussed in Chapter 2, feminist analyses that draw on understandings of biological sex or maternal bodies have incited criticism from other feminists who are anxious about the constraining effects of biology on women's opportunities.

In this account of essentialism, it may seem that analyses that rely on understandings of the nature of womanhood and gender as the products of socially constructed ideals and norms, rather than as biologically innate, would not fall foul of the criticism. Social characteristics, after all, tend to be much less immutable, more flexible and variable, and therefore less definitive and constraining. As a result, as set out in Chapter 3, some feminists have thought that shifting attention from the (apparently) biological category "woman" to the (apparently) social category "gender" would erase the problem of essentialism. But the essentialist charge associated with the problem of difference frequently also relates to assumptions about particular social patterns that are themselves presumed to be essential and universal to all women. For example, Lorde's criticisms of white feminisms relate to particular social aspects of white womanhood being taken as universal. Some theorists also interpret the views that all women feel trapped by their domestic responsibilities, are subject to sexual predation or tend to be nurturing and caring as essentialist in these terms. In light of the common employment of the sorts of terms that privilege white, middle-class, heterosexual conceptions of womanhood and exclude women of different races, ethnicities, classes, sexualities, abilities and so on, "essentialism" is often associated with these privileged perspectives.

Frequently, too, feminists have levelled the charge of essentialism more broadly at the use of generalized conceptions of womanhood or gender as analytic or methodological tools. This concern applies in particular to the adoption of gender, femininity or masculinity, and so on as self-evident categories of social analysis. The difficulty here relates not so much to any particular characteristics that a position may have (implicitly) essentialized but rather to applications of general categories that overlook diversity in damaging ways. Spelman's *Inessential Woman* (1988) details many of the ploys of these methodological essentialisms. In particular, she shows how analyses of oppression that understand gender oppression as distinctive from other forms of oppression, or that talk in terms of women "as women" – in abstraction from other aspects of their lives – fail to understand the entanglement of sexism with other forms of oppression and tacitly essentialize the interests and experiences of some, usually privileged, white middle-class women, rather than others. Even feminists who are sensitive to the social impacts of class and race, such as Beauvoir and Chodorow, readily slip into talking about the relations between men and women, and between women and their children, respectively, as if class, race, ethnic identity or sexual orientation made no difference to the truth of statements about "men and women" or "maternal relations" (see Spelman 1988: 62–6, 85–9). Another example of an essentialist device is talk about sexism in terms, usually tacit, of *white* male supremacy. Overcoming oppression in these terms, by giving women access to the halls of (white) men's power, may enhance the opportunities of white women but it would be unlikely to address racism and the situations of black women and men. Here, the neglect of black *males* in the analysis has the effect of taking the situation of white women in a white supremacist society as essential to understanding gender oppression. The experiences of black women and their concerns about racism are sidelined as inessential to the problem (see *ibid.*: 117–18).

All in all, the charge of essentialism – that theorizations of women's lives in terms of commonalities and generalizations are frequently flawed because they fail to understand the heterogeneity and power relativities of lived experience – has radically transformed contemporary feminisms. After all, with their focus on the emancipation and empowerment of the oppressed, feminist projects become hypocritical unless they strive to encompass the aspirations of all women. Charges that analyses focus either implicitly or explicitly on the experiences, interests and values of a particular group of women to the exclusion of those of other women seriously undermine this objective. Establishing itself as anti-essentialist has consequently become a dominant theme of feminist thought. (Indeed, some feminists even mark the anti-essentialist move to focus on "difference" in feminist thought as a new, "third wave" of feminism – sometimes also ambiguously referred to as "postfeminism" – in contrast to western women's "second-wave" aspirations for equality and first-wave struggles for women's suffrage.) Anti-essentialist feminisms hence draw attention to the diversity and intersecting nature of oppressions and the complexity, fragility and mutability of subjectivities and identities. In order to overcome false generalizations, they accept the political necessity of continuing recognition of the partiality and contingency of claims about womanhood and gender, and of vigilance concerning the notions of difference that they, at least implicitly, invoke as a crucial self-reflective requirement.

Anti-essentialist difficulties

However, as we have seen in previous chapters (as well as earlier in this chapter), the rejection of essentialism is often fraught with difficulties for feminist projects. The apparent tension between generalizing claims about women and the recognition of differences frequently seems to lead to a dead end. On the one hand, if all generalizations about women are inherently partial and exclusionary, then the terms of women's liberation seem to be similarly contaminated. In whose name can any version of feminism speak if all namings are incomplete and oppressive to those they omit? On the other hand, if all the differences among women are to be recognized, feminist projects face a slippery slope of endless fragmentation and proliferation of identities. How can women forge a movement from innumerable different voices? The tension develops from the recognition that feminist thought needs to become more nuanced and context-specific in its analyses in order to encompass the interests and values of all women; yet, as we shall discuss in Chapters 5 and 6, generalized understandings of womanhood are still important for social and political change. As a result, concern arises that the relativization of women's identities and subjectivities to the specificity of their sociohistorical contexts will undercut the possibility of any social criticism or political mobilization. The problem, differences among and within women, invites anti-essentialist responses but these responses themselves raise a new set of problems for feminist thinking.

In other words, anti-essentialist feminisms pose challenges relating to the nature of social knowledge and political resistance, and the connections between them: the relationship between theory and practice. As we have seen, for instance, some feminist activists have seen the development of anti-essentialism as an exercise in academic theoretical navel-gazing that fails to connect with such practical and political difficulties as increasing sexual violence and entrenched sexual inequality and discrimination, especially in non-western countries. (American philosopher Martha Nussbaum's strident criticism of Butler in "The Professor of Parody" [1999b] for her lofty abstractions and detachment from non-academic feminisms exemplifies this kind of criticism.) According to this sort of critique, privileged, western feminist theoreticians are engaged in some sort of make-work programme for themselves in the academy; their complex analyses of essentialism and invocations of psychoanalysis and poststructuralism have effectively abandoned the immense practical problems of women's oppression. Their (apparently) jargon-laden language also helps in fuelling the sociocultural backlash against feminist analyses.

For many of the activists critical of such abstractions the answer is to get out into the real world and start doing practice not theory. In part, this kind of response borrows from analyses of the divide between theory and practice that have continually dogged theoretical work more generally. But it also resonates with other more theoretical responses to feminist anti-essentialism that are concerned with the effects of scepticism about gender categories in abstraction from practical contexts of oppression and inequality. There is, in other words, a concern in relation to both critical social research and political action that anti-essentialist gender scepticism may become a totalizing rejection of all generalizations, as well as endorsing the absolute incommensurability of all individual identities.

Part of the difficulty here arises from accounts of the anti-essentialist response that turn the criticism of *false* generalizations into an in-principle criticism of *all* generalizations. After all, poststructuralist analyses of the logic of categorization seem to confirm the view that *a priori* use of any generalizing terms will have negative repercussions for some women. Such radical anti-essentialism, however, is a non-starter, for it makes essentialism unavoidable in any talk at all about women and men. Feminists who critically invoke anti-essentialism in these all-encompassing terms – as a charge against all generalized categories – undermine their own positions and the critical import of their analyses, for their criticisms apply to every viewpoint, including their own. In a similar way, some theorists read anti-essentialist emphases on the differences between and the uniqueness of individuals as claims about the absolute incommensurability of differences. But again this hyperbolic position makes essentialism unavoidable in all talk and indeed renders talk itself – meaningful communication across differences – nonsensical. Although it is certainly the case that differences between people prevent complete understanding, nevertheless some commonalities are necessary for any talk to get started in the first place.

Clarifying the mistakes of these radical understandings can avoid at least some of the difficulties anti-essentialist feminisms pose. But questions remain. How is feminist theorizing and research to proceed, given the way consideration of differences among and within women has unmasked problems of essentialism? How should feminists see the connections between different women that make understandings of gender politically important? What shape should feminist politics and feminist enquiry take in light of the complications of differing agendas, interests and values? As many of the topics we discuss in *Understanding Feminism* demonstrate, finding a path through these issues takes up much of feminist thought.

Rethinking the possibilities

As we have already seen, poststructuralist feminists respond to these difficulties in a variety of ways that shift understandings of the nature of political action. Some, such as Butler and British-Indian-American theorist Gayatri Spivak, have argued that theorists have articulated the logic of categorization not so much to draw attention to a mistake in feminist theorizing but as a warning of the dangers that generalizations can bring. In their eyes, the point is that generalizations, because they always exclude some possibilities, frequently result in abuses: the subordination and oppression of those who are left out. Consequently, continuous scrutiny and contesting of the terms of gender categories in politics and research are crucial to feminist work. As Butler puts it, "The task is to interrogate what the theoretical move that establishes foundations *authorizes*, and what precisely it excludes or forecloses" (1992: 7). In her turn, Spivak (1990) has influentially defended what she calls "strategic essentialism", a position that accepts that organization for political purposes necessarily entails uniting under a single banner and thereby some form of exclusion, but that this is simply a provisional necessity, not a categorical matter. This agenda resonates for many feminists. However, building it on a radical stance against any forms of homogenization and the continuous multiplication of differences within gender terms again raises doubts about the connections between theory and practice, and the structure of an effective feminist politics.

In a different vein, Kristeva has argued for the multiplication of differences within understandings of the concept of femininity as a strategy for resisting externally prescribed definitions and roles, including those of some versions of feminism. In this account, the locus of political action shifts to the specificity of individual subjects: to a subjectivist politics in which feminist resistance is about how each individual positions herself in relation to the social and cultural order in which she lives. That is, Kristeva's strategy is to give up the macropolitics of feminism for the micropolitics of a psychoanalytically sponsored individual transformation. Only then, she contends, can feminism "manage to rid itself of its belief in Woman, Her power, and Her writing and support instead the singularity of each woman, her complexities, her many languages, at the cost of a single horizon, of a single perspective" (1997: 366).

Nevertheless, although putting one's individual house in order is undoubtedly a large part of political change, the "community" of particular individuals that this move endorses seems to many to be a distant ideal that has little connection with addressing pervasive contexts of institutionally supported sexual abuse and exploitation. Accordingly, alternative approaches have centred on developing understandings of the structure of feminist communities and coalitions. That is, the focus shifts to working out how women can be held together in collective action, without losing sight of the political importance of their diverse histories and contexts, the multiple strands of commonality and differ-ence among them, and the inner complexity and tensions of individual identities. (In Chapter 6, we discuss a practical effort to engage in this sort of collective action in the context of global feminist activism.)

Other responses attempt to encapsulate the meanings that hold fem-inist research and political action together in terms of the history of intersecting social forces that have shaped understandings of gender. For example, British philosopher Alison Stone in her paper "Essen-tialism and Anti-essentialism in Feminist Philosophy" (2004) argues that women are identifiable through their acquisition and reworking of pre-established and historically shifting interpretations and practices of femininity. African-American philosopher Naomi Zack's *Inclusive Fem-inism* postulates that women share a relationship to the historical cat-egory of "individuals who are designated female from birth or biological mothers or primary sexual choice of men" (2005: 8). In her turn, taking a structuralist rather than an individualist approach, Young (2005) argues that gender is subtended by the three social axes of a sexual division of labour, normative heterosexuality and gendered hierarchies of power. But again, while these approaches may seem to solve the theoretical conundrum, their purchase in practical contexts is limited. Explaining group membership or the use of gender as an analytical category on these terms seems cumbersome at best and, at worst, beside the point.

Drawing on their cross-cultural experiences of feminist activism, Latin American feminists have provided some other important leads. Maria Lugones's collection of essays, *Pilgrimages/Peregrinajes* (2003a), for example, talks about the possibilities of affirming the complexity of identities and coalitions that are the result of various intermeshing "differences" within and between women. Critical of poststructuralist rejections of identity politics and the political significance of groups (despite some similarities in understandings of the nature of identity), Lugones describes the complexity of selves that are at the same time unified and multiplicitous, and coalitions of such selves that resist their multiple oppressions while working against tendencies to categorize and homogenize their affiliations. These are selves – like her Latina, woman, lesbian self – whose being contests their interlocking oppressions rather than simply representing the aggregation of separable and fragmented forms of oppression. On this view, the possibility for resistance and liberation arises from the hybridity and multiplicity of lives that activate the tensions and ambiguities of intermeshed differences and that defy forces of separation as well as univocality. In a memorable essay, Lugones recalls the activity of "curdling" when the ingredients in an emulsion (egg yolks and oil in mayonnaise, for example) tend to separate out but remain intermixed and impure. "Curdled" – and the Latina term, *mestizaje* – become a metaphor for resistance to the logic of control and purity:

> *Mestizaje* defies control through simultaneously asserting the impure, curdled multiple state and rejecting fragmentation into pure parts. In this play of assertion and rejection, the mestiza is unclassifiable, unmanageable. She has no pure parts to be "had", controlled. (Lugones 2003b: 123)

On this view, the problem of determining the nature of feminist group connections and political identifications that honour plurality and in-between-ness readily becomes prey to the abstraction of theoretical processes that seek to determine boundaries, and divide what is shared from what is not. For Lugones, community is to be understood as forged among concrete and complex subjects whose activation of their "nonreducible, cantankerous, fleshy, interrelated, positioned" selves (2003a: 196) resists pervasive and oppressive forces of homogenization and fragmentation. Resistant communities are open-ended and constantly shifting under the tensions of domination and resistance to domination.

Lugones's response to the problem of differences among and within women provides a rich understanding of the complexity of individual identities and the complexity of group interactions. It is not the end of the story, however, as the tensions between local analyses and challenges to structural power remain problematic and difficult to straddle. But it is emblematic of the necessity for feminist theory and practice to build complexity and the salience of intersecting oppressions into its core. It also shows how the interlinking of gender oppression with that of other differences pushes the compass of feminist projects to include resistance to all forms of social marginalization and exclusion. These issues – what could be called issues of individual and collective agency and responsibility – will be the focus of Chapters 5 and 6.

Summary of key points

- Mainstream feminisms (those privileging the concerns of white, middle-class women) have been criticized for their "false generalizations" and presumed common essences of womanhood and women's experiences of oppression, which ignore the many differences among women based on race, class, sexuality, abledness and so on.
- Charges of essentialism have also come from poststructuralists, who argue that the meanings of terms such as "woman" are contextual and subject to change over time, thus making attempts to generalize about the nature of womanhood both impossible and inherently exclusionary. Other theorists have criticized assumptions about the applicability of social "norms" to all women.
- The complex intersectionality of multiple identities and forms of oppression mean that a "pop-bead" approach (whereby accounts of each form are simply combined) is inadequate for achieving greater recognition of differences within feminisms. Creative approaches are required to dismantle the hierarchies of privilege and disadvantage inherent in such differences.
- Establishing itself as anti-essentialist has become a dominant concern of feminist thought, with some groups engaging in identity politics and separatism. However, such fragmentation may

undermine the power of collective action, and risks valuing theorization over practical change.

- Some feminists are now calling for feminisms that recognize both individuality and collectivity, and which are more fluid and resistant to oppressive forces of homogenization and fragmentation.

five

Agency

The call for women's agency

From our discussions so far, it seems clear that whenever and wherever the various forms of feminism are scratched, what shows is a desire and a call for women's agency, for a capacity for self-determination and autonomy according to which women are able to be effective against their own oppression. Although these terms – agency, self-determination, autonomy – are not quite interchangeable, they all point to women's desire for control over their own bodies and lives. This is their desire to be able to choose and act freely in accordance with their own objectives, to have some sense of entitlement to real choices and objectives, to be able to act against their subordination and, perhaps most importantly, to have a sense that they can "be themselves" or "be true to themselves". This is the desire that underpins Wollstonecraft's call for the rights of women, Beauvoir's call for women to no longer be constrained to domesticity, and even the Spice Girls' call for "girl power". It is the desire driving women's consciousness-raising activities, the proliferation of mantras for (women's) self-empowerment, and the current catch-phrase, "You go, girl".

This desire for effective agency thus drives the manifold projects of western feminisms, whether radical or liberal or socialist or psychoanalytic or poststructuralist, although in each case just what is understood as "agency" might be different. It also drives the work of third-world feminists and feminists of colour; although, as we saw in Chapter 4, they remind us of the complexity of agency once we become attuned to issues of race, ethnicity, class and geographical location as well as sex and gender. The desire for agency even drives the work of post-feminists and proponents of girl power in their promotion of (attractive and well-made-up) girl heroes who do their own "hunting, fighting and monster slaying" (Hopkins 2002: 3). Agency, however, despite going to the heart of feminist concern with oppression and the constraints on women's action, self-realization and freedom, has also been one of the most contested projects for feminists, at least with regard to what its criteria would actually need to be. Further, women's desire for agency may be seen as paradoxical in so far as many feminist analyses suggest that, owing to their social conditioning, women may lack the requisite abilities for taking control of their lives and resisting oppression.

This chapter is thus an investigation into agency and its position within feminist projects. More specifically, it is an investigation of who is seen to be a fully fledged agent and why, of some of the problems inherent in traditional understandings of agency, and how agency can be compromised. It further explores key feminist attempts to re-vision agency – to develop an effective agency from a feminist perspective – given the critique of traditional conceptions of self-determination and autonomy (especially with regard to how they overlook power inequalities and institutionalized oppressions), insights regarding multi-dimensionality outlined in anti-essentialist conceptions of identity, and renewed understandings of what it means to resist oppression and exercise agency in resistance to adverse socialization. Finally, after having considered these issues of individual agency, along with some of the associated processes and problems of subjectification, we shall outline some of the ways feminist thinkers have responded to questions concerning collective and political agency. After all, as Carol Gould has noted, effective women's agency requires not just self-government but "freedom from discrimination and domination", and the freedom to participate in the control of "the economic and social conditions of our lives" (1984: 5–6).

Traditional concepts of autonomous agency

If the attaining and recognition of effective agency is, as we have suggested, the very point of many feminist projects, then the question stands as to what agency is in so far as historically women have not been seen as possessing it. Most simply, in the western tradition of thought, agency is having the power and capacity to act as one chooses.

Linked to notions of self-determination and autonomy, agency denotes the exercise of free will and personal freedom, at least within the bounds of socially authorized actions. It also assumes certain capacities on the part of the agent. Specifically, the agent not only has to be able to make sense of and rank her own needs and desires, but must also have the self-esteem to recognize that she can rightfully have and pursue her own needs and desires. In addition, she has to be able to couple her needs and desires to possible actions and, more generally, see the possibility for action, as well as weighing up pros and cons and eventually deciding on specific actions. Overall, however, agency is tied to the idea that individuals are able to make their own decisions and that when they do so they are not unduly coerced or otherwise under someone else's control or influence. It further implies that there is a good fit between one's desires, choices and actions and one's individual identity, meaning that one's desires, choices and actions are one's own, neither uncharacteristic nor purposeless.

It should be obvious, then, that this conception of the autonomous agent has not always been applicable to women. Historically, women have not had access to the same range of choices as men, let alone the same range of possible actions. Think of how women cross-culturally have often not had full access to the public sphere, or to certain kinds of education or employment, and of the impact of what are often strong cultural and social expectations regarding motherhood and family duty and servicing the needs of men. Further, as we discuss in various ways throughout this book, women's choices have often not been made autonomously; women cross-culturally have not always been considered completely capable of making certain kinds of choices or completing certain kinds of actions either on their own or at all. Think here of that old mantra of men being more rational than women – women are supposed to be more intuitive and emotional, or at least less able to regulate their emotions and think objectively – or the notion common to many ethnic and religious traditions that women are to be led and to follow others. Further, women have not always been in the situation to make what are seen as fully autonomous choices in so far as they are characteristically bound by expectations and relations of interdependency, such as situations of caring for children and/or others where they accept the responsibility to consider others' needs and desires alongside (if not over) their own:

> As a woman, I feel I never understood that I was a person, that
> I could make decisions and I had a right to make decisions. I

always felt that that belonged to my father or my husband in some way, or church, which was always represented by a male clergyman. They were the three men in my life: father, husband, and clergyman, and they had much more to say about what I should or shouldn't do.   (Cited in Gilligan 1982: 67)

In addition, women have often not had full control over their own bodies, not because they are somehow more prone to their hormones or emotions than men (although of course that has been argued), but because of various forms of legislation, and social and cultural surveillance. As a result women have frequently not been considered to be autonomous agents, to possess the same level of self-determination and self-governance as men. And, of course, it goes without saying that these are some of the very conditions that sparked the manifold feminist demands for women's agency.

Problems with the traditional autonomous agent

A big question is whether the autonomous agent as traditionally understood actually exists. In response to this question, it has been argued that in order for someone to be completely autonomous she or he would surely need to be completely self-sufficient and unencumbered – rather like Robinson Crusoe – but further able to extricate herself or himself from all socialized norms and expectations. This is because socialization has been shown to impede autonomy in a range of ways. For instance, it can shape or curtail people's dreams and beliefs (including their beliefs about themselves), shape or constrain their development of certain skills and abilities, and enable or frustrate in very concrete ways their ability or freedom to realize their desires and carry out actions. Think, for instance, of how girls may be socialized to expect that they will get married ("every" girl dreams of marriage), have children ("every" girl wants babies), and play a significant role in servicing the needs of their husbands and households. Such expectations mean that girls – even if they have the chance – may not commit to developing or furthering their own careers (seeing life in the public domain not as intrinsically fulfilling but only as instrumentally valuable), instead, often encouraged by their families and culture, focusing on preparing themselves for finding a suitable marriage partner. This would seem to indicate that for someone to be really autonomous, they would need to have separated their essential self from all other influences, and to be sure that their decision-making was not driven in any way by such influences. Indeed, they would need to be able to exercise their reason and carry out decisions independently of even their own social expectations and involvements.

Autonomy in this unencumbered (and disembodied) sense would thereby seem to entail an impossibility in so far as human beings are socialized beings. People are reared in a social context of some sort or another, and remain, to at least some extent, involved in social relationships. Indeed, as New Zealand-American philosopher Annette Baier has noted, all individuals only become persons with their various subjective dreams and desires through their dependency on and relations with others. In her words, "Persons are essentially successors, heirs to other persons who formed and cared for them, and their personality is revealed both in their relations to others and in their response to their own recognized genesis" (1985: 85). This insight marks one of the most fundamental feminist critiques of traditional concepts of autonomy: that no individual, male or female, actually is this radically self-sufficient and unencumbered. Since all human beings grow up in social contexts and relationships, no one can be certain that they can identify and disregard every one of those expectations and norms that are part of their socialization and that have informed their identities and deep-seated values. Further, this critique makes the additional point that the traditional vision of autonomy has historically been underpinned by specific conceptions as to what is proper to masculinity, conceptions that are themselves socially constructed and maintained. For example, expectations of independence and self-sufficiency have, at least in the western world, tended to be more characteristic of the ways boys are socialized rather than girls. Conversely, girls have been typically enculturated into a "psychology of dependency and altruistic devotion to others", traits that are "traditionally associated with femininity" but are the very opposite of what is needed for autonomy (Meyers 2004: 4).

These issues seem to point to two possibilities for feminists: either the entire conception of and desire for autonomous agency is flawed and should be abandoned, or the conception of autonomous agency should be revisioned in such a way that the above critiques no longer apply. That is, the question is whether the ideal of autonomy can, in fact, be genuinely female- and feminist-friendly. At different times various feminists and other thinkers have held the first of these positions, rejecting the conception of autonomous agency. Arguments here have outlined autonomy in negative terms, as, for instance, that "thoroughly noxious concept" that "encourages us to believe that connecting and engaging with others limits us … and undermines our sense of self"

(Hoagland 1988: 144–5). Thinkers holding this view tend to affirm people's interconnectedness, their inherent sociality, and contend that it is only through their social connectedness that individuals – male and female – can discover what it truly is to be a human being. There is a range of projects exemplifying such a view, from revivals of ancient Greek understandings of the interrelatedness of persons with communities (in, for instance, virtue ethics), to what has come to be known as maternal thinking. From this latter perspective, the contention is that recognizing human beings' constitutive social embeddedness and interdependency – which, key thinkers argue, is exemplified in that "most central fundamental social relationship ... between mother or mothering person and child" (Held 1997: 634) – is essential for finding a way forward from increasingly pervasive and destructive assumptions that social relations and practices are simply instrumental to furthering the interests of unencumbered individuals. As American feminist philosopher Virginia Held has written, it is certainly worth looking to this relation between child and mothering person if human beings want to develop "a future more fit for our children than a global battleground for rational, egoistic entities trying, somehow, to restrain their antagonisms by fragile contracts" (1993: 204).

It should be clear, however, that this view really only demonstrates the rejection of the traditional conception of autonomy with its promotion of self-sufficient, unencumbered and hence impossible individuals. It does not help in suggesting ways to resist in contexts of oppression, and it does not seem useful in ascertaining what agency might mean for women in abusive situations or other instances of subordination. Importantly, then, the rejection of the traditional notion of the autonomous agent does not as such necessarily negate or exclude the possibility of revisioning conceptions of autonomy and the autonomous agent so that they are more female- and feminist-friendly. On this basis, collapsing the distinction between abandoning and revisioning traditional autonomy, several feminists argue that the general notion of autonomy is certainly still useful and that a female- and feminist-friendly understanding of autonomy is in fact possible.

Revisioning the traditional concept of the autonomous agent

Interestingly, in reconceiving agency many feminist thinkers have drawn on American psychologist Carol Gilligan's work on moral development. Basically, Gilligan has argued that the traditional conception of the autonomous agent is a clear exemplification of one of two common understandings (in the western world at least) of what it means to be a morally engaged individual. These two understandings, identified by Gilligan through the course of her research and set out in her influential work *In a Different Voice* (1982), are what she calls the rights or justice perspective and the care perspective, and they correlate, at least to some degree, with the moral understandings and decision-making of men and women respectively. That is, the rights or justice perspective – the typical moral perspective of the traditional autonomous agent – is, Gilligan found, more characteristic of men, while the care perspective is more characteristic of women's sense of moral agency. This is not to say that no men utilize the care perspective, and no women

---

Carol Gilligan (b. 1936)

Carol Gilligan is best known for her influential work *In a Different Voice* (1982). In response to early work with developmental psychologist Lawrence Kohlberg measuring the moral maturity of children, which was unable to explain why girls consistently scored lower than boys, Gilligan made the radical suggestion that it might be the Kohlberg test that was the problem rather than the girls' inherent moral immaturity. Gilligan noted that the traits of moral maturity at the top of Kohlberg's scale – autonomous reasoning from moral principles – correlated with the aims of boys' socialization while girls tended to incorporate more contextually specific modes of deliberation into their moral judgements. She argued that girls tend to speak using an "ethic of care" perspective, the "different voice" she contrasts with the mainstream "ethic of justice" voice of traditional moral theory. While she identified gendered correlations with these voices, Gilligan contended that this was due more to socialization than nature and that both voices were available to both genders, as well as being equally valuable. These ideas have been consolidated and developed in a range of further works, including *Mapping the Moral Domain* (edited with Janie Victoria Ward and Jill McLean Taylor, 1989), *Women, Girls, and Psychotherapy* (edited with Annie G. Rogers and Deborah L. Tolman, 1991), *Meeting at the Crossroads* (with Lyn Mikel Brown, 1992), *Between Voice and Silence* (with Jill McLean Taylor and Amy M. Sullivan, 1997), and *The Birth of Pleasure* (2002). She also published a work of fiction, *Kyra*, in 2008. Gilligan's theoretical work, especially her notion of the "ethic of care", has been highly influential for feminist work in ethics, epistemology and legal theory, although it has been criticized for its white, liberal and heteronormative assumptions. Her work has also been enormously influential in non-feminist spheres (some argue that this is owing to its continuities with dominant cultural assumptions) and in 1996 *Time* magazine listed her as one of the twenty-five most influential Americans.

the rights or justice perspective. Gilligan notes that, at least according to her findings in the late 1970s and 1980s, many individuals – men and women – seem to move between the two, but she also stresses that historically there has been a strong correlation between women and the care perspective.

With regard to these two perspectives, however, the key issues relevant here are as follows. While those utilizing the rights or justice perspective suppose that the self is rather like the traditional unencumbered autonomous agent, those utilizing the care perspective suppose the self to be primarily involved with and concerned for others. Hence, for those who use the care perspective, caring relations with others are intrinsic to their very process of decision-making and, indeed, to their sense of self as a whole. That is, caring relations with others are not something that people need to put aside when they come to make decisions that matter to them. This is a contested issue for feminists, however, as it means that the practice of care-based agency – and the fact of its stronger correlation with women than men – ends up looking much like the sort of practices that have traditionally been associated with women's supposedly inherent nature and the social roles of subordination and dependency that this is seen to justify: roles and practices that are considered to undermine the possibility of women's agency. Certainly Gilligan contends that these gender correlations are more a matter of socialization than nature or biology (Gilligan 1982: 7–8), a point she makes with reference to Chodorow's psychoanalytic account of the different socializations of boys and girls (previously mentioned in Chapter 2), but her discussion of care-based agency slips between describing it as "female" and as "more characteristic of female". Regardless of this – and regardless of the various challenges that have been directed at both Gilligan's and Chodorow's research – the care perspective has provided for many feminists a productive basis from which to rework the traditional understanding of autonomy.

Care-based agency and relational autonomy

More precisely, where Gilligan's prime concern was for the identification of the two perspectives – justice and care – and to argue for the validity of the care perspective, a range of other feminist thinkers have used her insights to argue for the significance of interconnectedness and caring interactions with others. In their view, it is imperative to develop an account of agency that actually relates to the context in which human beings live, where this context is one of dependency, socialization and involvement with others. After all, human beings are intrinsically dependent not just as social beings, but in terms of needing others to care for them when they are infants, when they are old and probably several times in the intervening period as well, to say nothing of those who need others to care for them all through their lives. On this basis, then, the care perspective's assumption that meaningful relations are at the heart of the self, and thereby need to be valued within its decision-making, is an appropriate starting-point. Agency, in this context, comes to point to decision-making that actually factors in human dependency and values social relations, and that responds to both contextual factors and the very specific needs and desires of others. However, while this understanding of agency does not necessarily have to be conceived of as female-specific, for many feminists it still seems uncomfortably close to mirroring the way women across a range of cultures have historically been socialized into an ethic of altruism and self-sacrifice where the needs and desires of others – especially men – are placed before one's own (necessarily selfish) needs and desires. In other words, it looks as if this supposedly gender-neutral account of agency ends up affirming and augmenting women's participation in their own oppression.

Saving care-based agency from an ethic of self-sacrifice that confirms women's dependent status has thus been one of the key problems for this attempt to rethink conceptions of autonomous agency, and has resulted in an array of different suggestions. Some feminists have argued, for instance, that genuine caring – which is typically exemplified by the bond between mothering person and child – simply does not equate to self-sacrifice in so far as, first, what the carer most wants is actually to secure the interests of the cared-for, and, secondly, all effective caring needs to include self-care. (With regard to the latter, presumably without self-care one will eventually not be able to function well in any relations.) However, even if these arguments hold, the notion of care-based agency seems problematic in other ways. For instance, some thinkers have argued that it ends up taking socialized feminine characteristics – altruism and social involvement, say – as if they were naturally present within people. (This is another example of how theories based on assumed social characteristics can still end up attracting the charge of essentialism.) Proponents of care-based relations and agency have responded in their turn that while the correlation between caring and people (women in particular) might certainly be no more than the outcome of socialization, this does not negate the importance of understanding agency in terms of people's constitutive embeddedness within caring relations. Society might do well, they suggest, to socialize men in this way as well as women.

There is a further point here, however. Basically, sustaining Gilligan's point that the care perspective is one of the two common (western) understandings of what it means to be morally engaged, care-based agency is understood here in moral terms. It stands for a relational moral agency able to explain and justify obligations to dependent or vulnerable others. What it does not seem to do, however, is provide any viable model of agency for the vulnerable and oppressed themselves. Nor does it seem able to challenge gender-differentiated expectations as to who takes on caring responsibilities or how society supports those who do the caring. (Remember here the lack of a clear distinction between practices of care-based agency and those of women socialized into traditional altruistic feminine characteristics.) After all, it is unlikely that those who benefit from these arrangements would ever see challenging them as part of their care-based obligations unless those who bear the burden push them to do so.

One response to this is to be found in the contemporary argument for "relational autonomy", an umbrella term that refers to a range of related perspectives, including that of care-based agency, but with the focus shifted from that of a morally significant relationality to that of a more neutral notion of relationality as interdependence. These perspectives, proponents of relational autonomy stress, share "the conviction that persons are socially embedded and that agents' identities are formed within the context of social relationships and shaped by a complex of intersecting social determinants, such as race, class, gender, and ethnicity" (Mackenzie & Stoljar 2000: 4). Indeed, proponents of relational autonomy argue that the recognition of this complexity will result in a much richer conception of agency and agents, one that recognizes and encompasses the point that people make their choices and carry out their decisions on the basis of far more than just a disengaged and unencumbered sense of self. Relational autonomy, in other words, is understood as an attempt to describe the actual rather than the ideal agent, and to understand what agency might look like once the notion of the unencumbered and disengaged self has been exposed for the illusion it is. Now although such descriptions have been undertaken across a broad range of perspectives and theoretical domains (including that of Gilligan's care perspective), and have led to diverse discussions of those features of agents that have received little or no coverage in accounts of the traditional autonomous agent – features such as "memory, imagination, and emotional dispositions and attitudes" (*ibid.*: 21) – there is one fairly typical characteristic of these accounts.

This is the shift from seeing autonomy or agency in terms of capacities and practices only possible for a certain kind of self – the traditional conception of the unencumbered self, say – to seeing it in terms of skills or competencies able to be developed by any/every self, albeit to varying degrees depending on the self's social environment. This is a procedural focus in so far as what matters – that is, what makes autonomy – is the exercise of a particular kind of self-reflection based on the use of specific skills or competencies. (As we shall discuss further below, American philosopher Diana Tietjens Meyers, in particular, talks of "autonomy competencies".) More specifically, autonomy in this sense can be summed up as consisting of three integrated sets of capacities: first, the possession of certain skills or competencies; secondly, the capacity for reflection based on these skills; and thirdly, the activation or exercise of those skills. And it should also be clear that the distinction between the second and third sets of capacities is key, entailing as it does the difference between being able to decide what attitude one will take to one's situation and being able to act with regard to the situation. This framework is thus an important development regarding understandings of autonomy in so far as it marks the recognition that a self can be autonomous and challenge its situation, at least to some extent, even under conditions of oppression. On this view the exercise of autonomy is certainly easier under conditions supportive of autonomy, but the lack of such conditions does not make autonomy impossible.

Autonomy competency and agency under oppression

Horrible as they are, social and economic structures that funnel individuals into a preordained status, that regiment their life trajectories, and that penalise nonconformity need not defeat autonomy. A social and economic environment that makes a wide range of attractive options available to all individuals is conducive to, not necessary for, autonomy. (Meyers 2004: 14)

As noted above, Meyers has set forth one of the clearest accounts of what autonomy competency might mean, along with what she sees as some of the hows and whys of the practice of autonomy under oppressive conditions. Hers is both a relational and procedural account of autonomy, and she stresses that because of this there can be no single blueprint for living an autonomous life. More specifically, Meyers contends that autonomy competency is nothing more than the capacity to use a "well-developed, well-coordinated repertoire" of skills in "self-discovery, self-definition, and self-direction" (*ibid*.: xvii) across a diverse range of both every-day and crisis situations. She adds that these situations may themselves either foster or be hostile to the exercising of autonomy, but stresses that the situations do not as such dictate whether autonomy is possible. (After all, if that were the case, people living in oppressive regimes, and women living in sexist societies, could be said to possess no autonomy at all and this is surely not the case.) In other words, Meyers proposes that, since it is based in skills that need to be learned and developed, autonomy competency is by no means an "all-or-nothing phenomenon" (*ibid*.: 8). Hence, along with the possibility that someone can and does live a fully autonomous life, she contends that "it must be possible for a life to contain pockets ... and threads of autonomy" (*ibid*.). All this would mean, then, that even under oppressive social circumstances (often thought to be autonomy-impairing) someone may be able to exercise control over her life in particular episodic situations: the choice of one goal over another, for instance. Further, she suggests that the exercise of autonomy in even very limited instances can assist in the development of greater autonomy competency.

These kinds of ideas have proved fruitful for many feminists, espe-cially the idea that autonomy is the development and practice of a certain kind of competency in the use of skills in self-discovery, self-definition and self-direction. Such a conception of autonomy has been particularly useful for resisting what many people call "victim" feminism: the idea that women's actions are best explained by their status as victims of oppression. An example of the latter would be when courts and others use the concept of "battered wife syndrome" to explain a woman's assault or murder of her abuser. Such an explanation strips women of their agency, their actions being explained not by their own intentionality or choice but by an unchallengeable socialization or psychological condi-tion (see Morrissey 2003). Nevertheless, this kind of focus on autonomy competency, or indeed on relational or care-based autonomy, is still problematic for many feminists. While such models are certainly cog-nizant of relationality, they still do not seem able to provide resources by which women can challenge systemic oppression. The main issue here is that these models conceive of autonomy in terms of an *individual's* competencies, meaning that agency is a matter for separate individuals rather than for individuals as members of groups, and it is the latter that is surely what is needed to effectively tackle systemic oppression.

In addition to the previous point, while Meyers's account of autonomy competency describes how autonomy might still be practised even in very limited ways within circumscribed conditions, the question remains as to whether choices made under such conditions could ever be autonomous in a meaningful sense. Certainly choices might be made via the exercise of relevant skills, but is this really enough for autonomy? Could autonomy really equate to carrying out choices that are just what would be expected on the basis of one's socialization? For instance, are women who choose to stay with violent partners really acting autonomously if they have been socialized to believe that they have no choice (it is not "right" to leave a spouse, there is no safe place to go)? Once again the problem of tackling systemic oppression becomes evident.

A focus on autonomy competency, however, is only one of the feminist strategies that theorists have explored with respect to conceptualizing the possibility of effective agency under oppression. Another tactic has been to develop a version of feminist agency capable of challenging the power inequalities that maintain women's subordination to and dependency on men, thereby considering women's agency in terms of their capacity to resist oppressive conditions and any co-option into oppressive practices. In this instance, one of the recurring strategies suggested by western middle-class feminists has been for women to demonstrate their agency by engaging in separatist initiatives. As outlined by Marilyn Frye, these initiatives can take many forms, but might include:

> Breaking up or avoiding close relationships or working relationships; forbidding someone to enter your house; excluding someone from your company or from your meeting; withdrawal from participation in some activity or institution, or avoidance of participation; avoidance of communications and influence from certain quarters (not listening to music with sexist lyrics, not watching TV); withholding commitment or support; rejection or rudeness toward obnoxious individuals ... Ceasing to be loyal to something or someone is a separation.
> (1997: 408)

As Frye continues, such initiatives have been seen by many feminists as some of the few ways open to women to develop a sense of agency and integrity that is not contingent on any of the masculinist assumptions underpinning traditional conceptions of autonomy and that also remains attuned to the idea that an effective notion of autonomy from a feminist perspective would be wary of seeing socialized choices as autonomous. More specifically, such initiatives suggest ways open to women to practise a counter-socialized agency in oppressive situations in so far as they mark the point where women decide to reject and opt out of prevailing practices. Further, they suggest women's exercise of agency in situations that might seem to have no real possibilities for action or for change. Examples such as the "marriage resistors" in early-twentieth-century southern China testify to the history of this form of female-based agency. Marriage resistance may have been a scandalous affront to Chinese tradition, but even the simplest act of "no-saying", as Frye has noted, marks the beginning of gaining some control that can lead to the possibility of self-definition, self-direction and self-governance (*ibid.*: 411–12).

One of the most controversial of such separatist proposals has been the call for lesbian separatism (also discussed in Chapter 4) that emanated from both radical and lesbian feminists. Although there are important differences between each of these groups, they share the basic assumption that it is only when women "begin disengaging from male-defined response patterns" that they can "realise [their] autonomy as [female] human beings" (Radicalesbians 1997: 156). In other words, this is to argue that women can only really express their agency successfully in woman-identified, woman-directed spaces and relationships, and that all hetero-spaces are inherently oppressive. (This sort of view and the question whether, as we discussed in Chapter 3, woman-identified spaces necessarily include any erotic components have led to some tension between lesbian theory and feminist theories that acknowledge that intimate relationships with men may be culturally, emotionally and/or economically important.)

The work of American lesbian theorists – such as Sarah Hoagland and Claudia Card – who suggest that lesbianism can provide constructive possibilities for conceiving of a feminist agency that is neither framed in terms of traditional masculine assumptions, nor stymied by being complicit with oppressive social contexts, provides a related argument. Hoagland, for example, notes that (lesbian) agency must always involve "the ability to go on under oppression: to continue to make choices, to act within the oppressive structure of our society and challenge oppression, to create meaning through our living" (1988: 13). Specifically, then, the kinds of lesbian agency envisaged by Hoagland and Card are concerned with ways of reclaiming and maintaining personal integrity in the face of oppressive conditions. This might involve what Card calls "taking responsibility for oneself" – standing behind one's own choices, actions, identity and self-definition – which, in the context of lesbianism, would need to include "coming out" as a lesbian (Card 1996: 141). Standing behind one's choices and definitions is, however, intrinsically risky given the fact that an individual's own definitions may not correspond to prevailing ones. Card reminds us through this example that all agency is an exercise in risk-taking and involves what she calls "moral luck" (*ibid.*: 150).

Such ideas, while they might have some resonances for middle-class, western (lesbian) feminists, are perhaps less productive for the many women in more oppressive cultures and women in more constrained situations (subsistence workers, sweatshop workers, victims of sex trafficking, etc.). In these latter instances, such choices may remain either outside the realm of possibility or constrained in some other way (despite Meyers-type positions on autonomy). For instance, in the context of the third world, as Indian feminist Uma Narayan points out, feminist criticism of and resistance to oppressive conditions and associated calls for women's agency can be read as a lack of respect for traditional culture and its associated practices. In other words, some people may read such moves as cultural disloyalty based on an inauthentic westernization (Narayan 1997: 397). Narayan contends that to avoid charges of westernization and cultural disloyalty any feminist strategies for resistance to traditional cultural practices that subordinate women (e.g. child marriage, arranged marriage, dowry-related harassment and death, veiling and *sati*) must work from within that culture. Acting against cultural oppression is never easy (as we have seen above) and it becomes even more fraught when outside (westernizing) forces heavily threaten that culture. (In Chapter 6 we take up the tension between western and postcolonial feminists' understandings of non-western cultures in relation to feminists' global responsibilities.)

Agency and the problem of essentialized identity

An important problem that emerges from these moves, however, and one that is clearly evident given our discussions in previous chapters, is that many of the feminist accounts that we have considered so far for the revisioning of agency and autonomy seem to end up basing agency on one or another aspect of some supposedly essential identity. For instance, we have seen arguments for women's agency based on them essentially being social and in relation, being (female) in oppressive conditions, being lesbian, being a "third-world" woman. Underlying these views, too, is the assumption that to be an autonomous agent one needs to possess some integrity as a self and some sense of being a self (not to mention being recognized and treated as a self). That is, one surely cannot make autonomous – in whatever sense – decisions if no one sees those decisions as owned by that decision-maker. (This, of course, is part of what Card means by "taking responsibility for oneself".) However, while feminist versions of agency do not assume (as the traditional conception of autonomy does) the existence of an independent, unitary and totalized self, we have also seen, especially in the previous three chapters, that there has been a growing questioning as to whether any claims about the integrity or coherence of one's identity can legitimately be made. More specifically, if it turns out that the self is internally fragmented, or worse, an illusion, what would this mean for conceptions of even the relational agent?

Many feminist thinkers see recognition of the multi-dimensionality of the self as an initial strategy for exploring this question. This is simply the recognition that it is impossible to describe accurately the social or relational self as made up of neatly integrated personal and social components or dimensions. Not only is this self not simply the sum of an individual's various relations with others and society, but people's "experience does not come neatly in segments, such that it is always possible to abstract what in one's experience is due to 'being a woman' from that which is due to 'being married', 'being middle class' and so forth" (Grimshaw 1986: 85). Hence feminist thinkers have generally come to contend that the various aspects or dimensions of the self interact in highly complex, occasionally conflicting, ways depending on the situation at hand. That is, the multi-dimensionality of the self is demonstrated not just by the fact that it inhabits different realms – including those to do with class, race, ethnicity, sexual orientation and so on – but also owing to the interaction of these different aspects in ways that are "sometimes compounding one another's effects and sometimes creating inner divisions and conflicts" (Meyers 2004: 15). Further, as Meyers stresses, these interactions may be neither completely determined nor recognized by the self in so far as they are also "significantly influenced by social systems of domination and subordination" (*ibid.*). For example, as we saw in the work of Lorde and Lugones in Chapter 4, proponents of multi-dimensionality or what is also called "intersectional identity" make the point that while class, race, ethnicity, sexual orientation and so forth may all impact on the self, it is next to impossible to trace their various effects back to their respective causes. This would seem to suggest that multi-dimensional or intersectional selves might find it difficult to achieve the self-knowledge, self-definition and self-direction necessary for effective agency, at least if agency is taken as having complete control over oneself. This, however, is perhaps too fast a dismissal of the possibility of agency for the multi-dimensional self. Meyers, for instance, argues that such dismissals rest on a misunderstanding of both self and agency in so far as there is no reason to understand either in "all or nothing" terms. And, as Lugones contends, it is certainly possible to resist effectively on some fronts even while one is caught up in oppressive systems on others.

Theorists working within the fields of psychoanalysis, postmodernism, poststructuralism and deconstruction (see, for instance, our discussion of Kristeva in Chapter 4) have also raised similar questions with regard to the integrity of the self. The starting-point for thinkers in all of these fields is, of course, Freud's insight that what people typically call "self" is at the very best fragmented, conflict-ridden, often self-deluded and thereby constitutively incapable of any real self-knowledge. From this point – which itself puts in question all of the traditional assumptions regarding the unified autonomous subject – many thinkers have gone on to argue what on first hearing confounds common sense: that the self may be no more than a discursive construction, that it cannot be found pure and independent beneath the effects of various social systems. Under this view, as Foucault has argued in particular, the self is more like the consolidated effect of all the discourses and social expectations that pre-date it. This in turn entails that the self is inextricable from its social discursive context, and that there can be no pre-cultural sense to any of the categories used to describe the self. For instance, as we have discussed in the previous chapters, categories such as "female" or "woman" have meaning only in terms of their discursive context. These views have, however, been seen as extremely problematic for attempts to theorize women's agency. For example, as American philosopher Linda Alcoff asks, "If the category 'woman' is fundamentally undecidable", then how can it be utilized to "demand legal abortions, adequate childcare, or wages based on comparable worth" (1997: 340)? (We shall see this issue emerge again in Chapter 6 when we explore questions of feminist responsibility.)

Nonetheless, what is seen as a problem here is perhaps again a matter of forgetting that the rejection of the traditional conception of the autonomous agent does not by itself entail the rejection of all conceptions of autonomy and agency. Certainly it is possible to argue that postmodern and poststructuralist critiques of the self problematize any attempt to develop a female-specific sense of agency (including a notion of effective feminist agency that is mindful of "women's" contexts of oppression), but it is important to remember that not all the feminist revisions of agency fall into this category. As we shall see below, some feminist thinkers have indeed taken these critiques of the self on board in their reworked understandings of agency.

Postmodern and poststructuralist-inspired revisionings of agency

One such understanding of agency inspired by postmodern and post-structuralist critiques of the self is to be found in the work of Butler, specifically her conception of "performative agency". (Another can be found in the work of Kristeva.) Now, as we discussed in Chapters 2 and 3, Butler's focus has been on reconceptualizing both subjectivity and gender from something that one is to something that one does, according to which they are both best understood as the effects of socially recognized practices being repeated over time. They are, in other words, "performative" in a way that does not pretend that there is anything like a pre-existing self who then chooses to perform as a self (making choices, performing actions, resisting oppressive conditions). Once again these are very difficult ideas, but the basic point is that people's activities create the particular personages they are rather than the other way round. (This is similar to the point made earlier, that relationality is not something a subject chooses; rather, the subject is a subject only because of her relationality.) Furthermore, Butler stresses that this does not happen in a vacuum. Rather, she argues that both subjectivity and gender (and the gender–sex complex) can only be formed and performed in terms of the available sociocultural expectations and discourses. Given these points, then – that the self does not pre-exist its various choices and actions and that it is perhaps only formed and performed with reference to existing sociocultural practices – what would this mean for the conception of agency? That is, what would a "performative agency" look like, given that "agency" here clearly does not mean the exercising of any traditional notion of autonomy (which assumes a pre-existing self)?

Although it might initially look as if there is no place for agency given Butler's poststructuralist argument concerning subjectivity and gendered identity, this is actually to move too fast. Indeed, Butler herself contends that agency – albeit a revised understanding of it – certainly exists for this self. As she puts it in *Gender Trouble*, although agency can no longer be understood in terms of an agent's choice of "whether to repeat", it might still be conceivable in terms of the issue of "how to repeat". That is, Butler reminds us that the carrying out of actions – even as they are framed by prevailing norms – always has the potential "to *displace* the very norms that enable the repetition itself" (1990: 148; see also 141). Agency, in other words, despite being the effect of socially determined practices, also resides in the possibility for inventive subversion and parody of those practices. Understood in this way, effective agency is that which draws attention to – or deconstructs – the social processes that produce (oppressive) normative expectations of individuals. Butler refers to the use of drag as exemplifying this notion of agency. Drag is a practice that is always and already inextricable from the gender norms for dressing that it contests, but at the same time it allows those norms to be shown up as a socially constructed set of constraints that simultaneously produces and sets the boundaries for gender identities.

Of course, engaging in such practices always runs the risk that their critical import will not be recognized or, more significantly, that they will bring seriously damaging repercussions. Using drag, for instance, might draw attention to dress codes and understandings of gender in some liberal societies, but in more oppressive societies it may be a non-starter because it is so transgressive that all it achieves is harsh punishment. We can see this dynamic playing out in a western context in the case, analysed by Australian theorist Belinda Morrissey in *When Women Kill* (2003), of Aileen Wuornos, an American lesbian and prostitute who killed seven men. (This case was also the subject of the film *Monster*.) Drawing on poststructuralist conceptions of agency, Morrissey argues that Wuornos's plea that she killed in self-defence – when the men whose sexual needs she was servicing brutally assaulted her – could not be recognized by the courts in part because it was so transgressive of heteronormative expectations of lesbians (women who have sex with other women, not men) and prostitutes (women who are subservient to the needs of their clients). More conventional conceptions of agency – those offered, for example, by Wuornos's prosecutor and the defence – interpreted her actions as those of either a cold-blooded but incomprehensible monster or a pure victim lacking any autonomy, with the result that she was sentenced to death for murder. The insight of Butler's poststructuralist understanding of agency here, however, is that no matter how oppressed an individual may be, their enactment (repetition) of the demands of the norms that constrain them simultaneously carries the possibility of drawing attention to and contesting the (oppressive) processes that have produced those norms. Effective agency in these terms may not be able to bring radical changes – indeed, as the case of Wuornos shows, radical transgressions are likely seriously to backfire – and for this reason may seem ephemeral and obscure. But such revisionings of agency remind us that although it is never possible to throw off the shackles of oppressive systems *tout court* (Wuornos's self-defensive actions could not on their own overturn the discriminatory strictures on lesbianism and prostitution in America), incremental challenges may accumulate to unmask the structures of oppression that shape women's lives.

What about collective agency?

Nevertheless, as we have seen so far (and as prefaced in Chapter 4), such anti-essentialist revisionings of subjectivity inspired by postmodernism and poststructuralism still seem to end up questioning the very possibility of effective feminist agency and sociopolitical action, in so far as they question the very categories of "self" and "woman". Again, as Alcoff asks, "What can we demand in the name of women if 'women' do not exist and demands in their name simply reinforce the myth that they do?" (1997: 340). Such questionings of agency thus seem highly problematic given the various pressures and constraints needing to be challenged by women. In addition, it seems clear that individual parodic and transgressive performances are also largely ineffective when it comes to challenging systems of oppression. That is, they may be helpful when – and if – they catch on, but they may still be reduced to an issue of style rather than political change. (Think, for instance, of how reports of the transgressive dress and practices on show at Gay and Lesbian Parades in the west typically talk about them in terms of colour and display rather than as calls for social and political change.) Finally, we also need to remember that the care-based, relational and competency conceptions of autonomy we explored previously also seem unable to challenge effectively systemic oppression.

One way to understand this problem is to recognize that while these various reconceptions of agency may be cognizant of relationality – or in the case of poststructuralist agency, cognizant of the social context of the self – they still see agency as the property of individuals rather than of individuals as members of groups or socially interconnected networks of cause and effect. And this perhaps is the problem: unless women understand themselves as members of groups, they will fail to see patterns of oppression, and they will fail to see that group or structural resistance is necessary to challenge structural oppression. Without the possibility of such resistance, women will take their failure to get promotion, say, as a personal rather than structural problem, with the result that systemic oppression will remain invisible. After all, as Marilyn Frye reminds us, to even "recognize a person as oppressed, one has to see that individual as belonging to a group of a certain sort" (1983: 8). Given these issues, we turn now to consider how feminists have tried to conceive of a form of agency able to challenge effectively group or structural oppression. More specifically, we consider issues surrounding the differences between individual and collective agency, key attempts by feminists to develop conceptions of collective or political agency, and what such attempts and conceptions have meant for minority groups or counter-cultures. (These issues are also central to Chapter 6.)

First, however, it is important to remember that with regard to this struggle to establish models for "women's" agency able to challenge systemic oppression, the debate as to whether there is in fact any coherent category not just of "woman" but of "women" is definitely still pertinent. Certainly, as has been discussed in previous chapters (and especially in Chapter 4), many early feminist arguments assumed that there was a coherent group "women", and that within this group individual women faced similar constraints, had similar needs and interests (even if unknown or unrecognized), and desired similar outcomes with regard to challenging existing oppressive conditions. On this view, women were construed as fighting for common goals – as exemplified in the social movement of "women's liberation" – and the name of the game was "solidarity" or "sisterhood": "We have been divided for so long, sisterly solidarity is important … This means always taking the woman's side and not being dismissive of each other" (York *et al.* 1991: 310). In this vein, early exercises in consciousness-raising were designed to expand women's understanding that many of the conflicts and problems they experienced individually were in fact problems that were common to other women, and that their difficulties were not simply personal matters but the effects of patterns of systematic oppression.

Such a view underpinned all of the collective action associated with the women's liberation movement. While not aimed directly at gender oppression, the Women's Peace Camp held at Greenham Common in Britain between 1981 and 2000 provides an exemplary case of the bonding and empowerment of agency through collective action. Protesting the nuclear policies of the United States and NATO within Britain, this action mobilized hundreds of thousands of women, both visitors and campers, and was clearly an attempt to bring about social change. Greenham was certainly an exercise in the development of agency at the individual level. As Sasha Roseneil reports:

> The experience of involvement in Greenham was one of empowerment and of transformation of self: housewives, mothers, and "grannies for peace" became feminists and lesbians; isolated young lesbians discovered community; jaded veterans of left politics found renewed energy and passionate commitment. (Roseneil 1995: 2)

Greenham also marked the construction (and reconstruction) of a collective identity and agency in so far as it was also always an instance of collective protest. It is, however, important to note that although as a collective action Greenham might suggest the development of a unified or totalized collective identity, this was far from the case. For instance, the very structure of the peace camp – being made up of eight separate camps – told against this, as did the fact that individual women became involved for a myriad of reasons, along with the strong ethos of anti-hierarchy and respect for diversity that underpinned this and other collective actions (see *ibid.*).

Despite the tentative and nuanced nature of much of its purported solidarity (see Segal 1999), as we discussed in Chapter 4 the women's liberation movement was heavily criticized for its assumptions of a coherent collective identity. And what was initially understood (by western, white, typically middle-class and heterosexual women) as the basis for collective action – some conception of women's common oppression and women's common identity – came inevitably to be seen as highly problematic. In bell hooks's words: "The idea of 'common oppression' was a false and corrupt platform disguising and mystifying the true nature of women's varied and complex reality" (1997: 485). Indeed, many feminists saw any attempt to conceive of a collective identity for women as problematic in so far as they understood it to be an essentializing move that assumed that all women share a set of gendered attributes that trump any differences between them to do with race, class, ethnicity, sexual orientation, disability and so forth. Although these assumptions are clearly false, difference-based counter-arguments contending that women should be understood as a strictly heterogeneous group have of course also proved to be problematic for feminists interested in collective action. After all, without some coherent notion of women as possessing some collective identity, feminist politics evaporates just as much as it might seem to do on the basis of poststructuralist insights. That is, it seems clear that a stress on commonalities of experience rather than differences is fundamental to the development of a political consciousness and engagement in the collective action and agency necessary for social transformation. This is a particularly pressing problem for those women who are most marginalized and oppressed: the poor, the sexually, racially and ethnically abused, the disabled and the economically exploited.

Feminist politics as coalition politics

In Chapter 4, our discussion of problems arising from feminist anti-essentialism took up the issue of how women might work together in collective action without undercutting the political importance of their individual specificity and diversity. Here, as there, the key point is that to be really successful under conditions of oppression, any concept of feminist politics – feminist collective agency – needs to include the potential for not only acting together with others, but being effective in so acting. This does not mean that women have to have identical experiences with other group members, or any kind of shared identity, but they do need to be able to understand themselves as acting in concert to achieve a shared goal. They need, in other words, to be more than just an aggregation of individuals. With regard to these requirements, we outlined in Chapter 4 the strategy Lugones developed from the perspective of community activism. Revisiting the issue in the context of the problem of collective agency raised by this chapter, a related possibility is that developed by thinkers inspired, at least in part, by poststructuralist insights. We can sum this up as the shift from "identity" to "coalition" politics, within which relationality perhaps marks a means of detecting patterns of oppression and creating possibilities for collective action against oppression, rather than being simply a source of obligations and responsibilities.

Here, starting from the assumption that there can be no essential integrity to any claims regarding identity – whether individual or collective – the argument is that categories such as "women" can still make sense and be used when they are understood as the result of strategic alliances or coalitions. (Also see, for instance, our outline of Spivak's conception of "strategic essentialism" in Chapter 4.) That is, while some thinkers "fear that positing a political coalition of *women* risks presuming that there must first be a natural class of women", this is to get it backwards; instead "it is coalition politics which constructs the category of women (and men) in the first place" (Fuss 1989: 36). Seen this way, the category "women" stands for a strategic unity or alliance – a relationality – that in no way assumes any essential or unified identity. This is the sort of view propounded by political thinker Chantal Mouffe when she argues for the reconception of both political agents and political struggle.

Specifically, Mouffe contends that any and every social agent – female or male – is irreducible to any essentialized and unified identity. Similar to conceptions of intersectionality, agents are understood as "constituted by an ensemble of 'subject positions'", making their identities "always contingent and precarious, temporarily fixed" (1995: 318). However, this does not mean that agents are unable to take part in projects of collective action aimed at achieving social change (such as feminist political projects, for example). After all, as Mouffe writes, "To deny the existence of an a priori necessary link between subject positions [and subjects] does not mean that there are not constant efforts to establish between them historical, contingent, and variable links" (*ibid*.: 319). Under this view, then, collective agency is all about the making and carrying out of

Although Belgian post-Marxist political theorist Chantal Mouffe is best known for her work in radical democracy and post-essentialist political theory, her insights into pluralism have been highly productive for feminist political thought. In particular, she has been seen as contributing to that strand of feminist political thought aimed at rethinking the divisive "friend–enemy" (us–them) distinction and the conflictual nature of politics in order to better understand the form and nature of coalitions and strategic alliances. Mouffe has outlined some of these possibilities in a well-known paper, "Feminism, Citizenship, and Radical Democratic Politics" (1995). Overall, however, Mouffe's key aim has been to propose and elaborate what she calls an agonistic model of democracy. Mouffe sees this as a fruitful alternative to the two dominant forms of democracy current in political theory: the aggregative (where preferences are aggregated without appeal to their justifications) and deliberative (where preferences are supported by reasons) models. The development of an alternative is imperative according to Mouffe, given the way increasing disaffection with democratic institutions in the world today is demonstrated by the growth in right-wing populism and Al-Qaeda forms of terrorism. She contends that neither the aggregative nor deliberative models of democracy seem able to respond to this disaffection effectively because of the priority they give to consensus. Mouffe's agonistic model, in contrast, accepts the antagonistic and pluralist dimension of the political, and accepts that consensus will always be riven by dissension. Mouffe has elaborated these ideas in an array of books including *Hegemony and Socialist Strategy* (with Ernesto Laclau, 1985), *The Return of the Political* (1993), *The Democratic Paradox* (2000) and *On the Political* (2005). She has also edited several texts in post-essentialist political theory, including the feminist-oriented *Feministische Perspektiven* (with Jürgen Trinks, 2000).

strategic alliances, what Mouffe also calls "articulations", which would mean that any sense of collective agency is also contingent, the result of historical alliances. It would also mean that any successful formation of collective agency can only attempt to achieve strategic and contextual ends. Nevertheless, Mouffe argues that this is a far more effective way to envisage feminist agency and all the various struggles it underpins than to try to find some "'true' form of feminist politics" (*ibid.*: 329).

Mouffe's point is that as long as feminists do not try to find or preserve any purportedly "'real' essence of womanhood" (*ibid.*) as the basis for feminist politics, then they will not end up with strategies that assume that one size fits all. In other words, she suggests that while conceptions of solidarity and collective action need to rest on some notion of common cause or common identity, this does not have to be based in biology or metaphysics or socialization as such. In her words:

> Feminism, for me, is the struggle for the equality of women. But this should not be understood as a struggle for realizing the equality of a definable empirical group with a common essence and identity, women, but rather as a struggle against the multiple forms in which the category "woman" is constructed in subordination. (*Ibid.*)

Although such a view would seem to answer the critiques regarding solidarity posed by thinkers such as bell hooks, there is still a further issue: can a coalition politics really be enough of a basis for feminist politics? More precisely, given that Mouffe actually envisages a coalition politics based on making strategic alliances, and that these will not necessarily see one subject position – sex or gender, say – as more crucial than any others, can this still be seen as a feminist politics? It seems that there is nothing to distinguish feminist political action from the manifold of democratic projects, something that has seemed to matter to a range of feminist thinkers. (Think, for instance, of how some feminists argue for keeping feminist politics separate from queer politics or even lesbian politics, and keeping women's spaces for naturally born women. And of how feminists of colour have struggled with the intersectionality of sex and gender issues with those of race, class and ethnicity.) Nonetheless, Mouffe contends that any "project of radical and plural democracy" has the potential to encompass the "pursuit of feminist goals and aims" (*ibid.*: 328, 329). (Such a point resonates with that made by American activist and academic Charlotte Bunch when she argues in "Women's Rights as Human Rights" [1990] that the concept of human rights can be transformed to take account of the specific needs and hopes of women. We explore this issue in Chapter 6.)

This brings us to the last issue we want to raise in this chapter, which is whether this kind of coalition politics can work effectively to protect the rights and agency of women in minority groups and counter-cultures. This has, of course, been highly problematic for feminists in so far as the majority of feminist projects and aims have ended up including some people while excluding others. For a start, however, it seems clear that any coalition politics would certainly allow for the agency of minority groups and counter-cultures better than some identity-based conceptions of collective agency. Indian-American feminist Chandra Talpade Mohanty, for example, talks about the way a "common context of struggle" powers the dynamic constituency of "women of colour" or "third-world women" rather than racial or colour identities (Mohanty 1991a: 7). On the other hand, while coalition politics does not assume the pre-existence of any identity, it does seem to assume the pre-existence of individual agency (and the potential to work productively across differences). That is, coalition politics requires that individuals or collectives possess and practise some degree of agency – skill in negotiation and compromise, for example – that is not simply dependent on their coalition membership or identity. However, as we have shown in this chapter, this is problematic. Not only are there questions around the criteria for individuals and agents, but there are also difficulties in understanding how groups are constituted, maintained and socially effective. These difficulties point to one of the central paradoxes of feminist projects: to present themselves as having potential for collective agency, they have to assume what they argue for – the agency of all the individuals that constitute them.

Summary of key points

- Agency – the power and capacity to act as one chooses – is central to feminist thought. However, feminists argue that traditional conceptions of the autonomous agent are not possible to realize, owing to socialization processes and people's interconnectedness.
- Care-based agency and relational autonomy take account of human interdependency and value social relations in decision-making. They also support viewing agency in terms of the development and exercise of skill-based competencies, enabling people to enact their agency even in oppressive conditions.
- Poststructuralist revisionings highlight the way agency is affected by socially determined practices. Under such conceptions, the self does not exist prior to its socialized choices and actions, but might be able to exercise some agency in the way it carries out those choices and actions.
- Feminists have not seen any of these revisionings of agency to be effective in challenging the systemic oppression of women, however, as they view agency in individual rather than in collective terms. The charge of essentialism often faces proposed collective forms of agency.
- To avoid charges of essentialism, some feminists have suggested that feminist collective agency should be viewed in coalition, rather than identity-based, terms.

six

Responsibility

What responsibilities do feminists have?

The preceding chapters have shown that understanding feminism entails understanding a variety of multi-sided areas of concern. Furthermore, as attention to these concerns is refined and diversified, and interacts with other movements of thought and changing sociopolitical contexts, it reshapes the grounds of concern and produces new complexities and difficulties. This dynamic of shifting ideas and continuously transforming understandings and practices is nowhere more evident than in the troubled field of sorting out the nature of feminist responsibility. At first sight, it would appear that feminists' responsibilities lie in understanding the bases of women's oppression and opposing positions and practices that support or contribute to that oppression. Feminists stand for challenging male bias in socioeconomic opportunities and understandings of embodiment, desire, linguistic usage, knowledge-making and other conceptual practices. But as we have seen, the work of understanding oppression and its multiple, changing and sometimes ambivalent expressions, along with the complex insights that understanding throws up, is far from straightforward. Women's oppression and feminist understandings of it do not trace out a neatly bounded terrain but instead draw feminists into a tangled and changing network of interlocking relations of domination and subordination.

Complicating this picture, the development of feminist thinking from early analyses of binary structures to a greater recognition of the instability of concepts and categories has diffused and fractured earlier confidence in collective social transformation. The unmasking of flawed generalizations by women of colour and other minority groups – lower-class women, lesbians, disabled women, older women and so on – and poststructuralist suspicion of universal categories, norms and identities have engendered considerable wariness about ideals of gender justice and responsibility. Indeed, to the frustration of many thinkers and activists, political projects directed towards improving women's material situations, since they risk unjust generalizations, have often ended up being avoided in favour of individualized expressions of cultural resistance.

In addition, nothing ever stands still: changing social, political, economic, cultural – and ecological – contexts inevitably affect feminist projects. In part feminisms are themselves accountable for shaping this environment. The gains (in the west at least) in women's formal opportunities to participate more fully in education, the workplace and politics, and in reproductive control and sexual expression have brought with them ambiguous outcomes and dissension: recognition that one size does not fit all, that liberation has many different meanings. But other changes in the late twentieth and early twenty-first centuries – increasing globalization and the march of corporate capitalism – have intensified the power hierarchies of racist, imperialist and patriarchal relations that feed off the exploitation of consumption, racial, ethnic and third-world subordinates and environmental resources, along with women's domestic and sexual service. As a result, inequalities and divisions between women have deepened everywhere.

What responsibilities do feminists have in light of this complexity? How should responsible feminists direct their energies when concepts of womanhood, gender and sex have no universal definitions and yet common patterns of discrimination against women occur locally and globally? How do feminists think and practise heterogeneity, multiplicity and difference without losing political and critical grip? What responsibilities do they have when oppressive gender relations are also caught up in systems of domination that unjustly subordinate people on the basis of their race, nationality, ethnicity, class, abledness, age and so on, and when the same conceptual logic threatens human relations with the natural environment that sustains us? And perhaps most importantly for a book written from the context of white, middle-class, predominantly Anglo-American feminism (although there is scant homogeneity here either!), what does responsibility mean for those feminists in more privileged situations with respect to that privilege and its effects on those who are more vulnerable?

These are the questions that shape this chapter. They arise out of the conviction that, despite its ongoing struggle with ever-increasing complexity, feminist thought is politically motivated thought that aims ultimately at understanding and eliminating oppressive sociopolitical relations. We propose to address the problem of responsibility, then, as a problem of political responsibility and we begin by taking up the issue as it emerges from the tension between feminist commitments both to multiplicity and difference, and to encompassing social change. From here we move on to consider feminist responses to issues concerning transnational responsibilities, especially given the increasing inequalities between western and non-western countries. The final sections of the chapter consider the connections between feminist and ecological responsibilities and then return to reflect on feminist insights concerning the concept of responsibility itself.

Poststructuralist and postfeminist responsibilities

Throughout this book we have talked about some of the effects of poststructuralist deconstructions of universal categories and norms on particular feminist problematics. Poststructuralism is, of course, a multifaceted movement and its loose appropriation under the term "postmodernism" is somewhat confusing. However, it is poststructuralist themes relating to the prioritizing of difference, the partial, the contradictory, the particular, against the illusion of a universal and unified female identity, that are most significant for the problem of responsibility.

As should be clear by now, feminist academics have used these ideas to draw attention to the problems of unreflective universalizations, the complex possibilities of social identities and relationships, and the difficulties of sociopolitical change. Criticisms of the "false certainties" of theories of oppression with their beliefs in women's shared interests – whether in achieving equality with men or recognition of the value of their difference – have helped to undo the parochialism of white middle-class accounts of what feminism stands for. Poststructuralist rejections of stable categories and emphases on multiple possibilities of meaning have further overturned taken-for-granted and oppressive understandings of womanhood and femininity. At the same time, they have freed up opportunities for occupying multiple diverse, anti-patriarchal, anti-heterosexist, queer and "in-between" positions. Women are encouraged to re-imagine their embodied possibilities, to resist totalizing socio-cultural discourses, by embracing the profusion of identities and spaces, and by exploring transgressive conceptions of femininity, sexuality and resistance on their own terms. But when "womanhood", "gender" and "sex" cannot be defined universally and individual subjects themselves are understood as internally fragmented, analyses of just where and how women are best positioned to resist the authority and power men commonly exert over them are sidelined. Standing up for equality and social justice and for political projects that oppose encompassing structures of oppression is viewed with suspicion. Organized resistance to relations of domination becomes highly problematic: always liable to reproduce the kinds of exclusionary identities and understandings it is trying to transcend. Not surprisingly, many feminists are troubled by these outcomes, often seeing poststructuralist themes as creating unbridgeable gaps between theory and politics, cultural expression and material change (see for instance Bell & Klein 1996).

I'm not a feminist, but …

The key point, then, is that for many feminists (especially those who prioritize activism), poststructuralist and postmodern themes have had dubious effects in mainstream culture (in the west at least) on notions of feminist responsibility. Here, the celebration of proliferating particularities of difference and the opening up of expressions of femininity have been reinforced by the understandings of a new generation of women (and men) that the sociopolitical work of feminism is done. For instance, a popular version of "postfeminism" claims that following equal access to education, employment and authority over their own affairs, women can have it all: they are no longer confined to the domestic sphere or burdened by the connection between sexuality and reproduction. Taking responsibility in this context of emancipation therefore simply means taking responsibility for oneself and throwing off the shackles of normalizing cultural expectations. (See Chapter 3 for a discussion of this in the context of desire and sexuality, where sexual transgression and pornography can exemplify expressions of individual empowerment that overturn orthodox gender categories.) These sorts of postfeminist views identify "old-style" (second-wave) feminisms on the other hand with decidedly unsexy bra-burning, strident attitudes and man-hating. They often see feminists' continuing focus on violence against women, sexual harassment, rape, affirmative action and comparable worth (equal pay for work of comparable value) as a form of irresponsible victimism: painting a picture of women as helpless and unable to take care of themselves. Think of Katie Roiphe's talk in *The Morning After* (1993) about "rape-crisis feminism" duping young women into believing they have been sexually exploited by men. Naomi Wolf's use of the contrasting terms "victim feminism" and "power feminism" in *Fire With Fire* (1993) runs along a similar line. (Wolf attributes "victim feminism" largely to academic feminism with its understanding of women as victims of patriarchy and patriarchal institutions, while she uses "power feminism" to refer to a "no-nonsense", real-world feminism that inspires women to take hold of their individual power and use it to achieve as much as men.) Some mainstream cultural movements, too, despite their tendencies to blame feminisms for assorted social problems – the break-up of the family, juvenile delinquency, sexualization of the culture and so forth – resonate with the new "power feminism". Anti-"political correctness" proponents, for example, readily castigate feminists as puritanical – and prudish – about language, about equality, about sexual harassment and pornography, while critics of "nanny states" and paternalism support views that feminism is "too extreme", "wants too much" and has "a chip on its shoulder".

Apart from the depoliticizing effect of individualist conceptions of liberation and responsibility, the force of these formulations is often diffusion, fragmentation and/or outright dismissal of feminisms (the familiar "I'm not a feminist but …"). It hardly needs mentioning that the personalization – and sexualization – of empowerment also fits especially well with the rampant lifestyle consumerism of postindustrial capitalism and some strands of patriarchalism (also see Hopkins 2002). Such views are not exactly a solid basis for radical change. Overall, this popular movement very effectively shifts attention away from social structures and concern for the poverty and marginalization of (other) women and other oppressed groups. Instead, individuals are encouraged to believe that their personalized, if market-endorsed, self-expressions of heterogeneity, sexual and gender transgressions are the mark of (feminist) responsibility.

Populism such as this is obviously a caricature of poststructuralist thought. Another version of postfeminism (sometimes also termed "third-wave" feminism) is described as being the outcome of "the shift within feminism from debates about equality to a focus on debates about difference" (Brooks 1997: 4). Far from a depoliticized framing, on this account postfeminism grapples with the challenges to feminist political consciousness wrought by the intersecting insights of poststructuralism, postmodernism and postcolonialism. From the perspective of feminist concern and activism on behalf of gender justice, however, it is not surprising that many view the focus on multiplicity and difference as creating a yawning gap between theory and politics, cultural expression and material change. As we have noted in earlier chapters, many feminists (and non-feminists) have dismissed poststructuralism (and postmodernism) for its often confusing and intractable language, the seemingly obsessive scrutiny of generalizations and its seeming disconnection with "reality". Some people also think that poststructuralism gives rise to a form of relativism and indeterminacy that actively undermines any political projects; they say that it results in an "anything goes", "all perspectives deserve the same respect" outlook. While these criticisms may be unjustified (as we discussed in Chapter 4), they speak to a tension in contemporary feminisms that is difficult to dispel.

Conceptually, however, poststructuralist insights are crucial to feminist projects. Feminists need to be attentive to the way their generalizations project perspectives that produce new exclusions. From an activist position, too, the sorts of individual transgressions and micropolitical activism that poststructuralism encourages can be useful, especially when they are novel, in drawing attention to oppressive relations and perhaps even building towards larger political movements. But in a world of increasing inequality where women still bear the major burden of child-rearing, nurturance and care, still suffer pervasive violence and make up the largest proportion of the poor, feminists must also engage people in social struggle against the structures of oppression that maintain these injustices. As British feminist Lynne Segal explained ten years ago, "Fearful of totalising generalisations we may be, and cautious we must be", but "the invocation of specific differences can serve broadly transformative ends … only as part of *some wider political project* seeking to dismantle these basic structures of domination" (1999: 34–5). Such a view still resonates today.

Transnational responsibilities

The effects of this (cluster of) tension(s) in feminist thought – particular–universal, theoretical–practical, cultural–material, individual–collective – are particularly troubled in relation to global feminism. It is a familiar complaint that most feminist theory does not include women from outside the developed west. Certainly the problems and developments in second-wave feminisms we have discussed in this book confirm this view. Their (almost) exclusive western focus is justification for women from non-western countries to see their concerns as outside the ambit of feminism. This is not terribly surprising. Western feminists' theories and activism have played a dominant role in putting feminisms on the map and it is to be expected that their work has been motivated (and constrained) by gender, class and race concerns that are close to home and/or understood from their own perspectives. But this is no excuse, of course, from the perspective of non-western women who are the most vulnerable and impoverished on the planet.

Increasing globalization, communication networks and immigration at the end of the twentieth and the beginning of the twenty-first centuries, along with economic inequalities and shifting fortunes of women worldwide, have all raised western feminists' concerns with global disparities in material wellbeing, cultural and political differences, and hierarchical structures of oppression. The United Nations Decade for Women (1976–85) helped to draw attention to the crucial role of women globally in economic and social development. By 2006, over ninety per cent of member countries of the United Nations had signed the "Convention on the Elimination of All Forms of Discrimination Against Women", a commitment to incorporate equality between women and men in their legal systems and to protect women against social, political and economic discrimination. Despite efforts to integrate women into policy goals, however, all over the world they are still worse off than their male counterparts. Women own less than one per cent of global property; seventy per cent of those in poverty are women; two-thirds of those who are illiterate are women; and women are paid less than men in all countries (Billson & Fluehr-Lobban 2005: 5–6). Violence against women – murder, rape, sexual abuse, trafficking, genital cutting, forced marriage, honour killings – remains a major impediment to achieving equality. Gender inequalities in wealth, education, employment and health in less industrialized, poorer nations are especially concerning and as a result many western feminists have been highly critical of the poverty, exploitative labour conditions, violence, sex trafficking and abuse suffered by women in these countries. In addition, gendered cultural practices such as genital cutting, honour killings, dowry murder and female infanticide, along with the more visible constraints of heavy veiling worn by women in countries such as Saudi Arabia and Afghanistan, also appal many feminists (and non-feminists).

Western feminist responses during the 1970s and 1980s to the injustices suffered by women in non-western countries were often influenced by radical feminists such as Daly, who understood the plight of women across the world through the singular focus of common patriarchal oppression. These feminists saw women in poor countries as victims of global patriarchal domination, albeit in a variety of forms depending on differing cultural and religious traditions. Under the rallying ideal "sisterhood is global", liberation of these women from their suffering was seen as a matter of extending the analyses and political practices already developed by western feminists. But positions such as this play into what Kumari Jayawardena has called "a Eurocentric view that the movement for women's liberation is not indigenous to Asia or Africa but has been a purely West European and North American phenomenon" (Jayawardena 1986: 2).

Other non-western and postcolonial feminists have mounted more direct and trenchant criticisms of these positions, seeing in them the arrogance of "the west will save the rest" attitude that has been a reinforcing theme of the colonial imperialism that is central to the oppression of women in poorer countries. These critiques have issued difficult challenges to contemporary western feminists' understandings of their global obligations.

Postcolonial positions

According to postcolonial feminist accounts, the tendency to isolate patriarchal practices as the source of gender inequality neglects the contexts of imperial rule that established white masculinity as the dominant norm in non-western countries, while simultaneously shap-

---

Kumari Jayawardena (b. 1931)
Feminist activist and political scientist, Kumari Jayawardena has chronicled the histories and complexities of movements for women's rights and feminist struggles in several countries in Asia and the Middle East. Her *Feminism and Nationalism in the Third World* (1986) traces the development of these movements in the late nineteenth and early twentieth centuries as part of nationalist resistance to imperialism, as well as resistance to traditional patriarchal and religious orthodoxies. Despite the exclusion of third-world women from the relations of ruling, preventing them from exercising equality and taking an active part in the development of their nations, their unique struggles against these forces provide evidence that feminism was not an ideological import from the west. In *The White Woman's Other Burden* (1995), Jayawardena undermines homogenized notions of colonial women by telling the stories of western women who crossed the boundaries of accepted gender, race and class positions for white women in South Asian colonies during the period of British rule and who took stands against colonial rule.

ing racial, sexual, cultural and national differentiations to reinforce that dominance. Insights such as those developed by women of colour and postmodernists in relation to the problem of differences among women (as discussed in Chapter 4) come to the fore again here. Feminist postcolonial theorists have argued that most western feminist engagements with the situation of women in less-developed countries have been based on essentialist generalizations that misunderstand the complexities of the gender, race, colonialist and cultural hierarchies within which their lives are situated. Definitions of womanhood based in white middle-class values will not be meaningful for women whose identities are complicated by struggles against multiple barriers.

Some of these thinkers criticize universalist feminisms for their global imposition of an abstract concept of gender that is not sensitive to the different ways local contexts understand it. Many women, for example, are suspicious of ideas that seem to pit women against men when they live in contexts where women and men are dependent on each other for their survival. Other critics are concerned about the way some western "difference" feminists identify the differences between western and non-western women in essentialist terms. Indian-American postcolonial feminist Chandra Talpade Mohanty, for example, argues that reliance on overly generalized assumptions about so-called "third-world" women has created a new binary within feminist thought that has the political effect of privileging western women as the reference point for representing and understanding the lives of poorer non-western women. "'The average third world woman'" is represented as "ignorant, poor, undereducated, tradition-bound, domestic, family-oriented, victimised" in contrast to the self-presentation of western women "as educated, as modern, as having control over their own bodies and sexualities, and the freedom to make their own decisions" (Mohanty 1991b: 56). In turn, in her influential essay, "Can the Subaltern Speak?", Spivak identifies contexts in which discussions concerning the "gendered subaltern" (the woman whose perspective lies outside dominant – feminist and non-feminist – understandings) use her as a vehicle for the representation of feminist and anti-imperialist positions without ever allowing her a voice of her own. Even the work of anti-essentialist feminists can unwittingly display this sort of oversight, as Spivak (1987) shows in a discussion of Kristeva's *About Chinese Women* (see Chapter 4 for more details of Kristeva's poststructuralist contribution to anti-essentialism). The Chinese women who are the objects of Kristeva's discussions are never heard representing their own understandings of their situations.

Oppressive relational practices that are now so familiar as a result of early feminist critiques of male domination, and women of colour's challenges to white feminisms – absence, silencing, tokenism, victimism, appropriation – are unmasked by postcolonial critics of western feminist attempts to address the problems of women in less-developed countries. As always, there are some exceptions to these practices and the critics in some cases may in their turn over-homogenize the "average western feminist". However, the tendency of western feminists to employ understandings of either identity or difference to shore up their own perspectives on the world, rather than empowering the lives of those whose experience is not simply the "other" of their own, is indisputable.

One of the central complicating features of this logic of domination, in the case of western feminist relations with women in postcolonial countries, concerns western feminists' failure to understand the effects of, and their own implication in, the imperialism and capitalism that have shaped the lives of postcolonial women. Westerners often attribute the restrictions, violence and subordination suffered by women in poorer countries to the specific cultural and religious practices of those countries. For instance, they see veiling and honour killings as an Islamic problem, and *sati* (the self-immolation of widows on their husbands' funeral pyres) and dowry murders as gendered injustices inherent in Hinduism. While undoubtedly there are gross violations of women's lives committed in the name of particular religious or cultural beliefs, the point that is often missed is that comparisons between western and non-western cultures that continually put the latter down frequently misunderstand the internal complexities of these different cultural practices and the interconnections between them wrought by colonialism.

For example, some cultural practices that are frequently criticized by westerners have been taken up with renewed vigour by their non-western practitioners precisely in order to shore up their national or religious identity against the often self-righteous intrusions of imperialist and westernized systems (e.g. genital cutting, veiling). Others have meanings for those who practise them that simply confound western and colonialist (mis)understandings of them (e.g. veiling – again! – used as a practice of privacy, piety or segregation). Still others are blown out of proportion by colonialist misrepresentations, despite their occurrence being extremely limited (e.g. *sati*). In addition, many injustices suffered by women in poorer countries result largely from servicing the demands of western inheritors of colonialist privilege (think sweatshop labour in China and sex trafficking in Thailand). Also significant is the fact that westerners, in their rush to condemn other cultures, often forget or underestimate pervasive sexist practices against women's bodies in their own cultures: domestic violence against women and the sexualization of young girls, for example. In all of these cases we can see the ways in which westerners, under the continuing effects of colonialist representations and practices, have misunderstood, stereotyped and disparaged non-western cultures, traditions and identities. Such analyses call for greater understanding of the multiple relations of oppression: collaborative understanding that is ever mindful of the traps of totalizing and reified concepts of "western" and "third world", "culture", "identity" and "tradition", and the misunderstandings of abstracted and universalized positions.

Liberal feminist universalism

Nevertheless, some liberal (equality-focused) feminists remain fearful that the call for more fine-grained, cross-cultural understanding of the particularities of specific configurations of culture (postcolonial feminist anti-essentialism) will result in a form of cultural relativism that, politically, amounts to little more than accepting the status quo for the least-well-off women globally. When there is so much impoverishment, violence, sexual and labour-force exploitation, pleas for more cultural sensitivity and understanding are difficult for some western feminists and non-feminists to accept. Okin has famously argued that "the problems of other women are 'similar to ours but more so'" (1994: 8). "Problems ... similar to ours", here, refers to the economic and social problems Okin has addressed in traditional family structures characteristic of her middle-class American culture. She sees the constrained and impoverished situations of non-western women as resulting from similar sorts of inegalitarian domestic and economic practices to those that western feminists have been dismantling at home. Nussbaum is also well known for extending liberal understandings of pluralism and respect in a cross-cultural humanism based on a universal accounting of human capabilities (e.g. 1999a). But how, then, is it possible to explain protests by third-world feminists about cultural insensitivity and stereotyping? For liberals like Okin and Nussbaum such protests underestimate the similarities between the gendered injustices suffered by women in developing countries and those in the west ("but more so"). And while they agree that it may be useful to discuss with women in poorer countries what they want, it is also important to recognize that these women may have unconsciously accepted the disadvantages of their cultural situations as normal or natural, and in so doing undermined the understanding and self-empowerment that is necessary universally in order to bring about change (Okin 1994). Western (and non-western) feminists, then, are charged with the responsibility to condemn these cultural injustices rather than engaging in what liberals see as rationalizing and politically passive, cultural understanding.

The continuity of liberal feminist analyses with dominant, non-feminist western positions on global justice has done much to help in foregrounding and legitimizing concern for the injustices and lack of autonomy suffered specifically by women in non-western countries. But despite their best intentions, they also play into (and out of) long-standing traditions of western dominance, self-righteousness and lack of understanding of other cultures. Think of the way the *burkha* has become, in the west, a symbol of gender oppression and a trigger for culture bashing (and a rationale for the invasion of Afghanistan). When feminism is associated with these sorts of responses, it readily evokes anti-feminist resistance from those it would help.

Are there responses to the pressing injustices suffered by women in non-western countries that can avoid this either/or bind, that is, being tarred with either politically quietist, cultural relativism or interfering and alienating western insensitivity? The difficulty here relates to articulating and enacting feminist responsibilities in ways that are both open to differences and critical of unjust differences, ways that are also alert to both the politically contested nature of discourses, categories and concepts, and the material struggles for survival of the most exploited people in the world.

Women's rights are human rights

One practical response that attempts to hold these often conflicting imperatives together has emerged from the movement for women's human rights. Some thinkers criticize human rights approaches to global injustice as the illegitimate product of westernization. However, as Bunch says, the concept of human rights "strikes deep chords of response among many", making the promotion of human rights "a useful framework for seeking redress of gender abuse" (1990: 486–7). Widespread cross-cultural dialogue among western and non-western feminists concerning abuses such as violence against women, sex trafficking and slavery has enabled this universalist framework to be used to direct attention to gender injustice in all its varied forms as a matter of "a politically constructed reality maintained by patriarchal interests, ideology, and institutions", rather than viewing it as "inevitable or natural" (*ibid*.: 491). (Such dialogue is, of course, also integral to what in Chapter 5 we saw Mouffe as promoting.) More specifically, the discourse of human rights, originally written from the perspective of western colonizers, is reformulated from the perspective of women's bodies in all their diversity and their actual needs for food, shelter, education and freedom from rape, war, violence and unwanted pregnancies. Active networking with women from countries around the world creates an international feminist collective, while simultaneously condemning global imperialism, racist, classist and ethnocentric relations of domination and subordination. Instead of western gatekeeping on rights, or reducing feminism to a single issue, the movement works on multiple fronts by supporting different cultures' own efforts to better themselves in order to reinforce equality. On this view, then, asking how feminist and working-class activists in Egypt, Afghanistan or Venezuela, for example, envisage a role for rights with all the messy accommodation and compromise that that involves is at the centre of internationalizing feminism rather than making proposals based on abstract conceptions. At the same time, the global focus on gender oppression opens the possibility for transforming the concept of human rights so that it can

---

Charlotte Bunch (b. 1942)

Charlotte Bunch became involved in women's liberation activism in the United States in the late 1960s. Against views that understood women's issues to be subcategories of other progressive movements, Bunch championed a vision of feminism as a distinctive perspective on the whole of society. At the same time, she understood opposition to racism, imperialism, class inequalities and heterosexism to be inevitable, although often conflicting, dimensions of feminist politics, and the grounds for forging coalitions and networks for the necessary structural change. Bunch is best known for her work in the global feminist movement, in particular her networking against trafficking in women and female sexual slavery, and her leadership on women's human rights. Her paper "Women's Rights as Human Rights: Toward a Re-Vision of Human Rights" (1990) explains how gender-related abuses of women's humanity – in particular sex discrimination and multiple forms of violence against females – are the most neglected of human rights abuses, and calls for a thoroughly feminist transformation of human rights that incorporates gender differentiation into the core of their conceptualization and application. Other writings include numerous articles, pamphlets and books, and her collection of essays from 1968–86, *Passionate Politics* (1987).

be more responsive to women's experience. As a result, unpacking and challenging specific contexts of intersecting power relations that keep in place traditional understandings of what is and what is not proper for women become the aims of politically responsible feminists.

The women's human rights movement, of course, has not sprung up out of nothing. It builds (in part) on insights from the criticisms of white feminisms made by women of colour in the 1970s and 1980s (see Chapter 4). Ethnically and racially oppressed women within the west – indigenous women, immigrant women, indentured labourers, slaves – have long understood the fateful effects of Eurocentric feminist analyses and the requirement to forge solidarities beyond the boundaries of race and nationality, north and south, west and east. The commitment to understanding and including the voices of all women on their own terms also embraces pluralizing themes associated with poststructuralist and postmodern feminisms. At the same time, it never loses sight of the fact that deep-seated understandings that women are of less value than men are a continuing worldwide problem.

Challenges to the international politico-economic order

Some alternative western feminist responses that are alert to the intricacies of this requirement argue that western complicity with the injustices experienced by women in poorer countries should be the target of western feminists' global responsibilities. Turning away from accepting the global responsibility problem as a dilemma of "colonial interference" versus "callous indifference" (Jaggar 2005: 186) – of "chasing oppression across the world" (*ibid.*: 189) or protesting the need for attentiveness to the complexities of sociocultural contexts – American feminist philosopher Alison Jaggar argues in her article "Global Responsibility and Western Feminism" that western feminists should "scrutinize our own complicity and power" (*ibid.*: 195). Western capitalism and imperialism are, after all, implicated at many levels in the creation and maintenance of inequalities and the oppression of women in poorer countries. For example, as we have already mentioned, the legacy of colonialism distorts western understandings of non-western cultures and in some cases has reinvigorated practices such as genital cutting and veiling as forms of national resistance. Jaggar cites some of the cases in which western powers have actively supported or even imposed "some of the most illiberal and gender-conservative regimes in the world" (e.g. in Saudi Arabia and currently in Afghanistan and Iraq), along with the impact of global economic development forces and neo-liberal principles of "free trade" – withdrawal from government social responsibilities and the abandonment of economic regulation in employment and environmental protection – on the livelihoods of women in non-western countries (*ibid.*: 190–93). As a result of these measures, many women have lost their traditional sources of income in local small-scale industries and agriculture. In addition, under the forces of global capitalism:

> Women have become the new industrial proletariat in labour intensive industries located in export-processing zones across the world. Especially in much of Asia, governments have often tempted multinational corporate investment with stereotypes of Asian women workers as tractable, hardworking, dexterous – and sexy. (*Ibid.*: 192)

While it might be argued that sweatshop labour provides these women with new opportunities and possibilities for autonomy, the arduous conditions under which they work often amount to little more than swapping servitude in patriarchal families for servitude to foreign corporations. According to this view, western feminists' responsibilities lie with struggles against the insidious, systematic and globally destructive effects of the political and economic orders that support their power and privilege. This is not to condone cultural practices that are oppressive to women or to be blind to those in non-western cultures who justify the continuation or adoption of oppressive practices in the name of resisting westernization. Rather, it is to acknowledge that feminists need to be active on many fronts, and that differently situated feminists have different opportunities and capacities to exercise responsibility.

Ecological responsibilities

One of the fronts that has been particularly important to feminists since the 1970s is the environment. At first sight this might appear a little surprising. The degradation of the environment may be a concern for everyone, but why should it be a specifically feminist issue? Do feminists not have enough on their plates already, dealing with all the multiple effects of gender hierarchies on women's lives and the specificities of other hierarchical relations – imperialist, race, class, cultural, and so on – that do not simply reduce to gender? Also, we have talked earlier in this book (see Chapters 1 and 2) about some of the negative implications of conceptual connections between women and nature. As was noted then, the identification of women with their bodies, and especially their bodily limitations, has often led to their exclusion from public life. Would it not be best, then, to argue that feminists should stay away from any such associations?

In the 1970s and 1980s, however, some western ecofeminists argued for a special positive affinity between women and nature. Their critique of male–female domination saw women holding a more benign and protective attitude to the natural world, compared with men's more aggressive and controlling character. Others have argued for a spiritual connection between women and nature, often drawing on prehistoric earth-centred spiritualities that offer inspiration for the empowerment of women and nature. Still others have argued that the gendered division of labour, in particular women's work in reproduction, nurturing and caring, gives women special insights into the cycles and interconnectedness of natural phenomena. (We have considered several of these positions in earlier chapters, especially Chapters 2 and 5.) On this view, the emancipation of women appears to become a condition of a sustainable relationship with the environment. Of course, such views make feminism an environmental issue rather than the other way round, and in this sense only indirectly call feminists into action on behalf of the environment. But they also run into problems as soon as understandings of women having an essential nature come under question. Whether women's affinity with nature is understood as biologically determined or socially constructed there is a danger that such perspectives may essentialize and naturalize both women and nature, limiting women's possibilities while ignoring the differences and inequalities between them. Some environmental feminists have even rejected the term "ecofeminism" in light of these problems.

How can feminists maintain that the environment is a feminist issue yet avoid the binds of the "women are closer to nature" stereotype? One response at the heart of many feminist positions arises from the insight that there is a deep connection (historical, material, conceptual) between the intersecting relations of patriarchal, imperialist, race, class and cultural domination that are central to feminist analyses and relations of human–environment domination. Concern with nature becomes a feminist issue because the ideologies that underlie the oppression of women are deeply enmeshed with those that underlie the domination of nature. (The sexual metaphors used by British philosopher of science Francis Bacon in the early seventeenth century are especially notorious here. Bacon famously identified nature as female and argued that she must be "'bound into service' and made a 'slave', put 'in constraint' and 'molded'" by "the new man of science" [Merchant 1980: 169].) In her book *Ecofeminist Philosophy* (2000), American philosopher Karen Warren sets out this concern in an ecofeminist argument for reconceiving feminism:

> (1) Feminism is, minimally, a movement to end sexism.
>
> But (2) Sexism is conceptually linked with naturism [unjustified domination of nonhuman nature].
>
> Thus, (3) Feminism is (also) a movement to end naturism.
>
> (2000: 56)

Warren goes on to explain that no matter how male bias or sexism and naturism (the unjustified domination of nature) are understood, in whatever specific locations and expressions, or what their elimination requires, or even what their feminist replacements should be, the conceptual link between the two forms of domination obliges feminist philosophers to extend their realm of responsibility to the elimination of biases against nature (*ibid.*: 63). In other words, any feminist position that does not extend itself to concern for the human domination of nature is inadequate.

In this sort of argument, much hangs on demonstrating the link between patriarchal oppression and the domination of nature. Not surprisingly, feminists have developed a range of positions. Ecofeminist philosophers such as Warren and Australian philosopher Val Plumwood focus on the organizing conceptual frameworks. Warren highlights what she sees as a common patriarchal oppressive framework with a "logic of domination" that justifies the power and privilege of gendered and natured hierarchical dualisms (male–female, human–nature), along with "the deep historical enmeshment of the concepts of women and nature" in the west that permeates and reinforces unjust "behaviours, policies, theories and institutions" (*ibid.*: 57–8). This "logic of domination" also gives moral approval to the now familiar attributes of dualistic thinking, licensing and normalizing the unjustified use of the dominant category's power and privilege over its subordinate. With their multiple intersecting relations, however, human and non-human "others" are disparately affected: there is no universal subject of oppression. In her turn, Plumwood (1993) talks about the "logic of colonization" and sees exclusion from "reason" as what commonly marks off dominated categories from the "master identity" in western culture. Sexual, racial, ethnic and environmental colonization and "inferiorization" are authorized by the association of the dominated with non-rational bodily attributes. Here, however, mastery rather than masculinity is at the core of these processes that systematically deny the dependencies between dualized categories and that devalue, exclude, instrumentalize and homogenize the "others" of the master identity. On this basis, Plumwood stresses that feminist responses to this logic that seek the inclusion of women in the category of the fully human collude with the dominator identity of mastery and fail to understand that humans are neither slaves to nor masters of nature. Instead she contends that women (and men) should challenge all unjust hierarchical "isms" (not just gendered "isms"), and affirm non-hierarchical differences and their interdependencies. Dualistic logics – male–female, reason–nature, western–non-western and so on – are distorted covers for dependency relationships and the interconnectedness of the differences they identify.

More materially oriented responses see the links between sexism and naturism through the intrinsic interconnectedness of human embodied life in its natural environment. According to such responses, patriarchal systems impose responsibility for the needs of human embodiment that must be met within the natural environment directly on women, with the result that damage to the environment disproportionately harms women. The specific responsibilities imposed on women vary, of course, with the context. In the west, for example, such responsibilities may mainly relate to childbearing and child-rearing, provision of food, bodily nurturance, health, security and care; in less-developed countries, women's tasks include mothering and nurturing, along with the agriculture, wood-gathering, water-fetching and so forth, which are more directly related to the environment. The material reality of ecologically embedded bodily requirements and the differential impacts of the gendered social order on men's and women's roles in relation to that reality, however, cut across these variations. Sexism and naturism – unjustified biases against women and nature – are linked in their misunderstanding of the nature and significance of human embodiment.

Feminists arguing from the perspectives of women in poorer countries who are engaged in subsistence labour have provided especially tangible evidence of these interlocking systems of domination. Here, as we have just mentioned, the immediate survival of women and the families they support depends directly on the environmental sustainability of their labour. Large-scale development projects that destroy forests, dam rivers and industrialize agriculture disrupt and displace the self-renewing function of women's work in the food chain. Indian ecofeminist Vandana Shiva and her German collaborator Maria Mies have argued that under the domination of western patriarchal imperialism, with its capitalist system of production and development, both women – their bodies and their labour – and nature have been simultaneously exploited (think sweatshop labour and terminator seeds). According to Shiva, the history of western agricultural development in India is a history of "maldevelopment" in which gender ideology and economic assumptions aimed exclusively at profits "have subjugated the more humane assumptions of economics as the provision of sustenance, to make for a crisis of poverty rooted in ecological devastation" (Shiva 1988: xviii). Both the organic, life-renewing work of nature and the work of women in sustaining the vital needs of their families are seen as unproductive and irrelevant by systems of reductive science and technology directed at profit-making commodity production.

Shiva's analysis is strongly influenced by the work of Mies, which ties understandings of human–environment relations to a Marxist–feminist analysis of capitalism. Capitalism, Mies insists, subtends systematic effects of colonialism, gender and naturism by feeding off western domination, the gendered division of labour and natural resources to create the wealth of ruling-class men. Exploitation of women, nature and less-developed countries, then, is part of a framework of global patriarchal and capitalist accumulation.

On this view, nature is a feminist issue most basically because women are disproportionately at risk from environmental destruction and

---

Vandana Shiva (b. 1952)

Originally trained as a physicist, Vandana Shiva is a leading environmentalist and contributor to feminist critiques of development in third-world countries. Shiva came to prominence for her activism with the women of the Chipko movement against the destruction of trees in her native India and subsequently has been particularly critical of the way reductive models of western science and patriarchal capitalist development have been used to exploit women and nature. Her prolific writings, including *Staying Alive* (1988), *Ecofeminism* (with Maria Mies, 1993), *Biopolitics* (edited with Ingunn Moser, 1995) and *Earth Democracy* (2005), draw attention to development practices – for example, biotechnology, genetic engineering, privatization of water, intellectual property rights regimes – that degrade ecological systems and impoverish women and their communities. Shiva argues that women's reproductive work in nurturing their communities and the biodiversity of their environments represents a feminine principle of partnership in the life force of nature, the recognition of which is necessary to overcoming destructive gendered systems.

because their work in sustaining domestic subsistence connects strongly with environmental issues. Feminists' responsibilities are ecofeminist, anti-imperialist, anti-racist, anti-classist responsibilities to struggle against the destructive forces of "white man's" patriarchal capitalism, with its allied scientific and technological, industrial and militarist systems, in defence of alternative, non-exploitative and sustainable women-based subsistence economies.

Philosophical analyses such as those of Warren and Plumwood articulate the conceptual links in the multiple relations of power within which women's disparate lives are situated. Important as these insights are, however, there are still many puzzles when it comes to appropriate change. Clearly, in contemporary pre-feminist societies, there is often no perfect ecofeminist action when intersecting relations of domination pull in different directions: when a woman's survival, for example, comes at the cost of affirming a sexist or homophobic culture and/or environmentally destructive practices. But it is also difficult to know how to bring about change. Against the interlocking structures of domination, individual understanding (or agency) is not enough on its own. Once again, the focus on the heterogeneity and non-generalizability of individual positions cuts away much of the ground for any collective action. Conversely, we might well ask whether Mies and Shiva's account of the interlocking causes of the domination of women and nature is not too totalizing. Does its narrative of exploitation neglect the imperatives of more context-specific feminist struggles? Mies and Shiva respond that "the activities of those women who have become the victims of the development process and who struggle to conserve their subsistence base" are not rooted in some abstract universalizing discourse. On the contrary, they are engaged in the task of maintaining the "life-sustaining networks and processes" necessary for the satisfaction of common human needs (Mies & Shiva 1993: 12–13). But we could ask (once again): is the link between women and nature too tight here? Are all women somehow caught up in this connection, whether they know and/or practise it or not? How can feminists hold together their responsibilities for ecological sustainability and a world that is a better place for all women (and men) in all their differences?

Rethinking feminist responsibilities

So where does all this leave the puzzles and problems of responsibility? It looks as if these differing responses to the problem of feminist responsibility continue to chase around in circles in an ongoing struggle to bring some kind of coherence and justice to an ever-intensifying tangle of different and shifting imperatives.

Despite these complexities, however, we can summarize several crucial themes that feminist understanding highlights through its continuing self-scrutiny. First, conceptual and discursive attempts to overcome inequality, injustice and environmental domination always require a reference point from which justice, equality and sustainability are measured. By necessity, this involves generalizations about human beings and the environment, and values that tend to smooth over the intricacies and complexities of their terrain. This process also cannot take place outside relations of power, relations of inclusion and exclusion that are likely to privilege some at the expense of others: white women over racially oppressed women, western women over third-world women, industrialized agriculture over subsistence agriculture (or vice versa), for example. Attempts to understand the complexity and the significance of particular contexts and differences, in order to undo the injustices of homogenized and distorting generalizations, tend to lose the critical possibility for identifying unjustified differences, disempowering identities and destructive contextual adaptations. Threaded through this problematic are the tensions between these discursive imperatives and the material struggles of everyday life for the most exploited people in the world. None of these tangled strands – equality, difference, discourse, materiality – is independent of the others. Understanding feminists' responsibilities in a way that favours any one of them has the potential to underplay or distort the others, and so requires constant self-monitoring, along with humility in face of inevitable partiality, and openness to learning from others.

Secondly, understanding oppression involves foregrounding the interconnections between different forms of domination, different structures of power and their effects. Gender, race, class, heteronormativity, ableism and naturism do not form a hierarchy of dominations but intersect and intermesh with each other. Each form of oppression involves all, but each works differently and has differing and sometimes conflicting effects. Treating feminist responsibility as isolated from antiracist, anti-imperialist or environmental responsibility, for example, is problematic because there is no unqualified form of male domination that oppresses women. Since women are oppressed in multiple ways, as particular kinds of women, feminist responsibility is necessarily linked with other responsibilities. But this does not dilute the significance of gendered hierarchies. Men's continuing power over women requires that feminists continue to expose the multiple effects of male domination on the everyday lives of women, while ensuring that the particularities of women's lives are not simply reduced to effects of gender. Maximizing the chances of change, then, entails broadening the base of those who desire change and can see how it is relevant to their lives, forging alliances with other progressive movements against racial, ethnic, class, heteronormative, ableist, naturist and other entrenched hierarchies of power.

Thirdly, openness and inclusivity, forging alliances and building solidarities are fraught with ambiguity and tension. Uplifting appeals to take responsibility across boundaries – white/black, first-world/third-world, settler/indigenous, abled/disabled, old/young, professional/homemaker, scientist/academic/activist – to engage in collaborative, cross-cultural dialogue are a familiar refrain of contemporary feminisms. But it is difficult to overestimate the messy work of compromise and negotiation. As we have seen, examples of the difficulties and failures to make connections without engaging in a power takeover of the multiplicity of perspectives, interests and values at stake abound in the history of feminist thought. This is the stuff of the multiple and diverse criticisms of "human" as a surrogate for man, "feminism" instead of white middle-class feminism, feminist universalism that overrides postcolonial understanding, and so on. Plurality must be written into the structures of theory and practice. But with plurality comes the potential for tension and ambiguity, tactical and strategic questions over who gives up what and why, and the requirement for continuous reassessment. There are no formulas here, but feminist understanding allows us to recognize the imperatives of plurality and its risks.

Fourthly, feminist responsibility is both individual and collective. One of the most important themes of feminist thought is its focus on the complex interconnections between persons. Not only are people's identities the products of the social relations in which they are enmeshed, but they are also dependent on others for their survival, care and nurturance. In other words, although everyone is a unique individual, everyone is also fundamentally interrelated with other people. Earlier sections of this chapter discussed the significance and problems of feminist responsibility understood as necessarily individual. As seen there, the focus on individual resistance foregrounds the importance of transgressive practices for showing up the constraints of gender orthodoxies while avoiding the dangers of essentialized positions. Yet the risks of depoliticization are manifold. In practice, it is a mistake to reduce politics to the personal and to expect transformative social change without some wider political movement against the structures of domination. Collective responsibility in this sense enjoins feminists to work together towards a shared end. A more subtle insight, however, is that it is people's interconnectedness that grounds collective responsibility. Their participation in social processes that create both opportunities and injustices is what powers their commitments and responses. Responsibility is not just collective because individuals cannot bring about change on their own but because people are diversely implicated in shared social practices.

Finally, differently situated individuals have different individual and shared responsibilities. This insight hardly needs further elaboration. It is clear by now that although individuals are all sustained through relations with others, as both oppressors and oppressed, they are differently positioned in relation to power and privilege, and so have different sorts and levels of responsibility. There are some taxing and uncomfortable lessons for western, middle-class heterosexual feminists, especially, to learn here. Deeply entrenched patterns of classism, racism, imperialism, heterosexism and naturism, along with intensifying inequalities and environmental degradation, chafe against their relatively powerful positions in the structures of oppression. The conditions of their "privilege" work simultaneously to systematically disempower other groups. Taking responsibility in this situation may be scary because it involves working against favoured processes that fulfil socially and individually cherished expectations of the good life, and giving up culturally normative and comfortable standards. This is "boundary crossing, from safe circle to wilderness … to the unsafe", as African-American legal theorist Patricia Williams writes in *The Alchemy of Race and Rights* (1991: 129), developing new habits and resisting temptations to go back to easy places. None of this lets poorer less-empowered women off the hook but it yet again underlines the enduring dynamic of feminist thought and struggle. Hard-won understandings at any one stage become the basis for new questions and new problems.

All of these insights point to the immense complexity of contemporary feminisms and the impossibility of encapsulating feminist thought in any tidy, unitary way (especially given that contemporary feminisms cannot by definition rest from responding to the diverse issues that women [and men] find pressing and socially important). This, of course, makes feminism an easy target for those who would take up any one strand in order to caricature and dismiss the whole. But it also shows that understanding feminism involves understanding one of the most diverse, creative and self-reflexive movements of modern thought.

Summary of key points

- Poststructuralist criticisms regarding the generalizations of mainstream feminisms, while encouraging greater recognition of differences, have often shifted western feminist thought from collective responsibility (dismantling structures of oppression) to individualized responsibility (taking responsibility for one's own empowerment).
- Global disparities and continued oppression of women in less-developed countries have attracted criticisms from western feminists. In turn, postcolonial feminists have criticized western feminism for its tendency to essentialize such issues in patriarchal terms, and for failing to scrutinize the role of imperialist and cultural factors.
- Some western feminists are concerned that calls for cultural sensitivity come at the expense of addressing very real issues faced by women in non-western countries. Such feminists have invoked the women's human rights movement as a means of redressing gender imbalances.
- Some feminists argue that feminisms should encompass ecological responsibilities. Some recognize a positive affinity between women and nature, while others contend that the domination of women and nature share common structures.
- Materially based conceptions focus on the relationship between women's wellbeing and environmental sustainability.
- Feminist responsibility requires recognition of tensions between theoretical and practical responses, between the need for plurality and the risks that this involves. It must also recognize the interconnections between all hierarchies of domination, not simply those that are gender based, and must be simultaneously individual and collective, as well as contextual.

Questions for discussion and revision

one Oppression

1. What significance has the public–private divide held for many feminists? What are the advantages and disadvantages to women of having the same access as men to the public sphere?
2. Explain the differences between the positions of equality and difference feminisms. Which of these positions do you prefer and why?
3. Explain the epistemological dimension to women's oppression. Why has this dimension been so hard for feminists to counter effectively?
4. Why have many feminists diagnosed language as one of the primary means of maintaining women's oppression and exploitation?

two Embodiment

1. What are dualist and binary modes of thought, and in what ways have they contributed to the subordination of women with regard to their embodiment as women?
2. What do some feminists see as Beauvoir's solution to the problem of women's perceived bodily constraints? Do you agree that such proposals to transcend the body are untenable?
3. Explain some of the problems with psychoanalytically inspired understandings of female embodiment. Do you think that the strategies poststructuralists have used to overcome these difficulties are successful?
4. Explain the feminist contention that social, cultural and legal norms and discourses concerning women's appearance and behaviour work to enable and maintain women's inferior status. Do you agree with this analysis?

three Sexuality and desire

1. What is meant by "patriarchal sexual economy" and "compulsory heterosexuality"? What, according to many feminists, have these assumptions meant for women's understanding of themselves?
2. Explain the distinction between "sex" and "gender", and the role it has played in feminist thinking.
3. Why has some of the questioning engaged in by queer, intersexed and transgendered thinkers troubled some feminists?

four Differences among and within women

1. Why have so many feminists argued that the terms "woman" and "women" can never accurately represent women's lived experiences of their subjectivities?
2. What does the term "intersectionality" mean, and how does it work as a response to the above problem?
3. Explain the meaning of the term "anti-essentialism" and clarify the advantages and disadvantages of anti-essentialism for feminist projects.

five Agency

1. What is the basis for the feminist argument that the traditional conception of the autonomous individual is a myth?
2. Why have many of the attempts to develop a female-friendly conception of autonomy still not been effective with regard to countering situations of women's systemic oppression?
3. Do you think that feminists need to be able to agree on what the category "women" refers to in order to argue successfully for the countering of women's systematic oppression?

six Responsibility

1. Why is it problematic to analyse the plight of women across the world simply in terms of a presumed common patriarchal oppression?
2. On what basis have some third-world feminists argued that western feminists are implicated in the imperialism and capitalism that have shaped the lives of postcolonial women?
3. What reasons have feminists given for the view that concern for the environment is a feminist responsibility? Do you agree with these analyses?
4. Explain the tension between individual and collective forms of feminist responsibility. How do you think this tension, and feminist responsibility, should best be managed?

Further reading

Feminist thought is a vast and contested field, with new work and new interpretations of existing work an ongoing occurrence. It is also a field that theorists are constantly reinterpreting with regard to its history, its future trajectories and its relations with an enormous range of theories, disciplines, policies and practical projects, not to mention that, as we have stressed throughout this book, there are multiple and conflicting feminisms rather than any single feminist project. This being so, the newcomer is liable to feel bewildered by the sheer quantity and variety of material falling under the descriptor of feminism. The listing that follows is a limited guide to this variety, consisting of books that are readily available and likely to be helpful to newcomers trying to understand the complex of related problems, attempted responses and past and future trajectories common to feminisms. Many of these books, as indeed does this one, possess their own bibliographies that will direct you to further, more specialized, reading.

General works on feminism

Margaret Walters's *Feminism: A Very Short Introduction* (Oxford: Oxford University Press, 2006) is, as the title suggests, a short introduction to the history of feminism that looks at its early roots with the rise of secularism in the west, examines key issues with the campaign for voting rights and the liberation of the 1960s, and analyses the current situation of women across Europe, in the United States and elsewhere in the world. For a more comprehensive introduction, see Rosemarie Putnam Tong's appropriately titled *Feminist Thought: A More Comprehensive Introduction*, 3rd edn (Boulder, CO: Westview, 2008), which provides clear critical examinations of the major schools of feminism, including liberal, radical, Marxist and socialist, psychoanalytic, care-focused and postcolonial feminisms, ecofeminism, and postmodern and third-wave feminisms. Two other useful texts are Mary Evans's *Introducing Contemporary Feminist Thought* (Cambridge: Polity, 1997) and Jennifer Mather Saul's *Feminism: Issues and Arguments* (Oxford: Oxford University Press, 2003). These works introduce readers to the impact of second-wave feminist thinking, with Evans considering its impact on academic disciplines (between the 1970s and the 1990s), framed in this case not by a focus on the various schools of feminist thought, but by the fundamental feminist distinction between the public and the private. Saul's work discusses feminist responses to such key topics as pornography, abortion, sexual harassment, feminine appearance and the politics of work and family. With regard to understanding feminist philosophy, a comprehensive and valuable guide can be found in Alison Stone's *An Introduction to Feminist Philosophy* (Cambridge: Polity, 2007), which explores the philosophical implications of concepts and debates that have arisen from feminist thought, including those concerning the nature of sex, gender and the body; the relation between gender, sexuality and sexual difference; whether there is anything that all women have in common; and the nature of birth and its centrality to human existence. A final useful introductory text is Jessica Valenti's *Full Frontal Feminism: A Young Woman's Guide to Why Feminism Matters* (Berkeley, CA: Seal Press, 2007) which, covering such topics as pop culture, health, reproductive rights, violence, education and relationships, delivers an argument aimed at young women as to why feminism should be an integral part of their lives.

Given the variety and scope of feminisms, there are innumerable primary texts. Anthologies of feminist writings therefore provide a handy means for attaining an overview of the field. Some useful anthologies are as follows. *The Second Wave: A Reader in Feminist Theory*, edited by Linda Nicholson (London: Routledge, 1997), is a historically organized collection of many of the essays that have made key contributions to second-wave feminist theory and that have generated extensive discussion. The collection presents the complex relationship between feminism and Marxism, the second wave's "gynocentric turn", the theoretical elaboration of differences among women and the essentialist debate. Another good collection, organized on interdisciplinary rather than historical grounds, is *Theorizing Feminisms: A Reader*, edited by Elizabeth Hackett and Sally Haslanger (Oxford: Oxford University Press, 2006). Underpinned by the questions "What is sexist oppression?" and "What ought to be done about it?", this collection includes sections considering approaches to (sameness, difference, dominance, postmodern, identity politics) and potential allies (postcolonial, neo-materialist, queer theory) of feminist thinking that include both theoretical essays and political and/or practical applications. *Feminist Theory Reader: Local and Global Perspectives*, edited by Carole R. McCann and Seung-Kyunk Kim (London: Routledge, 2002), incorporates the voices of women of colour and postcolonial scholars alongside classic works in western feminist theory. More so than the previous texts mentioned, this collection includes the conversations among postcolonial women and women of colour about issues of gender, race, colonialism and sexuality as paramount to understanding the concerns of feminism.

Works about feminist understandings of oppression

Women's Rights: The Public/Private Dichotomy, edited by Jurate Motiejunaite (New York: International Debate Education Association, 2005), is a helpful collection of essays exploring the impact of the public–private divide on women (and women's rights) throughout history and around the world. A good introduction to the ideas of the equality and difference debate is *Beyond Equality and Difference: Citizenship, Feminist Politics and Subjectivity*, edited by Gisela Bock and Susan James (London: Routledge, 1992). The essays in this collection deal with the meaning and use of these concepts in a range of contexts, including citizenship, maternity, justice and language. A comprehensive introduction to key issues in feminist epistemology – with chapters exploring such topics as objectivity, rationality, power and the subject – is to be found in Alessandra Tanesini's aptly named *An Introduction to Feminist Epistemologies* (Oxford: Blackwell, 1999). Varied discussions of feminist concerns with language are to be found in *Language and Liberation: Feminism, Philosophy, and Language*, edited by Christina Hendricks and Kelly Oliver (New York: SUNY Press, 1999).

Works about feminist understandings of embodiment

Feminist Theory and the Body: A Reader, edited by Janet Price and Margrit Shildrick (London: Routledge, 1999), is a wide-ranging collection exploring the historical developments and current controversies in feminist thought with regard to the body. Containing work from key theorists in this field, the text addresses a range of body-focused issues concerning beauty, race, cyberspace, transsexuality, reproductive technologies, illness, rape, plastic surgery and disabilities. Other useful collections include *Writing on the Body: Female Embodiment and Feminist Theory*, edited by Katie Conboy, Nadia Medina and Sarah Stanbury (New York: Columbia University Press, 1997), and *The Politics of Women's Bodies: Sexuality, Appearance, and Behaviour*, 2nd edn, edited by Rose Weitz (Oxford: Oxford University Press, 2002). Both of these collections explore the tensions between women's lived bodily experiences and the cultural meanings inscribed on the female body.

Works about feminist understandings of sexuality and desire

Veronique Mottier's *Sexuality: A Very Short Introduction* (Oxford: Oxford University Press, 2008) provides a general introduction to some of the assumptions and debates concerning sexuality in the modern world. Although this is not an explicitly feminist text, it does contain a chapter outlining the key feminist critiques regarding sexuality. The anthology *Feminism and Sexuality: A Reader*, edited by Stevi Jackson and Sue Scott (New York: Columbia University Press, 1996) gives an excellent overview of the feminist debates concerning sexuality and desire. This text introduces readers to key essays and debates on such issues as heterosexuality and lesbianism, sexual violence, pornography and prostitution, the sex trade and sex tourism, AIDS and cybersex. With a more specific focus, a comprehensive overview of feminists' debates regarding pornography – engaging with those who consume it, fight against it and work within it – is provided in *Feminism and Pornography*, edited by Drucilla Cornell (Oxford: Oxford University Press, 2000).

Works about feminist understandings of differences

For a good introduction to the debate within feminism regarding essentialism, Diana Fuss's *Essentially Speaking: Feminism, Nature and Difference* (London: Routledge, 1990) is particularly useful. Engaging with both essentialist and social constructionist arguments, Fuss outlines the importance of both with regard to better understanding issues of gender, race and ethnicity, and shows the pitfalls of a too rigidly held essence–construct opposition. Another good discussion of essentialist and anti-essentialist positions in feminist theory is Cressida J. Heyes's *Line Drawings: Defining Women through Feminist Practice* (Ithaca, NY: Cornell University Press, 2000). Like Fuss, Heyes notes the sterility of much of the debate between essentialism and social constructionism, and is concerned to find a route by which to travel beyond this debate.

With regard to understanding the critique of the white, middle-class, heterosexual and able-bodied bias in much of second-wave feminism, the following texts may be helpful. A good collection of essays setting out many of the interconnections between "race", racism, ethnicity and feminism is *Feminism and "Race"*, edited by Kum-Kum Bhavnani (Oxford: Oxford University Press, 2001). Another useful text is Chilla Bulbeck's *Re-orienting Western Feminisms: Women's Diversity in a Postcolonial World* (Cambridge: Cambridge University Press, 1997), which challenges the hegemony of western white feminism through a wide-ranging exploration of the lived experiences of "women of colour". *Feminism Meets Queer Theory*, edited by Elizabeth Weed and Naomi Schor (Bloomington, IN: Indiana University Press, 1997), is a helpful collection of essays and interviews detailing the intersectionality of feminist and queer theories. Susan Wendell's *The Rejected Body: Feminist Philosophical Reflections on Disability* (London: Routledge, 1996) outlines how feminist theorizing has typically been skewed toward non-disabled experience, and argues that the knowledge of people with disabilities must be integrated into feminist thinking. Finally, *Gendering Disability*, edited by Bonnie G. Smith and Beth Hutchison (Piscataway, NJ: Rutgers University Press, 2004), is an excellent collection of essays exploring the intersections between gender and disability (and ageing, race, intersex/queer) and the need for deeper dialogue.

Works about feminist understandings of autonomy and agency

Although not all of the entries are feminist-focused, *Relational Autonomy: Feminist Perspectives on Autonomy, Agency, and the Social Self*, edited by Catriona Mackenzie and Natalie Stoljar (Oxford: Oxford University Press, 2000), contains a number of helpful essays on some of the possible social and relational dimensions of individual autonomy. The introduction is particularly good at outlining the key feminist charges with regard to traditional understandings of autonomy. An interesting defence of the conception of autonomy from a feminist point of view is provided by feminist philosopher Marilyn Friedman in her *Autonomy, Gender, Politics* (Oxford: Oxford University Press, 2003). Martha Fineman's *The Autonomy Myth: A Theory of Dependency* (New York: New Press, 2004) conversely deconstructs the myth of autonomy, arguing that as we are inevitably dependent at various points in our lives, our public policies should reflect this. A clear introduction to the feminist ethics of care can be found in Grace Clement's *Care, Autonomy, and Justice: Feminism and the Ethic of Care* (Boulder, CO: Westview, 1996).

Works about feminist understandings of responsibility

A good introduction to the issue of feminist responsibility is bell hooks's *Feminism is for Everybody: Passionate Politics* (Cambridge, MA: South End Press, 2000). Here hooks calls for a genuine feminist politics able to remain free from divisive barriers, and able to connect with all those committed to equality, mutual respect and justice. *Decentering the Center: Philosophy for a Multicultural, Postcolonial and Feminist World*, edited by Una Narayan and Sandra Harding (Bloomington, IN: Indiana University Press, 2000), considers the implications of multicultural, global and postcolonial insights for feminist enquiries. Essays explore issues around family, rights, anti-racism, science, knowledge, experience, progress and modernity. Two texts that outline some of the struggles faced by feminists of colour with regard to advancing feminist understandings and ideals in a postcolonial world are Uma Narayan's *Dislocating Cultures: Identities, Traditions and Third World Feminism* (London: Routledge, 1997) and *Colonize This!: Young Women of Color on Today's Feminism*, edited by Daisy Hernández and Bushra Rehman (Berkeley, CA: Seal Press, 2002). Finally, for a comprehensive range of essays taking interdisciplinary and multicultural perspectives as well as considering philosophical implications and the academic and research significance of ecofeminism, see *Ecofeminism: Women, Culture, Nature*, edited by Karen J. Warren and Nisvan Erkel (Bloomington, IN: Indiana University Press, 1997).

References

Alcoff, Linda 1997. "Cultural Feminism versus Post-Structuralism: The Identity Crisis in Feminist Theory". In *The Second Wave: A Reader in Feminist Theory*, Linda Nicholson (ed.), 330–55. New York: Routledge.

Allende, Isabel 2008. "Elders Part 3 – Isabel Allende". In *Enough Rope with Andrew Denton*. Australia: ABC 1, 30 June 2008. Transcript available at www.abc.net.au/tv/enoughrope/transcripts/s2289911.htm [accessed February 2009].

Antony, Louise & Charlotte Witt (eds) 1993. *A Mind of One's Own: Feminist Essays on Reason and Objectivity*. Boulder, CO: Westview.

Anzaldúa, Gloria 1991. "To(o) Queer the Writer: Loca, Escrita Y Chicana". In *InVersions: Writings by Dykes, Queers and Lesbians*, Betsy Warland (ed.), 249–63. Vancouver: Press Gang.

Atwood, Margaret 1986. *The Handmaid's Tale*. Boston, MA: Houghton Mifflin.

Baier, Annette 1985. "Cartesian Persons". In her *Postures of the Mind: Essays on Mind and Morals*, 74–92. Minneapolis, MN: University of Minnesota Press.

Bartky, Sandra Lee 1990. *Femininity and Domination: Studies in the Phenomenology of Oppression*. New York: Routledge.

Bartky, Sandra Lee 2000. "Body Politics". In *A Companion to Feminist Philosophy*, Alison M. Jaggar & Iris Marion Young (eds), 321–9. Oxford: Blackwell.

Beauvoir, Simone de [1949] 1997. *The Second Sex*, H. M. Parshey (trans.). London: Vintage.

Bell, Diane & Renate Klein (eds) 1996. *Radically Speaking: Feminism Reclaimed*. Melbourne: Spinifex.

Berry, Bonnie 2007. *Beauty Bias: Discrimination and Social Power*. Westport, CT: Praeger.

Billson, Janet Mancini & Carolyn Fluehr-Lobban (eds) 2005. *Female Well-Being: Toward a Global Theory of Social Change*. London: Zed.

Bordo, Susan 1993. *Unbearable Weight: Feminism, Western Culture and the Body*. Los Angeles, CA: University of California Press.

Bordo, Susan 1997. "The Body and the Reproduction of Femininity". In *Writing on the Body: Female Embodiment and Feminist Theory*, Katie Conboy, Nadia Medina & Sarah Stanbury (eds), 90–110. New York: Columbia University Press.

Bornstein, Kate 1994. *Gender Outlaw: On Men, Women and the Rest of Us*. New York: Routledge.

Boston Women's Health Book Collective 1973. *Our Bodies, Ourselves: A Book by and for Women*. New York: Simon & Schuster.

Bouvard, Marguerite Guzman 1994. *Revolutionizing Motherhood: The Mothers of the Plaza de Mayo*. Lanham, MD: Rowman & Littlefield.

Brooks, Ann 1997. *Postfeminisms: Feminism, Cultural Theory and Cultural Forms*. London: Routledge.

Brownmiller, Susan 1975. *Against Our Will: Men, Women, and Rape*. New York: Simon & Schuster.

Bunch, Charlotte 1990. "Women's Rights as Human Rights: Toward a Re-Vision of Human Rights". *Human Rights Quarterly* **12**: 486–98.

Butler, Judith 1990. *Gender Trouble: Feminism and the Subversion of Identity*. New York: Routledge.

Butler, Judith 1992. "Contingent Foundations: Feminism and the Question of 'Postmodernism'". In *Feminists Theorize the Political*, Judith Butler & Joan W. Scott (eds), 3–21. New York: Routledge.

Butler, Judith 1993. *Bodies that Matter*. New York: Routledge.

Butler, Judith 1994. "Against Proper Objects". *differences: A Journal of Feminist Cultural Studies* **6**(2): 1–26.

Cameron, Deborah 1992. *Feminism and Linguistic Theory*, 2nd edn. London: Macmillan.

Card, Claudia 1996. "What Lesbians Do". In her *The Unnatural Lottery: Character and Moral Luck*, 140–62. Philadelphia, PA: Temple University Press.

Chodorow, Nancy 1978. *The Reproduction of Mothering: Psychoanalysis and the Sociology of Gender*. Berkeley, CA: University of California Press.

Cixous, Hélène 1981. "The Laugh of the Medusa". In *New French Feminisms: An Anthology*, Elaine Marks & Isabelle de Courtivron (eds), 245–64. New York: Schocken.

Cixous, Hélène 1986. "Sorties". In *The Newly Born Woman*, Hélène Cixous & Catherine Clément, Betsy Wing (trans.), 63–132. Minneapolis, MN: University of Minnesota Press.

Code, Lorraine 1993. "Taking Subjectivity into Account". In *Feminist Epistemologies*, Linda Alcoff & Elizabeth Potter (eds), 15–48. New York: Routledge.

Code, Lorraine 1998. "Epistemology". In *A Companion to Feminist Philosophy*, Alison M. Jaggar & Iris Marion Young (eds), 173–84. Oxford: Blackwell.

Cohen, Cathy 1997. "Punks, Bulldaggers, and Welfare Queens". *GLQ: A Journal of Lesbian and Gay Studies* **3**: 437–65.

Colapinto, John 2000. *As Nature Made Him: The Boy who was Raised as a Girl*. New York: HarperCollins.

Colebrook, Claire 1999. "A Grammar of Becoming: Strategy, Subjectivism, and Style". In *Becomings: Explorations in Time, Memory and Futures*, Elizabeth Grosz (ed.), 117–40. Ithaca, NY: Cornell University Press.

Collins, Patricia Hill 1990. *Black Feminist Thought: Knowledge, Consciousness, and the Politics of Empowerment*. London: Unwin Hyman.

Combahee River Collective 1977. "Combahee River Collective Statement". In *Home Girls: A Black Feminist Anthology*, Barbara Smith (ed.), 272–82. New York: Kitchen Table.

Connelly, Matthew 2008. *Fatal Misconception: The Struggle to Control World Population*. Cambridge, MA: Belknap Press of Harvard University Press.

Correa, Sônia & Rosalind Petchesky 2003. "Reproductive and Sexual Rights: A Feminist Perspective". In *Feminist Theory Reader: Local and Global Perspectives*, Carole R. McCann & Seung-Kyung Kim (eds), 88–102. New York: Routledge.

Crenshaw, Kimberle 1989. "Demarginalizing the Intersection of Race and Sex: A Black Feminist Critique of Antidiscrimination Doctrine, Feminist Theory and Antiracist Politics". *University of Chicago Legal Forum*, Volume 1989: Feminism in the Law: Theory, Practice and Criticism: 139–68.

Daly, Mary 1978. *Gyn/Ecology: The Metaethics of Radical Feminism*. Boston, MA: Beacon.

Daly, Mary & Jane Caputi 1987. *Webster's First Intergalactic Wickedary of the English Language*. Boston, MA: Beacon.

Delphy, Christine 2003. "Rethinking Sex and Gender". In *Feminist Theory Reader: Local and Global Perspectives*, Carole R. McCann & Seung-Kyung Kim (eds), 57–67. New York: Routledge.

Duggan, Lisa & Nan Hunter 1995. *Sex Wars: Sexual Dissent and Political Culture*. London: Routledge.

Faludi, Susan 1991. *Backlash: The Undeclared War Against American Women*. New York: Doubleday.

Fausto-Sterling, Anne 1985. *Myths of Gender*. New York: Basic Books.

Femenia, Nora Amalia 1987. "Argentina's Mothers of Plaza de Mayo: The Mourning Process from Junta to Democracy", Carlos Ariel Gil (trans.). *Feminist Studies* 13(10): 9–18.

Ferguson, Ann 1984. "Sex War: the Debate between Radical and Libertarian Feminists". *Signs* 10(1): 106–12.

Flax, Jane 1990. *Thinking Fragments: Psychoanalysis, Feminism, and Postmodernism in the Contemporary West*. Los Angeles, CA: University of California Press.

Fraser, Nancy 1997. "After the Family Wage: A Postindustrial Thought Experiment". In her *Justus Interruptus: Critical Reflections on the "Postsocialist" Condition*, 41–66. New York: Routledge.

Friedan, Betty [1963] 2001. *The Feminine Mystique*, with an introduction by Anna Quinlan. New York: Norton.

Frye, Marilyn 1983. *The Politics of Reality: Essays in Feminist Theory*. Trumansburg, NY: The Crossing Press.

Frye, Marilyn 1997. "Some Reflections on Separatism and Power". In *Feminist Social Thought*, Diana Tietjens Meyers (ed.), 407–14. New York: Routledge.

Funk, Rus Ervin 2004. "What does Pornography say about Me(n)?: How I Became an Anti-Pornography Activist". In *Not For Sale: Feminists Resisting Prostitution and Pornography*, Christine Stark & Rebecca Whisnant (eds), 331–51. Melbourne: Spinifex.

Fuss, Diana 1989. *Essentially Speaking*. New York: Routledge.

Garfinkel, Harold 1967. *Studies in Ethnomethodology*. Cambridge: Polity.

Gatens, Moira 1991. *Feminism and Philosophy: Perspectives on Difference and Equality*. Cambridge: Polity.

Gilbert, Michael A. "Miqqi Alicia" 2001. "A Sometime Woman: Gender Choice and Cross-Socialization". In *Unseen Genders: Beyond the Binaries*, Felicity Haynes & Tarquam McKenna (eds), 41–50. New York: Peter Lang.

Gilligan, Carol 1982. *In a Different Voice: Psychological Theory and Women's Development*. Cambridge, MA: Harvard University Press.

Gould, Carol (ed.) 1984. *Beyond Domination*. Totowa, NJ: Rowman & Allanheld.

Grimshaw, Jean 1986. *Philosophy and Feminist Thinking*. Minneapolis, MN: University of Minnesota Press.

Grosz, Elizabeth 1994. *Volatile Bodies: Toward a Corporeal Feminism*. St Leonards, NSW: Allen & Unwin.

Halperin, David 1995. *Saint Foucault: Towards a Gay Hagiography*. Oxford: Oxford University Press.

Haraway, Donna 1991a. *Simians, Cyborgs and Women: The Reinvention of Nature*. New York: Routledge.

Haraway, Donna 1991b, "Situated Knowledges". In her *Simians, Cyborgs and Women: The Reinvention of Nature*, 183–201. New York: Routledge.

Haraway, Donna 2004. "A Manifesto for Cyborgs: Science, Technology, and Socialist Feminism in the 1980s". In her *The Haraway Reader*, 7–45. New York: Routledge.

Harding, Sandra 1986. *The Science Question in Feminism*. Ithaca, NY: Cornell University Press.

Harding, Sandra 1993. "Rethinking Standpoint Epistemology: 'What is Strong Objectivity?'". In *Feminist Epistemologies*, Linda Alcoff & Elizabeth Potter (eds), 49–82. New York: Routledge.

Hartmann, Betsy 1987. *Reproductive Rights and Wrongs: The Global Politics of Population Control and Contraceptive Choice*. New York: Harper & Row.

Hartsock, Nancy 1983. "The Feminist Standpoint: Developing the Ground for a Specifically Feminist Historical Materialism". In *Discovering Reality: Feminist Perspectives on Epistemology, Metaphysics, Methodology, and Philosophy of Science*, Sandra Harding & Merrill B. Hintikka (eds), 283–310. Dordrecht: Reidel.

Hedley, Jane 1992. "Surviving to Speak New Language: Mary Daly and Adrienne Rich". *Hypatia* 7(2): 40–62.

Held, Virginia 1993. "Non-contractual Society: The Postpatriarchal Family as Model". In her *Feminist Morality: Transforming Culture, Society and Politics*, 192–214. Chicago, IL: University of Chicago Press.

Held, Virginia 1997. "Feminism and Moral Theory". In *Feminist Social Thought*, Diana Tietjens Meyers (ed.), 631–45. New York: Routledge.

Hird, Myra 2000. "Gender's Nature: Intersexuality, Transsexualism and the 'Sex'/'Gender' Binary". *Feminist Theory* 1(3): 347–64.

Hoagland, Sarah Lucia 1988. *Lesbian Ethics: Toward New Values*. Palo Alto, CA: Institute of Lesbian Studies.

Hochschild, Arlie 1989. *The Second Shift*. New York: Penguin.

hooks, bell 1981. *Ain't I a Woman: Black Women and Feminism*. Boston, MA: South End Press.

hooks, bell 1984. *Feminist Theory: From Margin to Center*. Boston, MA: South End Press.

hooks, bell 1997. "Sisterhood: Political Solidarity Between Women". In *Feminist Social Thought*, Diana Tietjens Meyers (ed.), 485–500. New York: Routledge.

Hopkins, Susan 2002. *Girl Heroes: The New Force in Popular Culture*. London: Pluto.

International Labour Office, 2000. *Gender! A Partnership of Equals*. Geneva: International Labour Office.

Ireland, Mardy S. 1993. *Reconceiving Women: Separating Motherhood from Female Identity*. New York: Guilford.

Irigaray, Luce 1977. "Women's Exile". *Ideology and Consciousness* 1: 62–7.

Irigaray, Luce 1985a. *Speculum of the Other Woman*, Gillian C. Gill (trans.). Ithaca, NY: Cornell University Press.

Irigaray, Luce 1985b. *This Sex Which is Not One*, C. Porter & C. Burke (trans.). Ithaca, NY: Cornell University Press.

Jaggar, Alison 2005. "Global Responsibility and Western Feminism". In *Feminist Interventions in Ethics and Politics: Feminist Ethics and Social Theory*, Barbara S. Andrew, Jean Keller & Lisa H Schwartzman (eds), 185–200. Lanham, MD: Rowman & Littlefield.

Jayawardena, Kumari 1986. *Feminism and Nationalism in the Third World*. London: Zed.

Jeffreys, Sheila 1990. *Anticlimax: A Feminist Perspective on the Sexual Revolution*. London: Women's Press.

Jensen, Robert 2004. "Blow Bangs and Cluster Bombs: The Cruelty of Men and Americans". In *Not For Sale: Feminists Resisting Prostitution and Pornography*, Christine Stark & Rebecca Whisnant (eds), 28–37. Melbourne: Spinifex.

Kaw, Eugenia 2003. "Medicalization of Racial Features: Asian-American Women and Cosmetic Surgery". In *The Politics of Women's Bodies: Sexuality, Appearance, and Behaviour*, Rose Weitz (ed.), 184–200. New York: Oxford University Press.

Kristeva, Julia 1977. *About Chinese Women*. London: Boyars.

Kristeva, Julia 1982. *Desire in Language: A Semiotic Approach to Literature and Art*. New York: Columbia University Press.

Kristeva, Julia 1996. "Woman is Never What We Say". In *Julia Kristeva Interviews*, Ross Mitchell Guberman (ed.), 95–102. New York: Columbia University Press.

Kristeva, Julia 1997. "Women's Time". In *The Portable Kristeva*, Kelly Oliver (ed.), 349–69. New York: Columbia University Press.

Lloyd, Genevieve 1984. *The Man of Reason: "Male" and "Female" in Western Philosophy*. Minneapolis, MN: University of Minnesota Press.

Lorde, Audre 1984a. "Age, Race, Class, and Sex: Women Redefining Difference". In her *Sister Outsider: Essays and Speeches by Audre Lorde*, 114–23. Freedom, CA: Crossing Press.

Lorde, Audre 1984b. "An Open Letter to Mary Daly". In her *Sister Outsider: Essays and Speeches by Audre Lorde*, 66–71. Freedom, CA: Crossing Press.

Lugones, Maria 2003a. *Pilgrimages/Peregrinajes: Theorizing Coalition Against Multiple Oppressions*. Lanham, MD: Rowman & Littlefield.

Lugones, Maria 2003b. "Purity, Impurity, and Separation". In her *Pilgrimages/Peregrinajes: Theorizing Coalition Against Multiple Oppressions*, 121–48. Lanham, MD: Rowman & Littlefield.

Mackenzie, Catriona & Natalie Stoljar 2000. "Introduction: Autonomy Refigured". In *Relational Autonomy: Feminist Perspectives on Autonomy, Agency, and the Social Self*, Catriona Mackenzie & Natalie Stoljar (eds), 3–31. New York: Oxford University Press.

MacKinnon, Catharine 1993. "Reflections on Sex Equality Under Law". In *American Feminist Thought at Century's End: A Reader*, L. Kauffman (ed.), 367–424. Oxford: Blackwell.

MacKinnon, Catharine 1997. "Sexuality". In *The Second Wave: A Reader in Feminist Theory*, Linda Nicholson (ed.), 158–80. New York: Routledge.

Markovic, Mihilo 1976. "Women's Liberation and Human Emancipation". In *Women and Philosophy: Toward a Theory of Liberation*, Carol Gould & Marx Wartofsky (eds), 145–67. New York: Capricorn.

Merchant, Carolyn 1980. *The Death of Nature: Women, Ecology and the Scientific Revolution*. San Francisco, CA: Harper & Row.

Meyers, Diana Tietjens 2004. *Being Yourself: Essays on Identity, Action and Social Life*. Lanham, MD: Rowman & Littlefield.

Mies, Maria & Vandana Shiva 1993. *Ecofeminism*. Melbourne: Spinifex.

Mill, John Stuart [1869] 1970. "The Subjection of Women". In John Stuart Mill and Harriet Taylor Mill, *Essays on Sex Equality*, Alice S. Rossi (ed.), 125–242. Chicago, IL: University of Chicago Press.

Miller, Casey & Kate Swift 1980. *The Handbook of Nonsexist Writing*. New York: Lippincott & Crowell.

Millett, Kate 1969. *Sexual Politics*. New York: Doubleday.

Mohanty, Chandra Talpade 1991a. "Cartographies of Struggle: Third World Women and the Politics of Feminism". In *Third World Women and the Politics of Feminism*, Chandra Talpade Mohanty, Ann Russo & Loudes Torres (eds), 1–47. Bloomington, IN: Indiana University Press.

Mohanty, Chandra Talpade 1991b. "Under Western Eyes: Feminist Scholarship and Colonial Discourses". In *Third World Women and the Politics of Feminism*, Chandra Talpade Mohanty, Ann Russo & Loudes Torres (eds), 51–80. Bloomington, IN: Indiana University Press.

Moi, Toril 1985. *Sexual/Textual Politics: Feminist Literary Theory*. London: Routledge.

Monro, Surya 2001, "Gender Love and Gender Freedom". In *Unseen Genders: Beyond the Binaries*, Felicity Haynes & Tarquam McKenna (eds), 157–65. New York: Peter Lang.

Morgan, Robin 1993. *The Word of a Woman: Selected Prose 1968–1992*. London: Virago.

Morris, Jenny 1991. *Pride Against Prejudice: Transforming Attitudes to Disability*. London: Women's Press.

Morris, Meaghan 1982. "A-mazing Grace: Notes on Mary Daly's Poetics". *Intervention* **16**: 70–92.

Morrissey, Belinda 2003. *When Women Kill: Questions of Agency and Subjectivity*. London: Routledge.

Mouffe, Chantal 1995. "Feminism, Citizenship, and Radical Democratic Politics". In *Social Postmodernism: Beyond Identity Politics*, Linda Nicholson & Steven Seidman (eds), 315–31. Cambridge: Cambridge University Press.

Narayan, Uma 1997. "Contesting Cultures: 'Westernization', Respect for Cultures, and Third-World Feminists". In *The Second Wave: A Reader in Feminist Theory*, Linda Nicholson (ed.), 396–414. New York: Routledge.

Nataf, Z. 1998. "Whatever I Feel ...". *New Internationalist* **300** (April): 22–5.

Nilsen, Alleen Pace 1984. "Winning the Great He/She Battle". *College English* **46**: 151–7.

Nussbaum, Martha 1999a. *Sex and Social Justice*. New York: Oxford University Press.

Nussbaum, Martha 1999b. "The Professor of Parody". *The New Republic* **220**(8): 37–45.

Nye, Andrea 1988. *Feminist Theory and the Philosophies of Man*. New York: Routledge.

Oakley, Ann 1985. *Sex, Gender and Society*. Aldershot: Gower.

Okin, Susan Moller 1989a. "Humanist Liberalism". In *Liberalism and the Moral Life*, Nancy Rosenblum (ed.), 39–53. Cambridge, MA: Harvard University Press.

Okin, Susan Moller 1989b. *Justice, Gender and the Family*. New York: Basic Books.

Okin, Susan Moller 1994. "Gender Inequality and Cultural Differences". *Political Theory* **22**(1): 5–24.

Okin, Susan Moller 1998. "Feminism and Political Theory". In *Philosophy in a Feminist Voice: Critiques and Reconstructions*, Janet A. Kourany (ed.), 116–44. Princeton, NJ: Princeton University Press.

Pateman, Carole 1989. "Feminist Critiques of the Public/Private Dichotomy". In her *The Disorder of Women*, 118–40. Palo Alto, CA: Stanford University Press.

Plato 1997a. *Apology*. In *Plato: Complete Works*, John M. Cooper & D. S. Hutchinson (eds). Indianapolis, IN: Hackett.

Plato 1997b. *Republic*. In *Plato: Complete Works*, John M. Cooper & D. S. Hutchinson (eds). Indianapolis, IN: Hackett.

Plumwood, Val 1993. *Feminism and the Mastery of Nature*. London: Routledge.

Questions Féministes Collective 1981. "Variations on Common Themes". In *New French Feminisms*, Elaine Marks & Isabelle de Courtivron (eds), 212–30. Brighton: Harvester.

Radicalesbians 1997. "The Woman Identified Woman". In *The Second Wave: A Reader in Feminist Theory*, Linda Nicholson (ed.), 153–7. New York: Routledge.

Raymond, Janice 1979. *The Transsexual Empire: The Making of the She-male*. Boston, MA: Beacon.

Reilly, Tom 2008. "Students Turn to Sex Work to Help Pay for University". *The Sunday Age*, 2 March. www.theage.com.au/news/national/students-turn-to-sex-work-to-help-pay-for-university/2008/03/01/1204227055215.html (accessed March 2009).

Rich, Adrienne 1977. *Of Woman Born: Motherhood as Experience and Institution*. London: Virago.

Rich, Adrienne 1984. "Compulsory Heterosexuality and Lesbian Existence". In *Desire: The Politics of Sexuality*, Ann Snitow, Christine Stansell & Sharon Thompson (eds), 212–41. London: Virago.

Roiphe, Katie 1993. *The Morning After: Sex, Fear and Feminism on Campus*. Boston, MA: Little Brown.

Roseneil, Sasha 1995. *Disarming Patriarchy: Feminism and Political Action at Greenham*. Buckingham: Open University Press.

Rousseau, J.-J. [1762] 1911. *Émile*, B. Foxley (trans.). London: Dent.

Rowbotham, Sheila, 1992. *Women in Movement: Feminism and Social Action*. New York: Routledge.

Rowland, Robyn 1996. "Politics of Intimacy: Heterosexuality, Love and Power". In *Radically Speaking: Feminism Reclaimed*, Diane Bell & Renate Klein (eds), 77–86. Melbourne: Spinifex.

Ruddick, Sara 1989. *Maternal Thinking: Toward a Politics of Peace*. Boston, MA: Beacon.

Saussure, Ferdinand de 1966. *Course in General Linguistics*, Wade Baskin (trans.). New York: McGraw-Hill.

Segal, Lynne 1999. *Why Feminism? Gender, Psychology, Politics*. Cambridge: Polity.

Shildrick, Margrit 1996. "Posthumanism and the Monstrous Body". *Body and Society* 2(1): 1–15.

Shiva, Vandana 1988. *Staying Alive: Women, Ecology and Survival in India*. New Delhi: Kali for Women.

Snitow, Ann, Christine Stansell & Sharon Thompson (eds) 1984. *Desire: The Politics of Sexuality*. London: Virago.

Spelman, Elizabeth 1988. *Inessential Woman: Problems of Exclusion in Feminist Thought*. Boston, MA: Beacon.

Spender, Dale 1980. *Man Made Language*. London: Routledge & Kegan Paul.

Spivak, Gayatri Chakravorty 1987. "French Feminism in an International Frame". In her *In Other Worlds: Essays in Cultural Politics*, 134–53. New York: Methuen.

Spivak, Gayatri Chakravorty 1988. "Can the Subaltern Speak?". In *Marxist Interpretations of Culture*, Cary Nelson & Lawrence Grossberg (eds), 271–313. Basingstoke: Macmillan.

Spivak, Gayatri Chakravorty 1990. "Criticism, Feminism and the Institution". In *The Post-Colonial Critic: Interviews, Strategies, Dialogues*, Sarah Harasym (ed.), 1–16. New York: Routledge.

Stark, Christine 2004. "Girls to Boyz: Sex Radical Women Promoting Prostitution, Pornography, and Sadomasochism". In *Not For Sale: Feminists Resisting Prostitution and Pornography*, Christine Stark & Rebecca Whisnant (eds), 278–91. Melbourne: Spinifex.

Stoltenberg, John 2004. "Pornography and International Human Rights". In *Not For Sale: Feminists Resisting Prostitution and Pornography*, Christine Stark & Rebecca Whisnant (eds), 400–409. Melbourne: Spinifex.

Stone, Alison 2004. "Essentialism and Anti-essentialism in Feminist Philosophy". *Journal of Moral Philosophy* 1(2): 135–53.

Summers, Anne 2003. *The End of Equality: Work, Babies and Women's Choices in 21st Century Australia*. Milsons Point, NSW: Random House Australia.

Thorne, Barrie & Nancy Henley (eds) 1975. *Language and Sex: Difference and Dominance*. Rowley, MA: Newbury House.

Thorne, Barrie, Cheris Kramerae & Nancy Henley (eds) 1983. *Language, Gender and Society*. Rowley, MA: Newbury House.

Vance, Carole S. (ed.) 1984. *Pleasure and Danger: Exploring Female Sexuality.* London: Routledge & Kegan Paul.

Waring, Marilyn 1990. *If Women Counted: A New Feminist Economics.* New York: HarperCollins.

Warren, Karen J. 2000. *Ecofeminist Philosophy: A Western Perspective on What it is and Why it Matters.* Lanham, MD: Rowman & Littlefield.

Wendell, Susan 1996. *The Rejected Body: Feminist Philosophical Reflections on Disability.* New York: Routledge.

Williams, Joan 2000. *Unbending Gender: Why Family and Work Conflict and What to Do About it.* Oxford: Oxford University Press.

Williams, Patricia 1991. *The Alchemy of Race and Rights: Diary of a Law Professor.* Cambridge, MA: Harvard University Press.

Williams, Wendy 1997. "The Equality Crisis: Some Reflections of Culture, Courts, and Feminism". In *The Second Wave: A Reader in Feminist Theory*, Linda Nicholson (ed.), 71–91. New York: Routledge.

Wittig, Monique 1992. "One is not Born a Woman". In her *The Straight Mind and Other Essays*, 9–20. Boston, MA: Beacon.

Wolf, Naomi 1990. *The Beauty Myth.* London: Chatto & Windus.

Wolf, Naomi 1993. *Fire With Fire: The New Female Power and How it will Change the 21st Century.* New York: Random House.

Wollstonecraft, Mary [1792] 1967. *A Vindication of the Rights of Woman*, Charles H. Hagelman (ed.). New York: Norton.

Woolf, Virginia 1929. *A Room of One's Own.* London: Hogarth Press.

York, J., D. Leonard, C. Liensol *et al.* 1991. "We are the Feminists that Women Warned Us About". In *A Reader in Feminist Knowledge*, S. Gunew (ed.), 308–11. London: Routledge.

Young, Iris Marion 1990. "Humanism, Gynocentrism, and Feminist Politics". In her *Throwing Like a Girl and Other Essays in Feminist Philosophy and Social Theory*, 73–91. Bloomington, IN: Indiana University Press

Young, Iris Marion 2005. "Lived Body vs. Gender: Reflections on Social Structure and Subjectivity". In her *On Female Body Experience: "Throwing Like a Girl" and Other Essays*, 12–26. Oxford: Oxford University Press.

Zack, Naomi 2005. *Inclusive Feminism: A Third Wave Theory of Women's Commonality.* Lanham, MD: Rowman & Littlefield.

Index